Cold War
Primary Sources

Cold War
Primary Sources

Sharon M. Hanes
and Richard C. Hanes

Lawrence W. Baker,
Project Editor

U.X.L
A part of Gale, Cengage Learning

GALE
CENGAGE Learning

Detroit • New York • San Francisco • New Haven, Conn • Waterville, Maine • London

Cold War: Primary Sources

Sharon M. Hanes and Richard C. Hanes

Project Editor
Lawrence W. Baker

Editorial
Sarah Hermsen, Matthew May, Diane Sawinski

Permissions
Shalice Shah-Caldwell

Imaging and Multimedia
Leitha Etheridge-Sims, Lezlie Light, Mike Logusz, Kelly A. Quin

Product Design
Pamela A. E. Galbreath, Jennifer Wahi

Composition
Evi Seoud

Manufacturing
Rita Wimberley

LIBRARY OF CONGRESS CATALOGING-IN-PUBLICATION DATA

Hanes, Sharon M.

  Cold war : primary sources / Sharon M. Hanes and Richard C. Hanes ; Lawrence W. Baker, editor.

    p. cm. — (UXL Cold War reference library)

Summary: More than thirty of the most important documents, papers, speeches, and communications during the Cold War by the major figures of the era. Includes bibliographical references and index.

    ISBN 0-7876-7666-7 (alk. paper)

  1. Cold War—Sources—Juvenile literature. 2. World politics—1945–1989—Sources—Juvenile literature. 3. United States—Foreign relations—Soviet Union—Sources—Juvenile literature. 4. Soviet Union—Foreign relations—United States—Sources—Juvenile literature. [1. Cold War—Sources. 2. World politics—1945–1989—Sources. 3. United States—Foreign relations—Soviet Union—Sources. 4. Soviet Union—Foreign relations—United States—Sources.] I. Hanes, Richard Clay, 1946– II. Baker, Lawrence W. III. Title. IV. Series.

  D839.3 .H36 2003
  327.73047′09′045—dc22   2003018988

Printed in the United States of America
6 7 8 9 10 11 14 13 12 11 10 09 08

Contents

Introduction

Sometimes single events alter the course of history; other times, a chain reaction of seemingly lesser occurrences changes the path of nations. The intense rivalry between the United States and the Soviet Union that emerged immediately after World War II (1939–45) followed the second pattern. Known as the Cold War, the rivalry grew out of mutual distrust between two starkly different societies: communist Soviet Union and the democratic West, which was led by the United States and included Western Europe. Communism is a political and economic system in which the Communist Party controls all aspects of citizens' lives and private ownership of property is banned. It is not compatible with America's democratic way of life. Democracy is a political system consisting of several political parties whose members are elected to various government offices by vote of the people. The rapidly growing rivalry between the two emerging post–World War II superpowers in 1945 would dominate world politics until 1991. Throughout much of the time, the Cold War was more a war of ideas than one of battlefield combat. Yet for generations, the Cold War affected almost every aspect of American life and those who lived in numerous other countries around the world.

The global rivalry was characterized by many things. Perhaps the most dramatic was the cost in lives and public funds. Millions of military personnel and civilians were killed in conflicts often set in Third World countries. This toll includes tens of thousands of American soldiers in the Korean War (1950–53) and Vietnam War (1954–75) and thousands of Soviet soldiers in Afghanistan. National budgets were stretched to support the nuclear arms races, military buildups, localized wars, and aid to friendly nations. On the international front, the United States often supported oppressive but strongly anti-communist military dictatorships. On the other hand, the Soviets frequently supported revolutionary movements seeking to overthrow established governments. Internal political developments within nations around the world were interpreted by the two superpowers—the Soviet Union and the United States—in terms of the Cold War rivalry. In many nations, including the Soviet-dominated Eastern European countries, basic human freedoms were lost. New international military and peacekeeping alliances were also formed, such as the United Nations (UN), the North Atlantic Treaty Organization (NATO), the Organization of American States (OAS), and the Warsaw Pact.

Effects of the Cold War were extensive on the home front, too. The U.S. government became more responsive to national security needs, including the sharpened efforts of the Federal Bureau of Investigation (FBI). Created were the Central Intelligence Agency (CIA), the National Security Council (NSC), and the Department of Defense. Suspicion of communist influences within the United States built some individual careers and destroyed others. The national education priorities of public schools were changed to emphasize science and engineering after the Soviets launched the satellite *Sputnik,* which itself launched the space race.

What would cause such a situation to develop and last for so long? One major factor was mistrust for each other. The communists were generally shunned by other nations, including the United States, since they gained power in Russia in 1917 then organized that country into the Soviet Union. The Soviets' insecurities loomed large. They feared another invasion from the West through Poland, as had happened through the centuries. On the other hand, the West was highly suspicious of the harsh closed society of Soviet communism. As a result, a move by one nation would bring a response by the other. Hard-liners on both sides believed long-term coexistence was not feasible.

A second major factor was that the U.S. and Soviet ideologies were dramatically at odds. The political, social, and economic systems of democratic United States and communist Soviet Union were essentially incompatible. Before the communist (or Bolshevik) revolution in 1917, the United States and Russia competed as they both sought to expand into the Pacific Northwest. In addition, Americans had a strong disdain for Russian oppression under their monarchy of the tsars. Otherwise, contact between the two growing powers was almost nonexistent until thrown together as allies in a common cause to defeat Germany and Japan in World War II.

It was during the meetings of the allied leaders in Yalta and Potsdam in 1945 when peaceful postwar cooperation was being sought that the collision course of the two new superpowers started becoming more evident. The end of World War II had brought the U.S. and Soviet armies face-to-face in central Europe in victory over the Germans. Yet the old mistrusts between communists and capitalists quickly dominated diplomatic relations. Capitalism is an economic system in which property and businesses are privately owned. Prices, production, and distribution of goods are determined by competition in a market relatively free of government intervention. A peace treaty ending World War II in Europe was blocked as the Soviets and the U.S.-led West carved out spheres of influence. Western Europe and Great Britain aligned with the United States and collectively was referred to as the "West"; Eastern Europe would be controlled by the Soviet Communist Party. The Soviet Union and its Eastern European satellite countries were collectively referred to as the "East." The two powers tested the resolve of each other in Germany, Iran, Turkey, and Greece in the late 1940s.

In 1949, the Soviets successfully tested an atomic bomb and Chinese communist forces overthrew the National Chinese government, and U.S. officials and American citizens feared a sweeping massive communist movement was overtaking the world. A "red scare" spread through America. The term "red" referred to communists, especially the Soviets. The public began to suspect that communists or communist sympathizers lurked in every corner of the nation.

Meanwhile, the superpower confrontations spread from Europe to other global areas: Asia, Africa, the Middle East, and Latin America. Most dramatic were the Korean and Vietnam wars, the Cuban Missile Crisis, and the military standoffs in Berlin, Germany. However, bloody conflicts erupted in many other areas as the United States and Soviet Union sought to expand their influence by supporting or opposing various movements.

In addition, a costly arms race lasted decades despite sporadic efforts at arms control agreements. The score card for the Cold War was kept in terms of how many nuclear weapons one country had aimed at the other. Finally, in the 1970s and 1980s, the Soviet Union could no longer keep up with the changing world economic trends. Its tightly controlled and highly inefficient industrial and agricultural systems could not compete in world markets while the government was still focusing its wealth on Cold War confrontations and the arms race. Developments in telecommunications also made it more difficult to maintain a closed society. Ideas were increasingly being exchanged despite longstanding political barriers. The door was finally cracked open in the communist European nations to more freedoms in the late 1980s through efforts at economic and social reform. Seizing the moment, the long suppressed populations of communist Eastern European nations and fifteen Soviet republics demanded political and economic freedom.

Through 1989, the various Eastern European nations replaced long-time communist leaders with noncommunist officials. By the end of 1991, the Soviet Communist Party had been banned from various Soviet republics, and the Soviet Union itself ceased to exist. After a decades-long rivalry, the end to the Cold War came swiftly and unexpectedly.

A new world order dawned in 1992 with a single superpower, the United States, and a vastly changed political landscape around much of the globe. Communism remained in China and Cuba, but Cold War legacies remained elsewhere. In the early 1990s, the United States was economically burdened with a massive national debt, the former Soviet republics were attempting a very difficult economic transition to a more capitalistic open market system, and Europe, starkly divided by the Cold War, was reunited once again and sought to establish a new union including both Eastern and Western European nations.

Reader's Guide

Cold War: Primary Sources* tells the story of the Cold War in the words of the people who lived and shaped it. The Cold War was the period in history from 1945 until 1991 that was dominated by the rivalry between the world's superpowers, the United States and the Soviet Union. Thirty-one excerpted documents provide a wide range of perspectives on this period of history. Included are excerpts from former British prime minister Winston Churchill's "Iron Curtain Speech," U.S. general Douglas MacArthur's address to the U.S. Congress, in which he uttered the famous lines, "Old soldiers never die, they just fade away"; "One Hundred Things You Should Know About Communism in the U.S.A." from the House Un-American Activities Committee (HUAC); and numerous speeches from Soviet leader Nikita Khrushchev and U.S. president John F. Kennedy.

Each excerpt presented in *Cold War: Primary Sources* includes the following additional material:

- An **introduction** places the document and its author in a historical context.

- **"Things to remember while reading ..."** offers readers important background information and directs them to central ideas in the text.

- **"What happened next ..."** provides an account of subsequent events, both in the Cold War and in the life of the author.

- **"Did you know ..."** provides significant and interesting facts about the document, the author, or the events discussed.

- **"Consider the following ..."** gives students and teachers research and activity ideas that pertain to the subject of the excerpt.

- **"For more information"** lists sources for further reading on the author, the topic, or the document.

Cold War: Primary Sources also features sidebars containing interesting facts about people and events related to the Cold War, nearly eighty photographs, a "Cold War Timeline" that lists significant dates and events of the Cold War era, and a cumulative subject index.

U•X•L Cold War Reference Library

Cold War: Primary Sources is only one component of the three-part U•X•L Cold War Reference Library. The other two titles in this set are:

- *Cold War: Almanac* (two volumes) presents a comprehensive overview of the period in American history from the end of World War II until the fall of communism in Eastern Europe and the Soviet Union and the actual dissolution of the Soviet Union itself. Its fifteen chapters are arranged chronologically and explore such topics as the origins of the Cold War, the beginning of the nuclear age, the arms race, espionage, anticommunist campaigns and political purges on the home fronts, détente, the Cuban Missile Crisis, the Berlin Airlift and the Berlin Wall, the Korean and Vietnam wars, and the ending of the Cold War. The *Almanac* also contains more than 140 black-and-white photographs and maps, "Words to Know" and "People to Know" boxes, a timeline, and an index.

- *Cold War: Biographies* (two volumes) presents the life stories of fifty individuals who played key roles in the Cold War superpower rivalry. Profiled are well-known figures such as Joseph Stalin, Harry Truman, Nikita Khrushchev, Henry Kissinger, John F. Kennedy, Mao Zedong, and Mikhail Gorbachev, as well as lesser-known individuals such as physicist and father of the Soviet atomic bomb Igor Kurchatov, British foreign minister Ernest Bevin, and longtime U.S. foreign policy analyst George F. Kennan.

- A cumulative index of all three titles in the U•X•L Cold War Reference Library is also available.

Acknowledgments

Special thanks to Catherine Filip, who typed much of the manuscript. Much appreciation also goes to copyeditor Theresa Murray, proofreader Wyn Hilty, indexer Dan Brannen, and typesetter Marco Di Vita of the Graphix Group for their fine work.

Dedication

To Aaron and Kara Hanes, that their children may learn about the events and ideas that shaped the world through the latter half of the twentieth century.

Comments and suggestions

We welcome your comments on *Cold War: Primary Sources* and suggestions for other topics to consider. Please write: Editors, *Cold War: Primary Sources*, U•X•L, 27500 Drake Rd., Farmington Hills, Michigan 48331-3535; call toll free: 1-800-877-4253; fax to 248-699-8097; or send e-mail via http://www.gale.com.

Cold War Timeline

September 1, 1939 Germany invades Poland, beginning World War II.

June 30, 1941 Germany invades the Soviet Union, drawing the Soviets into World War II.

December 7, 1941 Japan launches a surprise air attack on U.S. military installations at Pearl Harbor, Hawaii, drawing the United States into World War II.

November 1943 The three key allied leaders—U.S. president Franklin D. Roosevelt, British prime minister Winston Churchill, and Soviet premier Joseph Stalin—meet in

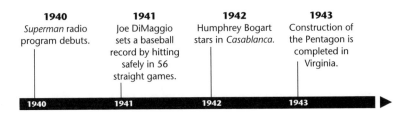

1940
Superman radio program debuts.

1941
Joe DiMaggio sets a baseball record by hitting safely in 56 straight games.

1942
Humphrey Bogart stars in *Casablanca.*

1943
Construction of the Pentagon is completed in Virginia.

1940   1941   1942   1943

Tehran, Iran, to discuss war strategies against Germany and Italy.

August-October 1944 An international conference held at Dumbarton Oaks in Washington, D.C., creates the beginning of the United Nations.

February 1945 The Yalta Conference is held in the Crimean region of the Soviet Union among the three key allied leaders, U.S. president Franklin D. Roosevelt, British prime minister Winston Churchill, and Soviet premier Joseph Stalin to discuss German surrender terms, a Soviet attack against Japanese forces, and the future of Eastern Europe.

April-June 1945 Fifty nations meet in San Francisco to write the UN charter.

April 12, 1945 U.S. president Franklin D. Roosevelt dies suddenly from a brain hemorrhage, leaving Vice President Harry S. Truman as the next U.S. president.

April 23, 1945 U.S. president Harry S. Truman personally criticizes Soviet foreign minister Vyacheslav Molotov for growing Soviet influence in Eastern Europe, setting the tone for escalating Cold War tensions.

May 7, 1945 Germany surrenders to allied forces, leaving Germany and its capital of Berlin divided into four military occupation zones with American, British, French, and Soviet forces.

July 16, 1945 The United States, through its top-secret Manhattan Project, successfully detonates the world's first atomic bomb under the leadership of nuclear physicist J. Robert Oppenheimer.

July-August 1945 The Big Three—U.S. president Harry S. Truman, British prime minister Winston Churchill,

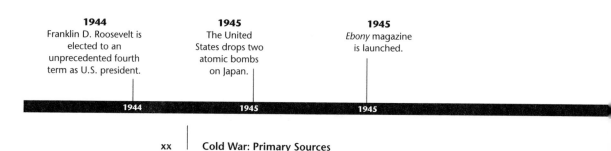

1944 Franklin D. Roosevelt is elected to an unprecedented fourth term as U.S. president.

1945 The United States drops two atomic bombs on Japan.

1945 *Ebony* magazine is launched.

1944   1945   1945

and Soviet premier Joseph Stalin meet in Potsdam, Germany, to discuss postwar conditions. On August 2, newly elected Clement R. Attlee replaces Churchill.

August 14, 1945 Japan surrenders, ending World War II, after the United States drops two atomic bombs on the cities of Hiroshima and Nagasaki.

February 9, 1946 Soviet leader Joseph Stalin delivers the "Two Camps" speech, declaring the incompatibility of communist Soviet Union with the West.

February 22, 1946 U.S. diplomat George F. Kennan sends the "Long Telegram" from Moscow to Washington, D.C., warning of the Soviet threat.

March 5, 1946 Former British prime minister Winston Churchill delivers the "Iron Curtain Speech" at Westminster College in Fulton, Missouri.

September 27, 1946 Nikolai V. Novikov, Soviet diplomat to the United States, sends a telegram to Moscow describing his perceptions of the United States's postwar intentions.

December 2, 1946 The United States, Great Britain, and France merge their German occupation zones to create what would become West Germany.

March 12, 1947 U.S. president Harry S. Truman announces the Truman Doctrine, which states that the United States will assist any nation in the world being threatened by communist expansion.

June 5, 1947 U.S. secretary of state George C. Marshall announces the Marshall Plan, an ambitious economic aid program to rebuild Western Europe from World War II destruction.

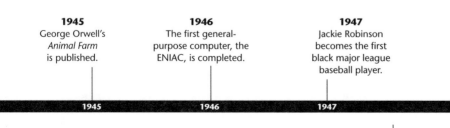

1945
George Orwell's
Animal Farm
is published.

1946
The first general-purpose computer, the ENIAC, is completed.

1947
Jackie Robinson becomes the first black major league baseball player.

1945   1946   1947

June 9, 1947 FBI director J. Edgar Hoover publishes an article titled "How to Fight Communism" in *Newsweek* magazine.

July 1947 U.S. diplomat George F. Kennan introduces the containment theory in the "X" article in *Foreign Affairs* magazine.

July 26, 1947 Congress passes the National Security Act, creating the Central Intelligence Agency (CIA) and the National Security Council (NSC).

October 1947 Actor Ronald Reagan and author Ayn Rand testify before the House Un-American Activities Committee (HUAC), a congressional group investigating communist influences in the United States.

December 5, 1947 The Soviets establish the Communist Information Bureau (Cominform) to promote the expansion of communism in the world.

1948 The House Un-American Activities Committee (HUAC) publishes "One Hundred Things You Should Know About Communism in the U.S.A.," alerting the public on how to guard against possible communist influences within the United States.

February 25, 1948 A communist coup in Czechoslovakia topples the last remaining democratic government in Eastern Europe.

March 14, 1948 Israel announces its independence as a new state in the Middle East.

March 17, 1948 U.S. president Harry S. Truman delivers a special message to the Congress on the Soviet threat to the freedom of Europe and urges congressional passage of the Marshall Plan.

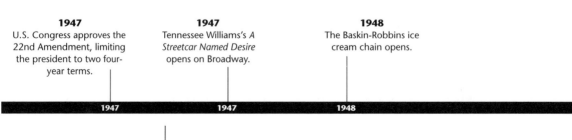

1947
U.S. Congress approves the 22nd Amendment, limiting the president to two four-year terms.

1947
Tennessee Williams's *A Streetcar Named Desire* opens on Broadway.

1948
The Baskin-Robbins ice cream chain opens.

1947   1947   1948

June 24, 1948 The Soviets begin a blockade of Berlin, leading to a massive airlift of daily supplies by the Western powers for the next eleven months.

April 4, 1949 The North Atlantic Treaty Organization (NATO), a military alliance involving Western Europe and the United States, comes into existence.

May 5, 1949 The West Germans establish the Federal Republic of Germany government.

May 12, 1949 The Soviet blockade of access routes to West Berlin is lifted.

May 30, 1949 Soviet-controlled East Germany establishes the German Democratic Republic.

August 29, 1949 The Soviet Union conducts its first successful atomic bomb test at the Semipalatinsk Test Site in northeastern Kazakhstan.

September 1949 Journalist Isaac Don Levine publishes an article titled "Our First Line of Defense" in *Plain Talk* magazine in opposition to the U.S. policy of allowing Mainland China to fall to the communists.

October 1, 1949 Communist forces under Mao Zedong gain victory in the Chinese civil war, and the People's Republic of China (PRC) is established, with Zhou Enlai its leader.

January 1950 The U.S. National Security Council issues "Report on Soviet Intentions (NSC-68)" under the leadership of Paul H. Nitze, proposing a large buildup of defense forces in the United States.

February 9, 1950 U.S. senator Joseph R. McCarthy of Wisconsin publicly claims in a speech in Wheeling, West

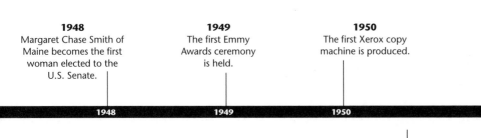

1948
Margaret Chase Smith of Maine becomes the first woman elected to the U.S. Senate.

1949
The first Emmy Awards ceremony is held.

1950
The first Xerox copy machine is produced.

1948   1949   1950

Virginia, to have a list of communists working in the U.S. government.

March 1, 1950 Chiang Kai-shek, former leader of nationalist China, which was defeated by communist forces, establishes the Republic of China (ROC) on the island of Taiwan.

April 7, 1950 U.S. security analyst Paul Nitze issues the secret National Security Council report 68 (NSC-68), calling for a dramatic buildup of U.S. military forces to combat the Soviet threat.

June 25, 1950 North Korea launches its armed forces against South Korea in an attempt to reunify Korea, leading to the three-year Korean War.

October 24, 1950 U.S. forces push the North Korean army back to the border with China, sparking a Chinese invasion one week later and forcing the United States into a hasty retreat.

April 11, 1951 U.S. president Harry S. Truman fires General Douglas MacArthur, the U.S. military commander in Korea, for publicly attacking the president's war strategy.

April 19, 1951 General Douglas MacArthur delivers his "Old Soldiers Never Die; They Just Fade Away" speech to a joint session of Congress, following his dismissal from his Korean War command by U.S. president Harry S. Truman.

June 21, 1951 The Korean War reaches a military stalemate at the original boundary between North and South Korea.

September 1, 1951 The United States, Australia, and New Zealand sign the ANZUS treaty, creating a military al-

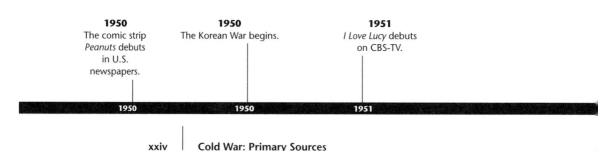

1950
The comic strip *Peanuts* debuts in U.S. newspapers.

1950
The Korean War begins.

1951
I Love Lucy debuts on CBS-TV.

1950   1950   1951

liance to contain communism in the Southwest Pacific region.

October 25, 1951 Winston Churchill wins reelection as British prime minister over Clement R. Attlee.

July 23, 1952 Former U.S. first lady Eleanor Roosevelt addresses the Democratic National Convention in Chicago, Illinois, on the importance of the United Nations.

October 3, 1952 Great Britain conducts its first atomic weapons test.

November 1, 1952 The United States tests the hydrogen bomb on the Marshall Islands in the Pacific Ocean.

November 4, 1952 Former military general Dwight D. Eisenhower is elected U.S. president.

March 5, 1953 After leading the Soviet Union for thirty years, Joseph Stalin dies of a stroke; Georgy Malenkov becomes the new Soviet leader.

April 16, 1953 U.S. president Dwight D. Eisenhower delivers his "Chance for Peace" address to the American Society of Newspaper Editors.

June 27, 1953 An armistice is signed, bringing a cease-fire to the Korean War.

August 12, 1953 The Soviet Union announces its first hydrogen bomb test.

December 8, 1953 U.S. president Dwight D. Eisenhower addresses the General Assembly of the United Nations on "Peaceful Uses of Atomic Energy."

May 7, 1954 The communist Viet Minh forces of Ho Chi Minh capture French forces at Dien Bien Phu, leading

1951
CBS offers the first color television broadcast.

1952
NBC-TV's *The Today Show* debuts.

1953
Lung cancer is attributed to cigarette smoking.

1951　　　　1952　　　　1953

to a partition of Vietnam and independence for North Vietnam under Ho's leadership.

September 8, 1954 The Southeast Asia Treaty Organization (SEATO) is formed.

December 2, 1954 The U.S. Senate votes to censure U.S. senator Joseph R. McCarthy of Wisconsin after his communist accusations proved to be unfounded.

February 8, 1955 Nikolai Bulganin replaces Georgy Malenkov as Soviet premier.

May 14, 1955 The Warsaw Pact, a military alliance of Soviet-controlled Eastern European nations, is established; the countries include Albania, Bulgaria, Czechoslovakia, East Germany, Hungary, Poland, and Romania.

November 22, 1955 Under the guidance of nuclear physicist Andrey Sakharov, the Soviets detonate their first true hydrogen bomb at the Semipalatinsk Test Site; Sakharov would be awarded several of the Soviet Union's highest honors.

February 24, 1956 Soviet leader Nikita Khrushchev gives his "Secret Speech," attacking the past brutal policies of the late Soviet leader Joseph Stalin.

October 31, 1956 British, French, and Israeli forces attack Egypt to regain control of the Suez Canal.

November 1, 1956 In Hungary, the Soviets crush an uprising against strict communist rule, killing many protestors.

March 7, 1957 The Eisenhower Doctrine, offering U.S. assistance to Middle East countries facing communist expansion threats, is approved by Congress.

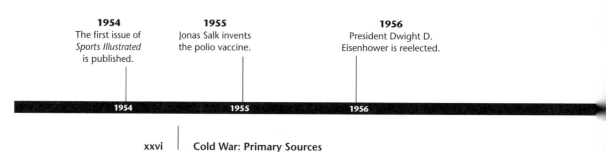

1954
The first issue of *Sports Illustrated* is published.

1955
Jonas Salk invents the polio vaccine.

1956
President Dwight D. Eisenhower is reelected.

1954   1955   1956

October 5, 1957 Shocking the world with their new technology, the Soviets launch into space *Sputnik,* the first man-made satellite.

1958 FBI director J. Edgar Hoover (1895–1972) writes *Masters of Deceit,* a book that educates the public about the threat of communism within the United States.

March 27, 1958 Nikita Khrushchev replaces Nikolai Bulganin as Soviet premier while remaining head of the Soviet Communist Party.

November 10, 1958 Soviet leader Nikita Khrushchev issues an ultimatum to the West to pull out of Berlin, but later backs down.

January 2, 1959 Revolutionary Fidel Castro assumes leadership of the Cuban government after toppling pro-U.S. dictator Fulgencio Batista y Zaldivar.

September 17, 1959 Soviet leader Nikita Khrushchev arrives in the United States to tour the country and meet with U.S. president Dwight D. Eisenhower.

September 28, 1959 Soviet leader Nikita Khrushchev delivers his "Peace and Progress Must Triumph in Our Time" speech to a Moscow audience upon returning from his trip to the United States.

May 1, 1960 The Soviets shoot down a U.S. spy plane over Russia piloted by Francis Gary Powers, leading to the cancellation of a planned summit meeting in Paris between Soviet leader Nikita Khrushchev and U.S. president Dwight D. Eisenhower.

November 8, 1960 U.S. senator John F. Kennedy of Massachusetts defeats Vice President Richard M. Nixon in the presidential election.

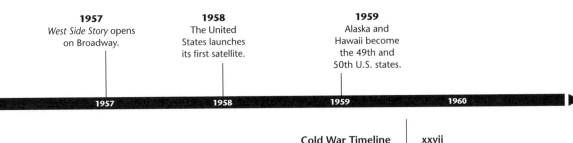

1957
West Side Story opens on Broadway.

1958
The United States launches its first satellite.

1959
Alaska and Hawaii become the 49th and 50th U.S. states.

1957   1958   1959   1960

March 1, 1961 U.S. president John F. Kennedy establishes the Peace Corps.

April 15, 1961 A U.S.-supported army of Cuban exiles launches an ill-fated invasion of Cuba, leading to U.S. humiliation in the world.

June 3, 1961 U.S. president John F. Kennedy meets with Soviet leader Nikita Khrushchev at a Vienna summit meeting to discuss the arms race and Berlin; Kennedy comes away shaken by Khrushchev's belligerence.

July 25, 1961 U.S. president John F. Kennedy speaks to the American people on the Berlin Crisis.

August 4, 1961 Soviet leader Nikita Khrushchev makes his "Secret Speech on the Berlin Crisis" speech, in response to U.S. president John F. Kennedy's July 25 address.

August 15, 1961 Under orders from Soviet leader Nikita Khrushchev, the Berlin Wall is constructed, stopping the flight of refugees from East Germany to West Berlin.

October 1962 The Cuban Missile Crisis occurs as the United States demands the Soviets remove nuclear missiles from Cuba.

October 22, 1962 U.S. president John F. Kennedy addresses the American people on the presence of Soviet nuclear arms in Cuba.

October 28, 1962 Soviet leader Nikita Khrushchev issues the "Communiqué to President Kennedy Accepting an End to the Missile Crisis."

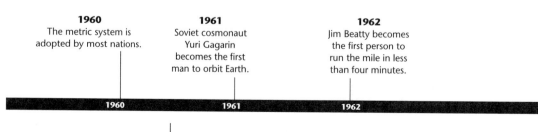

1960
The metric system is adopted by most nations.

1961
Soviet cosmonaut Yuri Gagarin becomes the first man to orbit Earth.

1962
Jim Beatty becomes the first person to run the mile in less than four minutes.

1960   1961   1962

January 1, 1963 Chinese communist leaders Mao Zedong and Zhou Enlai denounce Soviet leader Nikita Khrushchev's policies of peaceful coexistence with the West; the Soviets respond by denouncing the Chinese Communist Party.

June 26, 1963 U.S. president John F. Kennedy makes his famous proclamation of U.S. friendship with West Berliners in his "Remarks in the Rudolph Wild Platz, Berlin" speech.

August 5, 1963 The first arms control agreement, the Limited Test Ban Treaty, banning above-ground nuclear testing, is reached between the United States, Soviet Union, and Great Britain.

November 22, 1963 U.S. president John F. Kennedy is assassinated in Dallas, Texas, leaving Vice President Lyndon B. Johnson as the new U.S. president.

August 7, 1964 U.S. Congress passes the Gulf of Tonkin Resolution, authorizing U.S. president Lyndon B. Johnson to conduct whatever military operations he thinks appropriate in Southeast Asia.

October 15, 1964 Soviet leader Nikita Khrushchev is removed from Soviet leadership and replaced by Leonid Brezhnev as leader of the Soviet Communist Party and Aleksey Kosygin as Soviet premier.

October 16, 1964 China conducts its first nuclear weapons test.

November 3, 1964 Lyndon B. Johnson is elected U.S. president.

March 8, 1965 U.S. president Lyndon B. Johnson sends the first U.S. ground combat units to South Vietnam.

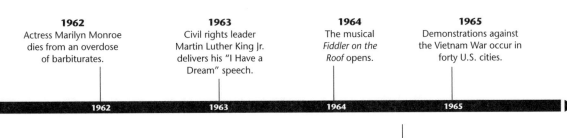

1962
Actress Marilyn Monroe dies from an overdose of barbiturates.

1963
Civil rights leader Martin Luther King Jr. delivers his "I Have a Dream" speech.

1964
The musical *Fiddler on the Roof* opens.

1965
Demonstrations against the Vietnam War occur in forty U.S. cities.

1962   1963   1964   1965

June 23, 1967 U.S. president Lyndon B. Johnson and Soviet premier Aleksey Kosygin meet in Glassboro, New Jersey, to discuss a peace settlement to the Vietnam War.

January 31, 1968 Communist forces inspired by the leadership of the ailing Ho Chi Minh launch the massive Tet Offensive against the U.S. and South Vietnamese armies, marking a turning point as American public opinion shifts in opposition to the Vietnam War.

July 15, 1968 Soviet leader Leonid Brezhnev announces the Brezhnev Doctrine, which allows for the use of force where necessary to ensure the maintenance of communist governments in Eastern European nations.

August 20, 1968 The Warsaw Pact forces a crackdown on a Czechoslovakia reform movement known as the "Prague Spring."

August 27, 1968 Antiwar riots rage in Chicago's streets outside the Democratic National Convention.

November 5, 1968 Richard M. Nixon defeats Vice President Hubert Humphrey in the U.S. presidential election.

1969 *Thirteen Days: A Memoir of the Cuban Missile Crisis,* by the late U.S. attorney general Robert F. Kennedy, is published.

March 18, 1969 The United States begins secret bombing of Cambodia to destroy North Vietnamese supply lines.

July 20, 1969 The United States lands the first men on the moon.

July 25, 1969 U.S. president Richard M. Nixon announces the Nixon Doctrine at a news conference in Guam,

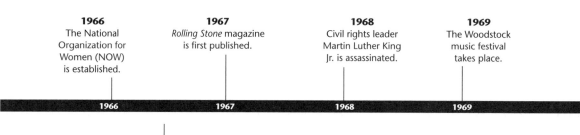

1966	**1967**	**1968**	**1969**
The National Organization for Women (NOW) is established.	*Rolling Stone* magazine is first published.	Civil rights leader Martin Luther King Jr. is assassinated.	The Woodstock music festival takes place.
1966	1967	1968	1969

stressing that the United States should be actively involved in Asia but not be the world's policeman and attempt to stifle any communist uprising.

October 15, 1969 Former West Berlin mayor Willy Brandt is elected chancellor of West Germany.

April 16, 1970 Strategic arms limitation talks, SALT, begin.

April 30, 1970 U.S. president Richard M. Nixon announces an invasion by U.S. forces of Cambodia to destroy North Vietnamese supply camps.

May 4, 1970 Four students are killed at Kent State University as Ohio National Guardsmen open fire on antiwar demonstrators.

October 25, 1971 The People's Republic of China (PRC) is admitted to the United Nations as the Republic of China (ROC) is expelled.

February 20, 1972 U.S. president Richard M. Nixon makes an historic trip to the People's Republic of China to discuss renewing relations between the two countries.

February 28, 1972 Following his historic visit to communist China, U.S. president Richard M. Nixon makes his "Remarks at Andrews Air Force Base on Returning from the People's Republic of China."

May 26, 1972 U.S. president Richard M. Nixon travels to Moscow to meet with Soviet leader Leonid Brezhnev to reach an agreement on the strategic arms limitation treaty, SALT I.

January 27, 1973 After intensive bombing of North Vietnamese cities the previous month, the United States and North Vietnam sign a peace treaty, ending U.S. involvement in Vietnam.

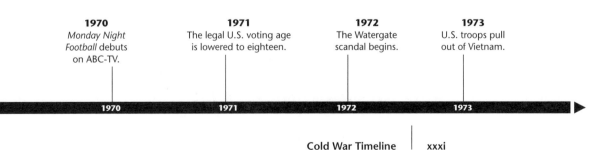

1970
Monday Night Football debuts on ABC-TV.

1971
The legal U.S. voting age is lowered to eighteen.

1972
The Watergate scandal begins.

1973
U.S. troops pull out of Vietnam.

1970   1971   1972   1973

June 27, 1973 Soviet leader Leonid Brezhnev journeys to Washington, D.C., to meet with U.S. president Richard M. Nixon to pursue détente.

June 27, 1974 U.S. president Richard M. Nixon travels to Moscow for another summit conference with Soviet leader Leonid Brezhnev.

August 9, 1974 Under threats of impeachment due to a political scandal, U.S. president Richard M. Nixon resigns as U.S. president and is replaced by Vice President Gerald R. Ford.

November 23, 1974 U.S. president Gerald R. Ford and Soviet leader Leonid Brezhnev meet in the Soviet city of Vladivostok.

April 30, 1975 In renewed fighting, North Vietnam captures South Vietnam and reunites the country.

August 1, 1975 Numerous nations sign the Helsinki Accords at the end of the Conference on Security and Cooperation in Europe.

November 2, 1976 Former Georgia governor Jimmy Carter defeats incumbent U.S. president Gerald R. Ford in the presidential election.

June 16, 1977 Soviet leader Leonid Brezhnev is elected president of the Soviet Union in addition to leader of the Soviet Communist Party.

December 25, 1977 Israeli prime minister Menachim Begin and Egyptian president Anwar Sadat begin peace negotiations in Egypt.

September 17, 1978 Israeli prime minister Menachim Begin and Egyptian president Anwar Sadat, meeting with

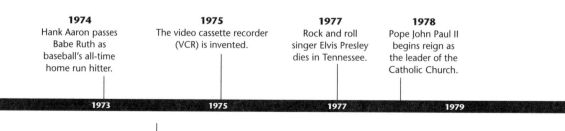

1974 Hank Aaron passes Babe Ruth as baseball's all-time home run hitter.

1975 The video cassette recorder (VCR) is invented.

1977 Rock and roll singer Elvis Presley dies in Tennessee.

1978 Pope John Paul II begins reign as the leader of the Catholic Church.

1973   1975   1977   1979

U.S. president Jimmy Carter at Camp David, reach an historic peace settlement between Israel and Egypt.

January 1, 1979 The United States and the People's Republic of China (PRC) establish diplomatic relations.

January 16, 1979 The shah of Iran is overthrown as the leader of Iran and is replaced by Islamic leader Ayatollah Ruhollah Khomeini.

June 18, 1979 U.S. president Jimmy Carter and Soviet leader Leonid Brezhnev sign the SALT II strategic arms limitation agreement in Vienna, Austria.

July 19, 1979 Sandinista rebels seize power in Nicaragua with Daniel Ortega becoming the new leader.

November 4, 1979 Islamic militants seize the U.S. embassy in Tehran, Iran, taking U.S. staff hostage.

December 26, 1979 Soviet forces invade Afghanistan to prop up an unpopular pro-Soviet government, leading to a decade of bloody fighting.

April 24, 1980 An attempted military rescue of American hostages in Iran ends with eight U.S. soldiers dead.

August 14, 1980 The Solidarity labor union protests the prices of goods in Poland.

November 4, 1980 Former California governor Ronald Reagan is elected president of the United States.

January 20, 1981 Iran releases the U.S. hostages as Ronald Reagan is being sworn in as the new U.S. president.

November 12, 1982 Yuri Andropov becomes the new Soviet leader after the death of Leonid Brezhnev two days earlier.

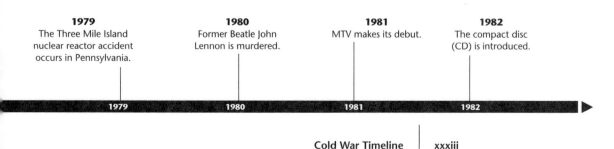

1979
The Three Mile Island nuclear reactor accident occurs in Pennsylvania.

1980
Former Beatle John Lennon is murdered.

1981
MTV makes its debut.

1982
The compact disc (CD) is introduced.

1979   1980   1981   1982

March 8, 1983 U.S. president Ronald Reagan calls the Soviet Union the "Evil Empire."

March 23, 1983 U.S. president Ronald Reagan announces the Strategic Defense Initiative (SDI).

September 1, 1983 A Soviet fighter shoots down Korean Airlines Flight 007 as it strays off-course over Soviet restricted airspace.

October 25, 1983 U.S. forces invade Grenada to end fighting between two pro-communist factions.

February 13, 1984 Konstantin Chernenko becomes the new Soviet leader after the death of Yuri Andropov four days earlier.

February 1985 The United States issues the Reagan Doctrine, which offers assistance to military dictatorships in defense against communist expansion.

March 11, 1985 Mikhail Gorbachev becomes the new Soviet leader after the death of Konstantin Chernenko the previous day.

October 11–12, 1986 Soviet leader Mikhail Gorbachev and U.S. president Ronald Reagan meet in Reykjavik, Iceland, and agree to seek the elimination of nuclear weapons.

October 13, 1986 U.S. president Ronald Reagan addresses the American public following his meeting with Soviet general secretary Mikhail Gorbachev in Iceland and describes historic nuclear arms reduction talks.

October 17, 1986 Congress approves aid to Contra rebels in Nicaragua.

November 3, 1986 The Iran-Contra affair is uncovered.

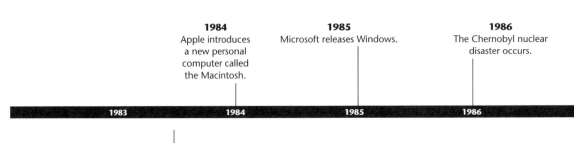

1984 Apple introduces a new personal computer called the Macintosh.

1985 Microsoft releases Windows.

1986 The Chernobyl nuclear disaster occurs.

1983   1984   1985   1986

December 8–10, 1987 U.S. president Ronald Reagan and Soviet leader Mikhail Gorbachev meet in Washington to sign the Intermediate Nuclear Forces Treaty (INF), removing thousands of missiles from Europe.

February 8, 1988 Soviet leader Mikhail Gorbachev announces the decision to begin withdrawing Soviet forces from Afghanistan.

May 29, 1988 U.S. president Ronald Reagan journeys to Moscow for a summit meeting with Soviet leader Mikhail Gorbachev.

November 8, 1988 U.S. vice president George Bush is elected president of the United States.

December 7, 1988 Soviet leader Mikhail Gorbachev addresses the United Nations General Assembly Session on major changes within the Soviet Union and foreign relations.

1989 In one nation after another in Eastern Europe, the communist leadership falls.

January 11, 1989 The Hungarian parliament adopts reforms granting greater personal freedoms to Hungarians, including allowing political parties and organizations.

January 18, 1989 The labor union Solidarity gains formal acceptance in Poland.

March 26, 1989 Open elections are held for the new Soviet Congress of People's Deputies, with the communists suffering major defeats; Boris Yeltsin wins the Moscow seat.

May 11, 1989 Soviet leader Mikhail Gorbachev announces major reductions of nuclear forces in Eastern Europe.

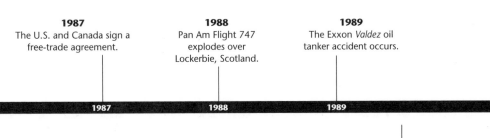

1987
The U.S. and Canada sign a free-trade agreement.

1988
Pan Am Flight 747 explodes over Lockerbie, Scotland.

1989
The Exxon *Valdez* oil tanker accident occurs.

1987   1988   1989

June 3–4, 1989 Chinese communist leaders order a military crackdown on pro-democracy demonstrations in Tiananmen Square, leading to many deaths.

June 4, 1989 The first Polish free elections lead to major victory by Solidarity.

October 7, 1989 The Hungarian communist party disbands.

October 23, 1989 Massive demonstrations begin against the East German communist government, involving hundreds of thousands of protesters and leading to the resignation of the East German leadership in early November.

November 10, 1989 East Germany begins dismantling the Berlin Wall; Bulgarian communist leadership resigns.

November 24, 1989 Czechoslovakia communist leaders resign.

December 1, 1989 Soviet leader Mikhail Gorbachev and U.S. president George Bush begin a three-day meeting on a ship in a Malta harbor to discuss rapid changes in Eastern Europe and the Soviet Union.

December 3, 1989 U.S. president George Bush and Soviet leader Mikhail Gorbachev make a joint statement on their discussions in the Malta Summit.

December 20, 1989 Lithuania votes for independence from the Soviet Union.

December 22, 1989 Romanian communist leader Nicolae Ceausescu is toppled and executed three days later.

March 1990 Lithuania declares independence from Moscow.

March 14, 1990 Mikhail Gorbachev is elected president of the Soviet Union.

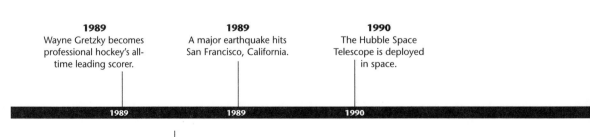

1989
Wayne Gretzky becomes professional hockey's all-time leading scorer.

1989
A major earthquake hits San Francisco, California.

1990
The Hubble Space Telescope is deployed in space.

1989   1989   1990

March 18, 1990 Open East German elections lead to a major defeat of Communist Party candidates.

May 29, 1990 Boris Yeltsin is elected president of the Russian republic.

May 30, 1990 Soviet leader Mikhail Gorbachev begins a summit meeting with U.S. president George Bush in Washington, D.C.

June 1990 Russia declares independence as the Russian Federation.

October 15, 1990 Soviet leader Mikhail Gorbachev is awarded the Nobel Peace Prize for his reforms that ended the Cold War.

November 14, 1990 Various nations sign the Charter of Paris for a New Europe, ending the economic and military division of Europe created by the Cold War.

July 1, 1991 The Warsaw Pact disbands.

August 19, 1991 Soviet communist hardliners attempt an unsuccessful coup of Soviet leader Mikhail Gorbachev, leading to the banning of the Communist Party in Russia and other Soviet republics.

August 20–September 9, 1991 The various Soviet republics declare their independence from the Soviet Union, including Estonia, Latvia, Lithuania, Ukraine, Belorussia, Moldovia, Azerbaijan, Uzbekistan, Kirgizia, and Tadzhikistan.

October 3, 1991 East and West Germany reunite as one nation.

December 8, 1991 Russia, Ukraine, and Belorussia create the Commonwealth of Independent States organization as an alliance replacing the Soviet Union.

1990
The animated sitcom *The Simpsons* debuts on the FOX network.

1991
The Persian Gulf War takes place.

1991
Clarence Thomas becomes a U.S. Supreme Court justice.

1990   1991   1991

December 25, 1991 Mikhail Gorbachev resigns as the Soviet president, and the Soviet Union ceases to exist.

January 28, 1992 In his State of the Union Address, U.S. president George Bush declares victory in the Cold War.

2000 Sergei Khrushchev, the son of the late Soviet leader Nikita Khrushchev, publishes *Nikita Khrushchev and the Creation of a Superpower.*

1992
Hurricane Andrew causes $15 billion in damage in Florida.

1997
Madeleine Albright becomes the first female U.S. secretary of state.

2001
Terrorists attack the World Trade Center and the Pentagon.

1992　　　　1997　　　　2001

Cold War
Primary Sources

Cold War Beginnings

The Cold War (1945–91), a war of differing systems of government, of mutual fear and distrust, did not begin like conventional wars, with guns blazing. The Cold War began on the heels of World War II (1939–45), and the principal opponents were the United States and the Soviet Union. The United States, with its democratic government and capitalist economy, operated very differently from the communist Soviet Union.

A democratic form of government consists of leaders elected directly by the general population. The candidates for election are supported by various political parties. Capitalism is an economic system based on competition in the marketplace. Prices, production, and distribution of goods are determined by the marketplace. Property and businesses are privately owned. Citizens enjoy many personal liberties, such as the freedom to worship as they choose.

Communism is a system of government in which a single party, the Communist Party, controls all aspects of society. Leaders are selected by the party. The party leaders centrally plan and control the economy. The communist system eliminates all private ownership of property. In theory, goods produced and wealth accumulated are shared equally by all. Religious practices are not tolerated under communism.

Communism came to Russia in 1917. Communism was based on the theories of Karl Marx (1818–1883), considered the founder of the revolutionary communist thought known as Marxism. A rising communist political party known as the Bolsheviks overthrew the Russian royalty, or the tsar, in the Bolshevik Revolution known as the October Revolution of 1917. Vladimir I. Lenin (1870–1924), who had founded the Communist Party, was the first communist dictator of Russia and served until his death in 1924.

Russia had no geographic buffer such as an ocean to protect it from the invading armies that generally came from countries to the west. Throughout history these invasions caused Russia to seek security from future threats. Joseph Stalin (1879–1953), a Bolshevik who became head of the Soviet communist state in 1929, was eager to expand the communist philosophy and extend its way of life to neighboring countries. But countries to the west were largely capitalist nations. Stalin was rebuffed by various foreign leaders and excluded from international diplomacy. The United States did not establish formal diplomatic relations with the Soviets until 1933. Even then, by the end of the 1930s, many Americans viewed the ruthless suppression of political, economic, and religious freedoms by Stalin with great contempt.

The capitalist United States was geographically separated by two great oceans. Desiring to avoid involvement in another European war after a bitter experience in World War I (1914–18), the United States had isolated itself. Neither the Soviet Union nor the United States was a world power before World War II.

The end of World War II marked the collapse of the traditional European powers of Great Britain, France, and Germany. The United States and the Soviet Union, with their vastly different forms of government and economics, emerged as the two superpowers of the world. Their ideologies, or differing political and social philosophies, immediately began to clash and the Cold War commenced. The United States was suspicious of Soviet intentions and sought to expand free-market capitalism and democracy throughout

Europe. The Soviets desired a substantial geographic divider from democratic Western Europe and against expanding American influence in European affairs. The two set their differences on a global stage. The United States and the democratic Western European countries became collectively referred to as the "West" or "Western influence." The Soviet Union and the Eastern European nations under communist control became known collectively as the "East."

The Cold War dominated the two powers' foreign policies, domestic priorities, and military planning for roughly the next forty-six years, having an impact on practically every nation on Earth. Various dates and events between 1945 and 1947 are identified as significant to the Cold War's beginning. Excerpts from three of the earliest communiqués, or reports, and speeches follow. They helped set the tone for the Cold War.

The first excerpt is from a 1946 telegram from George Kennan (1904–) titled "The Chargé in the Soviet Union

([Kennan) to the Secretary of State," commonly known as the "Long Telegram." The telegram made clear to American officials the thinking of Soviets and predicted future policies based on this Soviet philosophy. This famous telegram affected American foreign policy for decades through the Cold War. It was the basis of the U.S. policy of containment, a key U.S. Cold War policy to restrict the territorial growth of communist rule.

The second excerpt is from Winston Churchill's (1874–1965) "The Sinews of Peace," commonly known as the "Iron Curtain Speech." It was delivered on March 5, 1946, before the faculty and students of Westminster College in Fulton, Missouri. Churchill warned Americans of a descending Soviet "Iron Curtain" over Central and Eastern Europe. Behind the Iron Curtain, Soviet-dominated communist governments ruled over closed societies. (Closed societies are those in which the ruling communist party in each country, such as Poland and Bulgaria, dictates the production levels of industry and determine what may and may not be printed; the population is shielded from outside social and political influence.) Churchill contended only strong, assertive positions by the United States and Western European nations could stop the spread of communism.

The third excerpt, the "Novikov Telegram," was written by the Soviet ambassador, Nikolai Novikov, in Washington, D.C. Sent to Moscow on September 27, 1946, the telegram attempts to explain U.S. foreign policy to Stalin and other Soviet officials, much as Kennan had done for U.S. officials with his "Long Telegram." Soviet communiqués such as this became publicly available only after the breakup of the Soviet Union in 1991. Such fascinating Soviet archival materials (stored public or historical documents) are available through the Cold War International History Project at the Woodrow Wilson Center for Scholars in Washington, D.C. (available at http://wwics.si.edu).

George F. Kennan

Excerpt from the "Long Telegram"

Reprinted from *Foreign Relations of the United States (FRUS) 1946, Volume VI Eastern Europe; "The Soviet Union,"* published in 1969

O n February 3, 1946, U.S. newspaper reports stunned the American people. They revealed that a Soviet spy ring had been sending secrets from the U.S. atomic bomb project, "The Manhattan Project," to Moscow. Furthermore, on February 9, the evening before elections to the Supreme Soviet (the Soviet legislative body), Soviet leader Joseph Stalin (1879–1953) delivered his threatening "Two Camps" speech. The speech reflected traditional Marxist thought that the Soviet Union would inevitably have to wage war on capitalism. Stalin contended that capitalism and communism were incompatible. Alarmed and taken aback, U.S. State Department officials turned to the U.S. Embassy in Moscow. They wanted clarification of the speech and an explanation of why Stalin would have made it. George F. Kennan (1904–), the Soviet expert in the embassy, responded with an eight-thousand-word telegram. Kennan's official position was Chargé d'Affaires, that of a diplomat who is literally "in charge of affairs."

Kennan first apologized for the length of the document but stated an "analysis of our international environment" can hardly be expressed "in a single, brief message."

"In summary, we have here a political force committed fanatically to the belief that with US it is desirable and necessary that the internal harmony of our society be disrupted, our traditional way of life be destroyed, the international authority of our state be broken, if Soviet power is to be secure."

To do so, Kennan explained, would be "oversimplification"; so he asked his readers to bear with him in the lengthy telegram (hence the name the "Long Telegram"). Step by step, Kennan led his readers through a "post-war Soviet outlook"; a history of Soviet thought and why it evolved as it did, embracing the teachings of communism by Karl Marx (1818–1883); and his practical predictions of where Soviet policy in regard to the United States was going next.

The first two excerpted paragraphs show Kennan taking readers back to the start of communism, or Marxism, in Russia. He explained why its teachings were so believable to the Russians, a "peaceful agricultural people" constantly buffeted through history by various invaders.

After Kennan's insightful comments on Russian thought, the excerpt skips to the last part of the telegram, "Practical Deductions from Standpoint of U.S. Policy." Kennan used some of his most startling language, saying the Soviets will not feel secure until "our [the United States] traditional way of life [is] destroyed." He recognized that they were a very powerful nation despite their war losses; however, if the United States and Western European powers stood firm, he believed the Russians would back down. Strongly stressing education of the American public as to understanding the "Russian situation," Kennan stated "there is nothing as dangerous or as terrifying as the unknown." He also emphasized practical help for war-torn Europe to rebuild their countries and their lives because if the United States did not the Russians surely would.

Things to remember while reading "The Long Telegram":

- During the 1920s and 1930s, neither the capitalist United States nor the communist Soviet Union was a world power. They emerged as world powers only after World War II (1939–45).

- The United States and the Soviet Union were allies during World War II, joined in their common effort to defeat Nazi Germany. The Soviets suffered mightily at the hands of the Nazis but ultimately prevailed. The Red Army and Stalin were praised in Europe and the United States. After the war, most Americans, and even many U.S. officials, thought of Russians as a brave, suffering people and certainly had not considered warring against them.

- Kennan understood Stalin and the Soviets probably better than any other American. In the telegram, he urgently tried to impart this understanding to U.S. officials.

Excerpt from the "Long Telegram"

SECRET

Moscow, February 22, 1946—9 P.M.

[Received February 22—3:52 P.M.]

Neurotic: Emotionally unstable.

Instinctive: Inborn pattern of thought.

Nomadic: Roaming.

Marxism: Theories of struggle between social classes in a society developed by German philosopher Karl Marx that formed the basis of communism.

Equilibrium of separate: A generally equal division of powers of government such as in the United States between executive, judicial, and legislative branches.

Insoluble: Impossible to resolve.

Complete power of disposition: Total control.

Nationalism: Strong loyalty to one's own nation.

Underground methods: Spying.

Hitlerite: Reference to Nazi leader Adolf Hitler.

Schematic: Planned systematically.

Adventuristic: Launch aggressively.

Impervious to logic of reason: Hard to negotiate with or talk to.

*At bottom of Kremlin's **neurotic** view of world affairs is traditional and **instinctive** Russian sense of insecurity. Originally, this was insecurity of a peaceful agricultural people trying to live on vast exposed plain in neighborhood of fierce **nomadic** peoples. To this was added, as Russia came into contact with economically advanced West, fear of more competent, more powerful, more highly organized societies in that area....*

*It was no coincidence that **Marxism**, which had smoldered ineffectively for half a century in Western Europe, caught hold and blazed for first time in Russia. Only in this land which had never known a friendly neighbor or indeed any tolerant **equilibrium of separate powers** either internal or international, could a doctrine thrive which viewed economic conflicts of society as **insoluble** by peaceful means....*

Part 5: [Practical Deductions from Standpoint of US Policy]

*In summary, we have here a political force committed fanatically to the belief that with US it is desirable and necessary that the internal harmony of our society be disrupted, our traditional way of life be destroyed, the international authority of our state be broken, if Soviet power is to be secure. This political force has **complete power of disposition** over energies of one of world's greatest peoples and resources of world's richest national territory, and is borne along by deep and powerful currents of Russian **nationalism**. In addition, it has an elaborate and far flung apparatus for exertion of its influence in other countries, an apparatus of amazing flexibility and versatility, managed by people whose experience and skill in **underground methods** are presumably without parallel in history.... This is admittedly not a pleasant picture. Problem of how to cope with this force in [is] undoubtedly greatest task our diplomacy has ever faced and probably greatest it will ever have to face.... It should be approached with same thoroughness and care as solution of major strategic problem in war, and if necessary, with no smaller outlay in planning effort. I cannot attempt to suggest all answers here. But I would like to record my conviction that problem is within our power to solve—and that without recourse to any general military conflict. And in support of this conviction there are certain observations of a more encouraging nature I should like to make:*

*(1) Soviet power, unlike that of **Hitlerite** Germany, is neither **schematic** nor **adventuristic**. It does not work by fixed plans. It does not take unnecessary risks. **Impervious to logic of reason**,*

Contrasting Viewpoints: United States Versus the Soviet Union

The "X" article, originally titled "The Sources of Soviet Conduct," was published in the quarterly journal *Foreign Affairs* in July 1947. The author was George F. Kennan. Since Kennan was still a member of the U.S. State Department, and at the time the department did not wish to display an overt, or open, anti-Soviet policy, the article's author was simply noted as "X." However, readers soon figured out that the author was Kennan, and so it became known as his "X" article or "Article X."

In Article X, Kennan repeated and expanded parts of the "Long Telegram." He used the term "containment"—not allowing communism to spread further—several times when speaking of how to deal with the Soviet Union, who by that time seemed intent on spreading communism throughout Europe and perhaps the whole world. Kennan wrote:

> It is clear that the main element of any United States policy toward the Soviet Union must be that of a long-term patient but firm and vigilant containment of Russian expansive tendencies.... Soviet pressure against the free institutions of the western world is something that can be contained by the adroit [skillful] and vigilant application of Counter-force.... Soviet society may well contain deficiencies which will eventually weaken its own potential. This would of itself warrant the United States entering with reasonable confidence upon a policy of firm containment, designed to confront the Russians with unalterable counter-force at every point where they show signs of encroaching upon the interests of a peaceful and stable world.

With the "X" article, the policy of containment was firmly established. In many interviews with Kennan through the following decades, he constantly said this policy was completely misinterpreted by U.S. officials and in his estimation led to the unnecessary buildup of nuclear arms. He explained this misunderstanding was his fault but said he intended a diplomatic containment only. Kennan explained that the support of Western European nations through the Marshall Plan was the kind of policy he had in mind to help contain the spread of communism. (The Marshall Plan was a massive U.S. plan to promote Europe's economic recovery from the war; it was made available to all nations, though communist countries rejected it.)

In 1946 and 1947, the Soviets were in a greatly weakened postwar state. Kennan knew they had no desire to enter into more military conflicts and could be stopped by firm diplomacy. He never dreamed he had to say this—he thought that was obvious to all. Unfortunately, his containment policy was viewed as calling for military counterforce. Kennan was never able to change that viewpoint.

*and it is highly sensitive to **logic** of force. For this reason it can easily withdraw—and usually does—when strong resistance is encountered at any point. Thus, if the **adversary** has sufficient force and makes clear his readiness to use it, he rarely has to do so. If situations are properly handled there need be no prestige-engaging showdowns.*

*(2) **Gauged against** Western World as a whole, Soviets are still by far the weaker force. Thus, their success will really depend on degree of cohesion, firmness and vigor which Western World can muster. And this is factor which it is within our power to influence....*

For these reasons I think we may approach calmly and with good heart problem of how to deal with Russia....

(1) Our first step must be to apprehend, and recognize for what it is, the nature of the movement with which we are dealing. We must study it with same courage, detachment, objectivity, and same determination not to be emotionally provoked or unseated by it, with which doctor studies unruly and unreasonable individual.

(2) We must see that our public is educated to realities of Russian situation. I cannot over-emphasize importance of this. Press cannot do this alone. It must be done mainly by Government, which is necessarily more experienced and better informed on practical problems involved. In this we need not be deterred by [ugliness?] of picture. I am convinced that there would be far less hysterical anti-Sovietism in our country today if realities of this situation were better understood by our people. There is nothing as dangerous or as terrifying as the unknown....

*(3) Much depends on health and vigor of our own society. World communism is like **malignant parasite** which feeds only on diseased tissue. This is point at which domestic and foreign policies meet. Every courageous and incisive measure to solve internal problems of our own society, to improve self-confidence, discipline, morale and community spirit of our own people, is a diplomatic victory over Moscow worth a thousand diplomatic notes and joint **communiqués**....*

(4) We must formulate and put forward for other nations a much more positive and constructive picture of sort of world we would like to see than we have put forward in past. It is not enough to urge people to develop political processes similar to our own. Many foreign peoples, in Europe at least, are tired and frightened by

Logic: Threat.

Adversary: Enemy, such as the United States from the Soviet perspective.

Gauged against: Compared to.

Malignant parasite: One body that feeds on another until the one being assaulted dies.

Communiqués: Written messages.

"Report on the International Situation to the Cominform"

On September 22, 1947, Andrei Zhdanov (1896–1948) issued a report to counteract the "X" article. Zhdanov, a member of the Politburo, the key policy-making body in the Soviet Communist Party, gave the report to the first gathering of Cominform. Cominform had been established by the Soviet Union to promote communism internationally, and members included communist leaders from Soviet-dominated Eastern European countries.

Zhdanov stated that the Soviet Union had "always honored ... [its] obligations." The United States believed it clearly had not: since its forces still occupied the countries of Eastern Europe, the Soviet Union had imposed communist rule and not allowed free elections. Nevertheless. the world was in two distinct camps and set for the Cold War, as explained by Zhdanov:

> A new alignment of political forces has arisen. The more the war recedes into the past, the more distinct becomes two major friends in postwar international policy, corresponding to the division of the political forces operating on the international arena into two major camps: the imperialist ... on the one hand, and the anti-imperialist ... on the other....

Zhdanov defined the imperialist countries as the United States, Great Britain, France, Belgium, Holland, Turkey, Greece, China, and "Near Eastern" and "South American" countries. Imperialism refers to one nation extending its rule over another, often by force.

Zhdanov continued:

> The cardinal purpose of the imperialist camp is to strengthen imperialism, to hatch a new imperialist war, to combat [communism] ... and to support reactionary ... regimes and movements everywhere.... Soviet foreign policy proceeds from the fact of the coexistence for a long period of the two systems—capitalism and socialism [communism]. From this it follows that cooperation between the U.S.S.R. [Soviet Union] and countries with other systems is possible, provided that the principle of reciprocity [a mutual exchange] is observed and that obligations once assumed are honored. Everyone knows that the U.S.S.R. has always honored the obligations it has assumed. The Soviet Union has demonstrated its will and desire for cooperation.

Obviously, from the radically differing viewpoints of "Article X" and the report to the Cominform, the United States and the Soviet Union sat in opposing camps.

experiences of past, and are less interested in abstract freedom than in security. They are seeking guidance rather than responsibilities. We should be better able than Russians to give them this. And unless we do, Russians certainly will.

(5) Finally we must have courage and self-confidence to cling to our own methods and conceptions of human society. After all, the

Experiences: Wars.

greatest danger that can befall us in coping with this problem of Soviet communism, is that we shall allow ourselves to become like those with whom we are coping.

KENNAN

What happened next ...

As soon as the senior officials of the State Department read the telegram, its importance was obvious. It was distributed through many government offices in Washington and reported in the press. The transmission confirmed the worries of some U.S. officials that the Soviets could not be trusted as friends: U.S. foreign policy would have to change immediately.

The first evidence of change came in a situation with Iran. Since 1941, both British and Soviet forces occupied Iran in the Middle East, keeping an eye on its vast oil reserves. Both had agreed to withdraw all troops by March 1946. The British troops left, but seemingly confirming Kennan's predictions, the Soviets decided to stay. Secretary of State James Byrnes (1879–1972) condemned Soviet actions and on February 28 made a speech confirming the new tough stance and confrontational approach of the United States in its foreign policy. The speech is considered by many historians as a declaration of the Cold War. He sent the USS *Missouri,* the world's most powerful warship, into position by Turkey as a warning and demanded Moscow pull back its troops from Iran. After only a few weeks, the Iranian crisis was over. Just as Kennan had predicted, when the Soviets were faced with force, they pulled back.

On March 5, Winston Churchill (1874–1965) delivered his famous "Iron Curtain Speech" (see next excerpt) in the state of Missouri with U.S. president Harry S. Truman (1884–1972; served 1945–53) at his side. Churchill warned the still-disbelieving Americans that indeed the Soviets were occupying large territories in Eastern Europe with no intention of leaving. Americans still wondered if Kennan and

Churchill could indeed be correct, and their fear of spreading communism increased greatly.

In July 1947, Kennan authored "The Sources of Soviet Conduct," which became known as the "X" article (see box). The "X" article restated some points of the "Long Telegram" and expanded others. The term "confrontational" that Secretary Byrnes had spoken of in 1946 turned with the "X" article's publication into a "policy of containment," or not allowing communism to spread and take over any more countries. The policy of containment essentially remained the basis of U.S. foreign policy throughout the Cold War.

Did you know ...

- During the 1930s and World War II, Kennan saw the United States appease the Soviets, making concession after concession to the Soviet government as the two countries cooperated to defeat Germany's Adolf Hitler

(1889–1945) and his Nazi army. Kennan was dismayed at his nation's lack of firmness with the Soviets and its eagerness to please Joseph Stalin.

• According to Kennan, his policy of containment had been misunderstood from the start. He had meant political or diplomatic containment, not military containment. In his view, the misunderstanding led to an unnecessary nuclear arms race.

• The Iran flare-up and resolution foreshadowed just how accurate Kennan's overall assessment of the Soviet viewpoint in the "Long Telegram" was. The Soviets would constantly test and push the United States until it stopped short, stood firm, and generally threatened military action. At that point, the Soviets would back down. In reality, neither the Soviets nor the United States wanted to start a superpower war. This pattern continued through much of the Cold War.

Consider the following ...

• Explain what Kennan meant by "there is nothing as dangerous or as terrifying as the unknown." In reality, few Americans studied or came to understand the Soviets as Kennan had hoped. Research and report on the resulting "Red Scare" that swept America between 1947 and 1954.

• Consider the first two paragraphs of the Kennan excerpt. If you had lived in an agricultural society that through history had been invaded by aggressive groups, where would your security level be? Do you think the Russian insecurities that directed their Cold War policies were justified? Why, for how long, and to what extent? If you do not think they were justified, why not?

For More Information

Books

Foreign Relations of the United States (FRUS) 1946, Volume VI, Eastern Europe; "The Soviet Union." Washington, DC: U.S. Government Printing Office, 1969.

Isaacson, Walter, and Evan Thomas. *The Wise Men: Six Friends and the World They Made: Acheson, Bohlen, Kennan, Harriman, Lovett, McCloy.* New York: Simon and Schuster, 1986.

Kennan, George F., and John Lukacs. *George F. Kennan and the Origins of Containment, 1944–1946: The Kennan-Lukacs Correspondence.* Columbia: University of Missouri Press, 1997.

Miscamble, Wilson D. *George F. Kennan and the Making of American Foreign Policy, 1947–1950.* Princeton, NJ: Princeton University Press, 1992.

Web Sites

"A CNN Perspectives Series. Episode 4: Berlin." *CNN Interactive.* http://www.CNN.com/SPECIALS/cold.war/episodes/04/documents/cominform.html (accessed on September 10, 2003).

Kennan Institute for Advanced Russian Studies. http://www.kennan.yar.ru/news/25anniv/gfk.htm (accessed on September 10, 2003).

Winston Churchill

Excerpt from the "Iron Curtain Speech" (also known as the "Sinews of Peace speech"), March 5, 1946

Reprinted from *'Iron Curtain' Speech Fifty Years Later,* **published in 1999**

"From Stettin in the Baltic to Trieste in the Adriatic, an iron curtain has descended across the Continent. Behind that line lie all the capitals of the ancient states of Central and Eastern Europe.... All these famous cities and the populations around them lie in ... the Soviet sphere, and all are subject ... to Soviet influence ... and ... [an] increasing measure of control from Moscow."

On March 5, 1946, wearing his top hat and cape and smoking a cigar, former British prime minister Winston Churchill (1874–1965) traveled with U.S. president Harry S. Truman (1884–1972; served 1945–53) to the American Midwest to Fulton, Missouri. In Fulton, he visited the campus of small Westminster College and delivered his famous "Iron Curtain Speech," also known as the "Sinews of Peace" speech.

Having led Great Britain through its dark days during World War II (1939–45), in July 1945, Churchill was defeated in a general election by British Labor Party candidate Clement Attlee (1883–1967). Attlee had proposed a planned economy and nationalization (in which the government takes ownership) of several British industries. The British approved of these proposals as a correct approach to rebuild Britain, and Churchill lost the election and found himself retired at seventy-one years of age. In his book *The Gathering Storm*, Churchill bluntly stated that having successfully brought Britain through World War II, he "was immediately dismissed by the British electorate from all further conduct of their affairs." Churchill could have become disheartened and

16

sullen, simply fading from view. However, Churchill's brilliant international insightfulness continued to influence the world. He immediately set about writing his massive five-volume history of World War II.

By early 1946, he was greatly troubled by the refusal of Soviet troops to leave the Eastern European countries they had occupied after driving out the German army. He saw Soviet influence beginning to control the people and governments of Eastern Europe. Churchill believed that only with the pulling together of the United States, Britain, and Western European nations could the Soviets be stopped from overrunning all of Europe. To warn the world, Churchill delivered his "Iron Curtain Speech."

First, Churchill greeted his audience. He told them the thoughts he would express in his speech were his alone and did not represent any official stance. In the 1940s, war and tyranny were the two most disturbing menaces in the world. (Tyranny means unrestrained, oppressive rule by a government over a people.) Churchill said that while the United States and Britain enjoyed liberties, other countries were suddenly being overwhelmed with tyranny. Eloquently, Churchill lamented, "From Stettin in the Baltic to Trieste in the Adriatic, an iron curtain has descended across the Continent [over Central and Eastern Europe]." The word iron brought to mind something that could not be penetrated. So a curtain of iron had closed and trapped millions behind it.

Former British prime minister Winston Churchill, author of the "Iron Curtain Speech."

Things to remember while reading the excerpt from the "Iron Curtain Speech":

- By early 1945, European leaders, rather than praising the Soviet army and Soviet leader Joseph Stalin (1879–1953) for their hard-won victories against Nazi Germany in World War II, were feeling increasingly threatened by the growing Soviet presence in Eastern Europe.

- The Soviets so far had failed to hold free elections in Eastern European countries they had freed from Nazi Germany's control. Yet at the Yalta Conference in February 1945, Stalin had agreed with U.S. president Franklin D. Roosevelt (1882–1945; served 1933–45) and Britain's Churchill to allow the elections so that the countries could establish new governments.

- The "Iron Curtain Speech" was delivered only a couple of weeks after George F. Kennan (1904–) had startled Washington officials with the "Long Telegram." Kennan's telegram stated that the United States had best wake up and confront the Soviets from a position of power.

Excerpt from the "Iron Curtain Speech"

President McCluer, ladies and gentlemen, and last, but certainly not least, President of the United States of America,

I am very glad, indeed, to come to Westminster College this afternoon....

It is also an honour, ladies and gentlemen, perhaps almost unique, for a private visitor to be introduced to an academic audience by the President of the United States. Amid his heavy burdens, duties, and responsibilities ... the President has traveled a thousand miles to dignify and magnify our meeting here to-day and to give me an opportunity of addressing this kindred nation, as well as my own countrymen across the ocean, and perhaps some other countries too. The President has told you that it is his wish, as I am sure it is yours, that I should have full liberty to give my true and faithful counsel in these anxious and baffling times. I shall certainly avail myself of this freedom, and feel the more right to do so because any private ambitions I may have cherished in my younger days have been satisfied beyond my wildest dreams. Let me, however, make it clear that I have no official mission or status of any kind. I speak only for myself. There is nothing here but what you see.

President McCluer: Franc L. McCluer, president of Westminster College.

I can therefore allow my mind, with the experience of a lifetime, to play over the problems which beset us on the morrow of our absolute victory in arms, and to try to make sure with what strength I have what has been gained with so much sacrifice and suffering shall be preserved for the future glory and safety of mankind.

*Ladies and gentlemen, the United States stands at this time at the **pinnacle** of world power. It is a solemn moment for the American democracy. For with primacy in power is also joined an awe-inspiring accountability to the future....*

A shadow has fallen upon the scenes so lately lighted by the Allied victory. Nobody knows what Soviet Russia and its Communist international organization [Comintern] *intends to do in the immediate future, or what are the limits, if any, to their expansive and **proselytizing** tendencies. I have a strong admiration and regard for the valiant Russian people and for my wartime comrade, Marshal Stalin. There is deep sympathy and goodwill in Britain— and I doubt not here also—towards the people of all the Russians*

Soviet leader Joseph Stalin, U.S. president Franklin D. Roosevelt, and British prime minister Winston Churchill at the Tehran Conference, 1943.
Reproduced by permission of AP/Wide World Photos.

Pinnacle: Highest point.

Proselytizing: Attempts to convert another to one's own beliefs.

and a resolve to persevere through many differences and rebuffs in establishing lasting friendships. We understand the Russian need to be secure on her western frontiers by the removal of all possibility of German aggression. We welcome Russia to her rightful place among the leading nations of the world. We welcome her flag upon the seas. Above all, we welcome, or should welcome, constant, frequent and growing contacts between the Russian people and our own peoples on both sides of the Atlantic. It is my duty however, for I am sure you would wish me to state the facts as I see them to you, to place before you certain facts about the present position in Europe.

From Stettin [a Polish port city on the Baltic Sea] *in the Baltic to Trieste* [a city at the northeasternmost point of the Adriatic Sea] *in the Adriatic, an iron curtain has descended across the Continent. Behind that line lie all the capitals of the ancient states of Central and Eastern Europe. Warsaw, Berlin, Prague, Vienna, Budapest, Belgrade, Bucharest and Sofia, all these famous cities and the populations around them lie in what I must call the* **Soviet sphere**, *and all are subject in one form or another, not only to Soviet influence but to a very high and, in some cases, increasing measure of control from Moscow. Athens alone—Greece with its ... glories—is free to decide its future at an election under British, American and French observation. The Russian-dominated Polish Government has been encouraged to make enormous and wrongful inroads upon Germany* [move the Polish western boundary into Germany], *and mass* **expulsions** *of millions of Germans on a scale grievous and undreamed-of are now taking place. The Communist parties, which were very small in all these Eastern States of Europe, have been raised to* **pre-eminence** *and power far beyond their numbers and are seeking everywhere to obtain* **totalitarian** *control. Police governments are prevailing in nearly every case, and so far, except in Czechoslovakia, there is no true democracy....*

I have, however, felt bound to portray the shadow which, alike in the west and in the east, falls upon the world. I was a minister at the time of the **Versailles Treaty**.... *In those days there were high hopes and unbounded confidence that the wars were over and that the* **League of Nations** *would become all-powerful. I do not see or feel that same confidence or even the same hopes in the* **haggard** *world at the present time....*

From what I have seen of our Russian friends and Allies during the war, I am convinced that there is nothing they admire so much

Soviet sphere: Region of Soviet influence.

Expulsions: Forced removal from homes.

Pre-eminence: Prominence.

Totalitarian: Complete or total.

Versailles Treaty: Peace treaty that ended World War I.

League of Nations: An international organization formed after World War I to seek peaceful resolutions to international conflicts.

Haggard: Weary.

*as strength, and there is nothing for which they have less respect than for weakness, especially military weakness.... If the Western Democracies stand together in strict adherence to the principles of the United Nations Charter, their influence for furthering those principles will be immense and no one is likely to **molest** them. If, however, they become divided or falter in their duty and if these all-important years are allowed to slip away, then indeed catastrophe may overwhelm us all.*

Last time [in the 1930s as Hitler came to power in Germany] *I saw it all coming and I cried aloud to my own fellow-countrymen and to the world, but no one paid any attention. Up till the year 1933, or even 1935, Germany might have been saved from the awful fate which has overtaken her and we might all have been spared the miseries Hitler let loose upon mankind. There never was a war in history easier to prevent by timely action than the one which has just **desolated** such great areas of the globe. It could have been prevented in my belief without the firing of a single shot, and Germany might be powerful, prosperous and honored today; but no one would listen and one by one we were all sucked into the awful whirlpool. We surely, ladies and gentlemen: I put it to you, surely, we must not let that happen again. This can only be achieved by reaching now, in 1946— this year, 1946—by reaching a good understanding on all points with Russia under the general authority of the United Nations Organization, and by the maintenance of that good understanding through many peaceful years, by the world instrument, supported by the whole strength of the English-speaking world and all its connections. There is the solution which I respectfully offer to you in this Address to which I have given the title "The Sinews of Peace."*

*Let no man underrate the abiding power of the British Empire and Commonwealth. Because you see the 46 millions in our island harassed about their food supply, of which they only grow one half, even in wartime, or because we have difficulty in restarting our industries and export trade after six years of passionate war effort, do not suppose we shall not come through these dark years of **privation** as we have come through the glorious years of agony* [World War II], *do not suppose that half a century from now, you will not see 70 or 80 millions of Britons spread about the world, united in defence of our traditions and our way of life, and of the world causes which you and we **espouse**. If the population of the English-speaking Commonwealths be added to that of the United States, with all that such co-operation implies in the air, on the sea, all over the globe, and in science and in industry, and in moral force, there*

Molest: Hassle.

Desolated: Destroyed.

Privation: Lack of usual comforts or necessities.

Espouse: Embrace.

U.S. president Harry S. Truman, Soviet leader Joseph Stalin, and British prime minister Winston Churchill, meet at the Potsdam Conference in July 1945. *Reproduced by permission of the Harry S. Truman Library.*

Sedate: Calm.

Sober: Serious.

Arbitrary: Based purely on one's own decision.

will be no quivering, precarious balance of power to offer its temptation to ambition or adventure. On the contrary, there will be an overwhelming assurance of security. If we adhere faithfully to the Charter of the United Nations and walk forward in **sedate** and **sober** strength, seeking no one's land or treasure, seeking to lay no **arbitrary** control upon the thoughts of men, if all British moral and material forces and convictions are joined with your own in fraternal association, the highroads of the future will be clear, not only for us but for all, not only for our time, but for a century to come.

What happened next ...

Joseph Stalin denounced the "Iron Curtain Speech" as baseless. He said it only proved that hostility was building in Western Europe and the United States against the Soviets and communism. He charged Churchill with "warmongering," or stirring up emotions in favor of war. Nevertheless, with the "Long Telegram" and now the "Iron Curtain Speech" fresh in everyone's mind, the U.S. State Department applied exceedingly strong pressure on the Soviets to move their occupying troops out of oil-rich Iran in the Middle East. The Soviets responded by pulling out their troops by May in exchange for the U.S. promise to allow them access to Iranian oil. In actuality, that promise was never fulfilled. Iran was the first test of wills between the United States and the Soviet Union as the Cold War began.

Through the summer of 1946, the Soviet Union pulled back significantly from interaction with the West. Stalin halted efforts to secure a $1 billion loan from the United States, rejected Soviet membership in the World Bank and International Monetary Fund, and purged any pro-Western sympathizers from the Soviet government. In June 1946, the Soviets totally rejected a U.S. plan for international control of atomic energy.

During the summer, White House aides continually impressed upon President Truman the need to exhibit American strength before the Soviets and to not compromise or make any concessions. The White House now spoke of Stalin's ultimate goal as world domination. The U.S. anti-Soviet policy solidified. Truman said he was "tired of babying the Soviets." Even Truman's mother, in an infamous message, told her Harry it was time to get tough on the Soviets.

Did you know ...

- Churchill was a skilled, productive writer. His words captured readers' full attention. Likewise, when he rose to deliver a speech, audiences were riveted to every word.

- In the days immediately following Churchill's speech, most of the U.S. press considered the speech too extreme and reported on it in that perspective. The American public had not yet come to the conclusion that their wartime ally, the Soviet Union, posed any problems. Realizing this and ever mindful of public opinion, President Truman declined to comment on the speech to the press.

- The term "Iron Curtain" came into the general U.S. vocabulary. It was used extensively throughout the rest of the twentieth century to refer to the ruthless Soviet domination of Eastern Europe.

Consider the following …

- In the speech, whom did Churchill compare Stalin to in the pre–World War II days of the 1930s? What similarities caused him to make the comparison?
- What did Churchill predict the Western powers needed to do to stop Soviet aggression?
- Comparing Churchill's "Iron Curtain Speech" and George Kennan's "Long Telegram," look for similarities of how to halt the aggression between the Western and Eastern powers.

For More Information

Books

Bialer, Seweryn, and Michael Mandelbaum. *The Global Rivals*. New York: A. A. Knopf, 1988.

Edmonds, Robin. *The Big Three: Churchill, Roosevelt, and Stalin in Peace and War*. New York: Norton, 1991.

Harbutt, Fraser J. *The Iron Curtain: Churchill, America, and the Origins of the Cold War*. New York: Oxford University Press, 1986.

Keegan, John. *Winston Churchill*. New York: Viking, 2002.

Larnes, Klaus. *Churchill's Cold War: The Politics of Personal Diplomacy*. New Haven, CT: Yale University Press, 2002.

Muller, James W., ed. *'Iron Curtain' Speech Fifty Years Later*. Columbia: University of Missouri Press, 1999.

Nikolai V. Novikov

Excerpt from the "Novikov Telegram," September 27, 1946
Available at *Cold War International History Project* (Web site)

Nikolai V. Novikov, Soviet ambassador to Washington, D.C., wrote and sent the "Novikov Telegram" to Moscow on September 27, 1946. In the telegram, which, like the famous telegram of U.S. advisor George F. Kennan (1904–), was "long," Novikov analyzed U.S. foreign policy in much the same way Kennan analyzed Soviet foreign policy, his "Long Telegram."

Novikov declared that the United States was striving for "world supremacy." He suggested that because Europe was so devastated by World War II (1939–45), the United States would "infiltrate" countries with offers of aid to rebuild. This strategy, according to Novikov, fit with U.S. plans for world domination. More proof was found, he suggested, in the large U.S. peacetime military force and in the establishment of U.S. bases worldwide. Novikov mentioned the "Iron Curtain Speech" of former British prime minister Winston Churchill (1874–1965), noting that Churchill called for a strong British-U.S. military alliance. Novikov attributed America's new hard-line policy to a new U.S. president, Harry S. Truman (1884–1972; served 1945–53), who was less cooperative than

"Careful note should be taken of the fact that the preparation by the United States for a future is being conducted with the prospect of war against the Soviet Union, which in the eyes of the American imperialists is the main obstacle in the path of the United States to world domination."

his late predecessor, Franklin D. Roosevelt (1882–1945; served 1933–45). Novikov ended his telegram with the prediction that the United States was planning a Third World War that would be waged against the Soviet Union.

Things to remember while reading the "Novikov Telegram":

- When Novikov used the word democratic, he was actually referring to the communistic world. For example, his "strengthening of democratic tendencies" means strengthening of communist tendencies. It was a characteristic of postwar communism to refer to their "communistic" policies as "democratic" policies.

- Novikov believed that the policies of the United States were expansive and aiming for world domination.

- Novikov's analysis was written approximately six months after Kennan's "Long Telegram" and Churchill's "Iron Curtain Speech." Both called for a tough stance against the Soviet Union. The United States had adopted such a position by the time of Novikov's telegram.

Excerpt from the "Novikov Telegram"

*The foreign policy of the United States, which reflects the **imperialist** tendencies ... is characterized in the postwar period by a striving for world supremacy. This is the real meaning of the many statements by President [Harry] Truman and other representatives of American ruling circles: that the United States has the right to lead the world. All the forces of American diplomacy—the army, the air force, the navy, industry, and science—are enlisted in the service of this foreign policy. For this purpose broad plans for expansion have been developed and are being implemented through diplomacy and the establishment of a system of naval and air bases stretching far beyond the boundaries of the United States, through the arms race, and through the creation of ever newer types of weapons....*

Imperialist: Extending the rule of one nation over another.

*Europe has come out of the war with a completely **dislocated** economy, and the economic devastation that occurred in the course of the war cannot be overcome in a short time. All of the countries of Europe and Asia are experiencing a colossal need for consumer goods, industrial and transportation equipment, etc. Such a situation provides American **monopolistic capital** with prospects for enormous shipments of goods and the importation of capital into these countries—a circumstance that would permit it to **infiltrate** their national economies.*

Such a development would mean a serious strengthening of the economic position of the United States in the whole world and would be a stage on the road to world domination by the United States.

On the other hand, we have seen a failure of calculations on the part of U.S. circles which assumed that the Soviet Union would be destroyed in the war or would come out of it so weakened that it would be forced to go begging to the United States for economic assistance. Had that happened, they would have been able to dictate conditions

Soviet diplomats Nikolai Novikov, Andrei Vishinsky, and Vyacheslav Molotov. *Reproduced by permission of the Corbis Corporation.*

Dislocated: Functioning unsatisfactorily.

Monopolistic capital: The only nation with money to invest.

Infiltrate: Take over parts of.

permitting the United States to carry out its expansion in Europe and Asia without hindrance from the USSR [the Soviet Union].

*In actuality, despite all of the economic difficulties of the post-war period connected with the enormous losses inflicted by the war and the German **fascist** occupation, the Soviet Union continues to remain economically independent of the outside world and is rebuilding its national economy with its own forces....*

*The enormous relative weight of the USSR in international affairs in general and in the European countries in particular, the independence of its foreign policy, and the economic and political assistance that it provides to neighboring countries, both allies and former enemies, has led to the growth of the political influence of the Soviet Union in these countries and to the further strengthening of **democratic** tendencies in them.*

Such a situation in Eastern and Southeastern Europe cannot help but be regarded by the American imperialists as an obstacle in the path of the expansionist policy of the United States.

The foreign policy of the United States is not determined at present by the circles in the Democratic party that (as was the case during [Franklin] *Roosevelt's lifetime) strive to strengthen the cooperation of the three great powers that constituted the basis of the **anti-Hitler coalition** during the war. The **ascendance** to power of President Truman, a politically unstable person but with certain conservative tendencies, and the subsequent appointment of* [James] *Byrnes as Secretary of State meant a strengthening of the influence on U.S. foreign policy of the most **reactionary** circles of the Democratic party....*

Obvious indications of the U.S. effort to establish world dominance are also to be found in the increase in military potential in peacetime and in the establishment of a large number of naval and air bases both in the United States and beyond its borders....

All of these facts show clearly that a decisive role in the realization of plans for world dominance by the United States is played by its armed forces....

The ruling circles of the United States obviously have a sympathetic attitude toward the idea of a military alliance with England, but at the present time the matter has not yet culminated in an official alliance. [Winston] *Churchill's speech in Fulton calling for the conclusion of an Anglo-American military alliance for the purpose of*

Fascist: Dictatorial.

Democratic: In this context, communistic.

Anti-Hitler coalition: The combination of nations opposing Nazi Germany led by Adolf Hitler.

Ascendance: Rise.

Reactionary: Desire to go back to previous conditions.

establishing joint domination over the world was therefore not sup-ported officially by Truman or Byrnes, although Truman by his pres-ence [during the "Iron Curtain Speech"] did indirectly sanction Churchill's appeal.

Even if the United States does not go so far as to conclude a military alliance with England just now, in practice they still main-tain very close contact on military questions....

*The numerous and extremely hostile statements by American government, political, and military figures with regard to the Soviet Union and its foreign policy are very characteristic of the current re-lationship between the ruling circles of the United States and the USSR. These statements are echoed in an even more unrestrained tone by the overwhelming majority of the American **press organs.** Talk about a "third war," meaning a war against the Soviet Union, even a direct call for this war—with the threat of using the atomic bomb—such is the content of the statements on relations with the Soviet Union by reactionaries at public meetings and in the press....*

*The basic goal of this anti-Soviet campaign of American "public opinion" is to exert political pressure on the Soviet Union and com-pel it to make concessions. Another, no less important goal of the campaign is the attempt to create an atmosphere of **war psychosis** among the masses, who are weary of war, thus making it easier for the U.S. government to carry out measures for the maintenance of high military potential. It was in this very atmosphere that the law on universal military service in peacetime was passed by congress, that the huge military budget was adopted, and that plans are being worked out for the construction of an extensive system of naval and air bases.*

*Of course, all of these measures for maintaining a highly mili-tary potential are not goals in themselves. They are only intended to prepare the conditions for winning world supremacy in a new war, the date for which, to be sure, cannot be determined now by anyone, but which is contemplated by the most **bellicose** circles of American imperialism.*

Careful note should be taken of the fact that the preparation by the United States for a future is being conducted with the prospect of war against the Soviet Union, which in the eyes of the American imperialists is the main obstacle in the path of the United States to world domination. This is indicated by facts such as the tactical training of the American army for war with the Soviet Union as the

Press organs: Media.

War psychosis: Fear of more war.

Bellicose: Hostile.

future opponent, the siting of American strategic bases in regions from which it is possible to launch strikes on Soviet territory, intensified training and strengthening of Arctic regions as close approaches to the USSR, and attempts to prepare Germany and Japan to use those countries in a war against the USSR.

What happened next …

The "Novikov Telegram" was studied carefully by Stalin and other leaders in the Soviet Communist Party. Adding credibility to the telegram's messages was the U.S. establishment of the Truman Doctrine and the Marshall Plan in 1947. The Truman Doctrine promised to help any country fighting the establishment of communism in their lands. The Marshall Plan was devised to aid any European country with their rebuilding effort. Stalin forbade any Eastern European country behind the "Iron Curtain" to take advantage of Marshall Plan aid.

Did you know …

- Novikov concluded that President Truman was not open to cooperation with the Soviet Union and was intolerant of individuals within his closest government circles not totally supportive of his anti-Soviet perspective. This proved correct when Truman fired Secretary of Commerce Henry A. Wallace (1888–1965) on September 20, 1946, because he opposed the get-tough policy.

- Many documents such as the "Novikov Telegram" began to be released from Soviet document archives only after the 1991 breakup of the Soviet Union. Until then, there were virtually no documents that looked at the Cold War from the Soviet point of view.

Consider the following …

- According to Novikov, how could the U.S. economy benefit from postwar economic devastation in Europe? Has this same pattern occurred in more recent times, such as in the 1990s and early 2000s?

- List the reasons that led Novikov to his conclusion that the United States was aiming for world supremacy.

- What role in the Cold War did Novikov attribute to the "press organs"? What were the chief "press organs" in the mid-1940s?

- Go to the Cold War International History Project at http://wwics.si.edu to learn more about the latest Soviet documents released and translated into English for Americans to study.

For More Information

Books

Antonov-Ovseyenko, Anton. *The Time of Stalin: Portrait of a Tyranny.* New York: Harper & Row Publishers, 1980.

Crockatt, Richard. *The Fifty Years War: The United States and the Soviet Union in World Politics, 1941–1991.* London: Routledge, 1995.

Lewis, Jonathan, and Phillip Whitehead. *Stalin: A Time for Judgement.* New York: Pantheon Books, 1990.

Paterson, Thomas G. *On Every Front: The Making of the Cold War.* New York: Norton, 1979.

Ulam, Adam B. *Stalin: The Man and His Era.* New York: The Viking Press, 1973.

Web site:

Cold War International History Project. http://wwics.si.edu/index.cfm?fuseaction=topics.home&topic_id=1409 (accessed on September 22, 2003).

2 Confrontation Builds

A clear announcement of a new U.S. policy toward the Soviets came in early 1947, triggered by events in the eastern Mediterranean. In Greece, civil war raged between communist-backed resistance fighters and forces from Great Britain that were attempting to support British influence in Greece. Turkey had also been under British influence during World War II (1939–45) and in need of the British aid offered. On February 21, 1947, the British, greatly weakened by the expenses of World War II, announced in a message from London to Washington they could no longer send military and economic aid to Greece or Turkey. The British revealed that they would leave Greece and Turkey in six weeks, and they hoped the United States would assume responsibility for aid to the two countries.

U.S. administrative officials, including Secretary of State George C. Marshall (1880–1959) and Under-secretary Dean Acheson (1893–1971), huddled with U.S. congressional leaders. Deciding that the United States must replace the British presence, on March 12, 1947, U.S. president Harry S. Truman (1884–1972; served 1945–53) addressed Congress.

The first excerpt in this chapter is from a "Special Message to the Congress on Greece and Turkey: The Truman Doctrine," published in the *Public Papers of the Presidents of the United States: Harry S. Truman, 1947*. The Truman Doctrine proposed to aid any country in the world where free peoples were threatened by the spread of communism.

Not only were the communists gaining toeholds in Greece and Turkey but also in France and Italy. The economies of France and Italy were still suffering from the disruptions caused by World War II. When Secretary Marshall visited Europe in April 1947, he was astonished at the conditions of poverty that he saw. On June 5, Marshall gave a speech at Harvard University in which he introduced a new massive plan of U.S. aid to help Europe's economic recovery. The second excerpt in this chapter is titled "Remarks by the Honorable George C. Marshall, Secretary of State, at Harvard University on June 5, 1947." This speech is published in the 1972 document *Foreign Relations of the United States (FRUS), Volume III, 1947: The British Commonwealth; Europe*. The proposed plan quickly became known as the Marshall Plan.

The third excerpt in this chapter is from the "Special Message to the Congress on the Threat to the Freedom of Europe, March 17, 1948." This message is published in *Public Papers of the Presidents of the United States: Harry S. Truman, January 1 to December 31, 1948*. The message was delivered to rally Congress to pass the Marshall Plan.

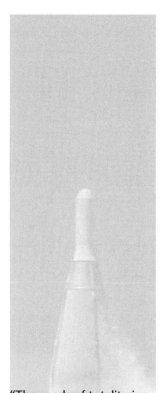

Harry S. Truman

Excerpt from "Special Message to the Congress on Greece and Turkey: The Truman Doctrine, March 12, 1947"

Published in *Public Papers of the Presidents of the United States: Harry S. Truman, 1947*, published in 1963

"The seeds of totalitarian regimes are nurtured by misery and want. They spread and grow in the evil soil of poverty and strife. They reach their full growth when the hope of a people for a better life has died. We must keep that hope alive."

With the British planning to pull out of Greece by March 31, 1947, both President Harry S. Truman (1884–1972; served 1945–53) and Secretary of State George C. Marshall (1880–1959) recognized the urgent need for the United States to step in and to aid the Greek government. Greece had been left destitute after World War II (1939–45). Its infrastructure (railroads, ports, highways, etc.) and economy were destroyed. The Greek government and small Greek army, without British support, would surely fall to the National Popular Liberation Army (ELAS) fighters. ELAS was dominated by communists promising the people a better life. ELAS had been fighting against the Greek army backed up by British troops since 1944. Although the United States assumed that Joseph Stalin (1879–1953) and the Soviets were supporting ELAS, they were not. Marshal Josip Tito (1892–1980), communist leader of Yugoslavia, was behind ELAS, sending supplies to them across Greece's northern border.

Turkey was also attempting to move away from the disruption of war and to rebuild a strong nation. Turkey had sought financial aid from both Great Britain and the United

States. With Great Britain halting all support, the United States would have to provide a great deal of additional aid. If no aid was kept up, communist rebels in Turkey might cause unrest and even overthrow the government.

The overwhelming fear of the United States and Western European nations was well described by U.S. undersecretary of state Dean Acheson (1893–1971). Quoted in media corporation CNN's 1998 book *Cold War: An Illustrated History, 1945–1991*, Acheson explained, "Like apples in a barrel infected by one rotten one, the corruption [communist takeover] of Greece would infect Iran to the east. It would also carry infection [communism] to Africa through Asia Minor and Egypt, and to Europe through Italy." At the time, the phrase "domino theory" or "domino effect" had not been coined. It would enter the American vocabulary a few years later. Acheson was saying that if one or two countries fell to the communists, such as Greece and Turkey, then all of Western Europe, the Middle East, and even Africa could fall

U.S. president Harry S. Truman, speaking before a joint session of Congress, March 12, 1947, urging aid for Greece and Turkey. *Reproduced by permission of AP/Wide World Photos.*

like dominos to the communists. Although the term had not yet been spoken, this domino idea would influence American thinking for decades.

On March 12, 1947, President Truman delivered a stirring address to a joint session of Congress. He explained the conditions in Greece and Turkey and warned that the people of weakened countries "have recently had totalitarian [Soviet-backed communist] regimes forced upon them against their will." He described the regimes as filled with "terror and oppression." Then Truman proposed the idea that dominated U.S. foreign policy for the next twenty-five years, the Truman Doctrine: "I believe that it must be the policy of the United States to support free peoples who are resisting attempted subjugation [control] by armed minorities [communist rebels] or by outside pressures [as the Soviet Union]." Truman asked for $400 million in aid for Greece and Turkey.

Things to remember while reading the excerpt from the Truman Doctrine:

- President Truman set up his speech to deliver a simple good-guy-versus-bad-guy scenario, freedom and democracy versus suppression under communism.

- People who were hungry and poor with little hope for a better tomorrow were particularly susceptible to communist influence.

- Joseph Stalin was constantly taking advantage of weakness in postwar countries to pressure for control by communist parties. He had been successful in most Eastern European nations except, at that time, for Czechoslovakia.

Excerpt from "Special Message to the Congress on Greece and Turkey: The Truman Doctrine, March 12, 1947"

Mr. President, Mr. Speaker, Members of the Congress of the United States:

The gravity of the situation which confronts the world today necessitates my appearance before a joint session of the Congress....

The United States has received from the Greek Government an urgent appeal for financial and economic assistance ... assistance is imperative if Greece is to survive as a free nation....

*When forces of liberation entered Greece they found that the retreating Germans had destroyed virtually all the railways, roads, port facilities, communications, and merchant marine. More than a thousand villages had been burned. Eighty-five percent of the children were **tubercular**. Livestock, poultry, and draft animals had almost disappeared. **Inflation** had wiped out practically all savings.*

As a result of these tragic conditions, a militant minority, exploiting human want and misery, was able to create political chaos which, until now, has made economic recovery impossible....

The very existence of the Greek state is today threatened by the terrorist activities of several thousand armed men, led by Communists, who defy the government's authority at a number of points, particularly along the northern boundaries....

Meanwhile, the Greek Government is unable to cope with the situation. The Greek army is small and poorly equipped. It needs supplies and equipment if it is to restore authority to the government throughout Greek Territory....

The United States must supply this assistance. We have already extended to Greece certain types of relief and economic aid but these are inadequate.

There is no other country to which democratic Greece can turn.

No other nation is willing and able to provide the necessary support for a democratic Greek government.

*The British Government, which has been helping Greece, can give no further financial or economic aid after March 31. Great Britain finds itself under the necessity of reducing or **liquidating** its commitments in several parts of the world, including Greece....*

The Greek Government has been operating in an atmosphere of chaos and extremism. It has made mistakes. The extension of aid by this country does not mean that the United States condones everything that the Greek Government has done or will do....

Greece's neighbor, Turkey, also deserves our attention....

Tubercular: Suffering from tuberculosis, a disease of the lungs.

Inflation: Prices of goods rise faster than wages.

Liquidating: Ending.

*Turkey now needs our support. Since the war Turkey has sought additional financial assistance from Great Britain and the United States for the purpose of effecting that **modernization** necessary for the maintenance of its **national integrity**.*

That integrity is essential to the preservation of order in the Middle East.

The British Government has informed us that, owing to its own difficulties, it can no longer extend financial or economic aid to Turkey.

As in the case of Greece, if Turkey is to have the assistance it needs, the United States must supply it. We are the only country able to provide that help....

*One of the primary objectives of the foreign policy of the United States is the creation of conditions in which we and other nations will be able to work out a way of life free from **coercion**. This was a fundamental issue in the war with Germany and Japan. Our victory was won over countries which sought to impose their will, and their way of life, upon other nations.*

*To ensure the peaceful development of nations, free from coercion, the United States has taken a leading part in establishing the United Nations. The United Nations is designed to make possible lasting freedom and independence for all its members. We shall not realize our objectives, however, unless we are willing to help free peoples to maintain their national integrity against aggressive movements that seek to impose upon them **totalitarian regimes**. This is no more than a frank recognition that totalitarian regimes imposed upon free peoples, by direct or indirect aggression, undermine the foundations of international peace and hence the security of the United States.*

*The peoples of a number of countries of the world have recently had totalitarian regimes forced upon them against their will. The Government of the United States has made frequent protests against coercion and **intimidation**, in violation of the **Yalta agreement**, in Poland, Rumania, and Bulgaria. I must also state that in a number of other countries there have been similar developments.*

At the present moment in world history nearly every nation must choose between alternative ways of life. The choice is too often not a free one.

*One way of life is based upon the will of a minority forcibly imposed upon the majority. It relies upon terror and **oppression**, a con-*

Modernization: Updated improvement.

National integrity: Independence.

Coercion: Unwanted pressure and influence from outsiders.

Totalitarian regimes: Governments such as dictatorships that exert total control over their citizens.

Intimidation: Forced fear.

Yalta agreement: An accord reached in Yalta, Germany, in 1944 between Allied leaders Joseph Stalin, Winston Churchill, and Franklin D. Roosevelt on how to manage lands conquered by Germany during World War II.

Oppression: Unjust power.

trolled press and radio, fixed elections, and the **suppression** of personal freedoms.

I believe that it must be the policy of the United States to support free peoples who are resisting attempted **subjugation** by armed minorities or by outside pressures.

I believe that our help should be primarily through economic and financial aid which is essential to economic stability and orderly political processes.

Suppression: Removal.

Subjugation: Complete control.

It is necessary only to glance at a map to realize that the survival and integrity of the Greek nation are of grave importance in a much wider situation. If Greece should fall under the control of an armed minority, the effect upon its neighbor, Turkey, would be immediate and serious. Confusion and disorder might well spread throughout the entire Middle East.

Moreover, the disappearance of Greece as an independent state would have a profound effect upon those countries in Europe whose peoples are struggling against great difficulties to maintain their freedoms and their independence while they repair the damages of war.

I therefore ask the Congress to provide authority for assistance to Greece and Turkey in the amount of $400,000,000 for the period ending June 30, 1948. In addition to funds, I ask the Congress to authorize the detail of American civilian and military personnel to Greece and Turkey, at the request of those countries, to assist in the tasks of reconstruction, and for the purpose of supervising the use of such financial and material assistance as may be furnished.

This is a serious course upon which we embark. I would not recommend it except that the alternative is much more serious.

The seeds of totalitarian regimes are nurtured by misery and want. They spread and grow in the evil soil of poverty and strife. They reach their full growth when the hope of a people for a better life has died.

We must keep that hope alive.

What happened next ...

A stunned and sober Congress overwhelmingly passed the aid package for Greece and Turkey. An anticommunist, anti-Soviet feeling spread through government and the American public.

George C. Marshall was in Moscow for a meeting at the time of the speech. He remained there for six weeks trying to break a stalemate over how to handle postwar Germany. The United States, Great Britain, France, and the Soviet Union had never reached agreement. As a result, a peace treaty involving the future of defeated Germany had never been signed. Again they came to no agreement. Leaving Moscow at the end of April, Marshall feared Stalin believed no treaty was needed because it was only a matter of time before all of Western Europe, weakened by war, fell under Soviet domination. Marshall urgently devised a plan, the Marshall Plan, to prop up European economies (see the next two excerpts).

The civil war in Greece stumbled along until roughly the end of 1949. Yugoslavia's Marshal Tito tired of aiding the rebels of ELAS. ELAS could garner no support from Stalin. Stalin's interests were elsewhere, and he had no desire to fight a battle with the United States over Greece. Greece remained a free, democratic nation.

Did you know ...
- George F. Kennan (1904–), author of the "Long Telegram" (an eight-thousand-word telegram that warned that the Soviet leaders could not be trusted and recommended that the United States give up its isolationist attitude and take on more of a leadership role with regard to international politics), strongly supported the Truman Doctrine and declared Greece could be pivotal to the Cold War.

- With the adoption of the Truman Doctrine, the U.S. Congress had given the U.S. government approval to intervene in the internal political affairs of other distant countries.

- The domino effect, although not called that in the Truman speech, would be the basis for U.S. intervention in the Vietnam War (1954–75) in the 1960s.

Consider the following ...
- Why would peoples experiencing poverty and hardship be susceptible to communist thought? Research early Bolshevik or communist doctrine and the appeal to peasants and workers.

- How did the overall attitudes in the Truman Doctrine affect the Cold War? Did they heat it up or cool it down?

- If communist takeovers were threatened in other parts of the world such as in Asia or Africa or Latin America, did the Truman Doctrine apply to those areas as well? Or was the intent of the Truman Doctrine to apply aid only to European countries threatened by the spread of communism?

For More Information

Books

Collins, David R. *Harry S. Truman: People's President*. New York: Chelsea Juniors, 1991.

Donovan, Robert J. *Conflict and Crisis: The Presidency of Harry S. Truman, 1945–1948*. Columbia: University of Missouri Press, 1994.

Farley, Karin C. *Harry Truman: The Man From Independence*. Englewood Cliffs, NJ: Julian Messner, 1989.

Isaacs, Jeremy, and Taylor Downing, eds. *Cold War: An Illustrated History, 1945–1991*. New York: Little, Brown & Company, 1998.

McCullough, David G. *Truman*. New York: Simon and Schuster, 1992.

Public Papers of the Presidents of the United States: Harry S. Truman, 1947. Washington, DC: U.S. Government Printing Office, 1963.

Walker, Martin. *The Cold War: A History (Owl Book)*. New York: Henry Holt & Company, Inc., 1995.

Web Site

Truman Presidential Museum & Library. http://www.trumanlibrary.org (accessed on September 10, 2003).

George C. Marshall

Excerpt from "Remarks by the Honorable George C. Marshall, Secretary of State, at Harvard University on June 5, 1947"

Published in *Foreign Relations of the United States (FRUS), Volume III, 1947: The British Commonwealth; Europe*, published in 1972

Following the passage of the Truman Doctrine in March 1947, Secretary of State George C. Marshall (1880–1959) put the staff of the State Department to work planning an overall economic recovery program for Europe. By April 1947, communist parties were gaining strength in France and Italy. Postwar Western European economies were in danger of collapsing with resulting political chaos, ripe for communist intervention. Although George Kennan (1904–), author of the "Long Telegram," was in charge of policy planning at the State Department, it was Under-secretary of State Will Clayton (1880–1966) who stressed to Marshall that France and Italy could be lost within a very short time period—weeks or months. Kennan wanted to direct the recovery planning over the next four to five years. Clayton said it was most important to address "starvation" and "chaos" immediately. Marshall, sharing Clayton's concern, saw that a plan was pulled together in a few short weeks.

Marshall was due to receive an honorary degree at Harvard University on June 5 and would be provided time for a short speech. This is where the Marshall Plan was first

> "Our policy is directed not against any country or doctrine but against hunger, poverty, desperation and chaos. Its purpose should be the revival of a working economy in the world so as to permit the emergence of political and social conditions in which free institutions can exist."

revealed. It had all been pulled together so fast that few immediately realized they had just heard a plan that would rebuild Western Europe, allow those countries' economies to expand through the 1950s and 1960s, and effectively halt the spread of communism in Europe.

U.S. secretary of state George C. Marshall.
Courtesy of the Library of Congress.

Things to remember while reading "Remarks by the Honorable George C. Marshall, Secretary of State, at Harvard University on June 5, 1947":

• Marshall offered the plan to all nations in Europe, including communist-controlled countries—even including the Soviet Union.

• The Marshall Plan was not a complete, finished plan of action. On the contrary, the nations that decided to take advantage would meet and develop an assessment of their needs and then propose how the plan should work.

Excerpt from "Remarks by the Honorable George C. Marshall, Secretary of State, at Harvard University on June 5, 1947"

Press Release Issued by the Department of State, June 4, 1947

I need not tell you gentlemen that the world situation is very serious. That must be apparent to all intelligent people. I think one difficulty is that the problem is one of such enormous complexity that the very mass of facts presented to the public by press and radio make it exceedingly difficult for the man in the street to reach a clear appraisement of the situation. Furthermore, the people of

Cominform, Molotov Plan, Comecon

In reaction to the Marshall Plan, the Soviets held a meeting with Eastern European nations on September 22, 1947. That was the same day the European nations participating in the plan had their proposals of their needs ready to go to Washington. The Eastern European nations, at Stalin's order, formed the Communist Information Bureau (Cominform) to create a tighter bond between the Soviet Union and its Eastern European satellite states. ("Satellite states" was the term coined in the new space age of the 1950s to describe the smaller Eastern European countries controlled politically and economically by the Soviet Union.) Cominform's primary mission was to combat the spread of American capitalism and imperialism (taking control of other countries).

Named after Soviet foreign minister V. M. Molotov, the Molotov Plan provided economic assistance for Eastern European countries. The Soviet Union established a series of trade agreements between itself and the Eastern European countries.

Expanding agreements of the Molotov Plan, the Soviets founded the Council of Mutual Economic Assistance (Comecon) in January 1949. Comecon closely tied Eastern European economies to the Soviet Union's economy. To maximize production of certain products or food, each country was assigned a specific product or crop. Participating in Comecon were the Soviet Union, Bulgaria, Czechoslovakia, Hungary, Poland, Romania, Yugoslavia, and even the communist parties in France and Italy.

---

*this country are distant from the troubled areas of the earth and it is hard for them to comprehend the plight and **consequent reactions** of the long-suffering peoples, and the effect of those reactions on their governments in connection with our efforts to promote peace in the world.*

*In considering the requirements for the rehabilitation of Europe, the physical loss of life, the visible destruction of cities, factories, mines and railroads was correctly estimated, but it has become obvious during recent months that this visible destruction was probably less serious than the **dislocation of the entire fabric** of European economy. For the past ten years conditions have been highly abnormal. The feverish preparation for war and the more feverish maintenance of the war effort engulfed all aspects of national economies. Machinery has fallen into disrepair or is entirely obsolete. Under the **arbitrary** and destructive Nazi rule, virtually every possible enterprise was geared into the German war machine. Long-standing*

Consequent reactions: Responses to new conditions, such as poverty.

Dislocation of the entire fabric: Complete disruption.

Arbitrary: Without reason.

commercial ties, private institutions, banks, insurance companies and shipping companies disappeared, through loss of **capital**, absorption through **nationalization** or by simple destruction. In many countries, confidence in the local currency has been severely shaken. The breakdown of the business structure of Europe during the war was complete. Recovery has been seriously retarded by the fact that two years after the close of hostilities a peace settlement with Germany and Austria has not been agreed upon. But even given a more prompt solution of these difficult problems, the **rehabilitation** of the economic structure of Europe quite evidently will require a much longer time and greater effort than had been foreseen.

There is a phase of this matter which is both interesting and serious. The farmer has always produced the foodstuffs to exchange with the city dweller for the other necessities of life. This division of labor is the basis of modern civilization. At the present time it is threatened with breakdown. The town and city industries are not producing adequate goods to exchange with the food-producing farmer. Raw materials and fuel are in short supply. Machinery is lacking or worn out. The farmer or the peasant cannot find the goods for sale which he desires to purchase. So the sale of his farm produce for money which he cannot use seems to him an unprofitable transaction. He, therefore, has withdrawn many fields from crop cultivation and is using them for grazing. He feeds more grain to stock and finds for himself and his family an ample supply of food, however short he may be on clothing and the other ordinary gadgets of civilization. Meanwhile people in the cities are short of food and fuel. So the governments are forced to use their foreign money and **credits** to **procure** these necessities abroad. This process exhausts funds which are urgently needed for reconstruction. Thus a very serious situation is rapidly developing which bodes no good for the world. The modern system of the division of labor upon which the exchange of products is based is in danger of breaking down.

The truth of the matter is that Europe's requirements for the next three or four years of foreign food and other essential products—principally from America—are so much greater than her present ability to pay that she must have substantial additional help, or face economic, social and political deterioration of a very grave character.

The remedy lies in breaking the vicious circle and restoring the confidence of the European people in the economic future of their own countries and of Europe as a whole....

Capital: Wealth in money and property.

Nationalization: Ownership by government.

Rehabilitation: Restoration to a good condition.

Credits: Loans.

Procure: Purchase.

*Aside from the demoralizing effect on the world at large and the possibilities of disturbances arising as a result of the desperation of the people concerned, the consequences to the economy of the United States would be apparent to all. It is logical that the United States should do whatever it is able to do to assist in the return of normal economic health in the world, without which there can be no political stability and no assured peace. Our policy is directed not against any country or doctrine but against hunger, poverty, desperation and chaos. Its purpose should be the revival of a working economy in the world so as to permit the emergence of political and social conditions in which free institutions can exist. Such assistance, I am convinced, must not be on a piece-meal basis as various crises develop. Any assistance that this Government may render in the future should provide a cure rather than a mere **palliative**. Any government that is willing to assist in the task of recovery will find full cooperation, I am sure, on the part of the United States Government. Any government which maneuvers to block the recovery of other countries cannot expect help from us. Furthermore, governments, political parties or groups which seek to **perpetuate** human misery in order to profit therefrom politically or otherwise will encounter the opposition of the United States.*

*It is already evident that, before the United States Government can proceed much further in its efforts to **alleviate** the situation and help start the European world on its way to recovery, there must be some agreement among the countries of Europe as to the requirements of the situation and the part those countries themselves will take…. It would be neither fitting nor **efficacious** for this Government to undertake to draw up **unilaterally** a program designed to place Europe on its feet economically. This is the business of the Europeans. The initiative, I think, must come from Europe. The role of this country should consist of friendly aid in the drafting of a European program and of later support of such a program so far as it may be practical for us to do so. The program should be a joint one, agreed to by a number, if not all European nations….*

With foresight, and a willingness on the part of our people to face up to the vast responsibility which history has clearly placed upon our country, the difficulties I have outlined can and will be overcome.

Palliative: A quick fix without actually solving the main problem.

Perpetuate: Continue.

Alleviate: Bring relief to.

Efficacious: Capable of reaching the desired result.

Unilaterally: Without advice from other countries.

What happened next ...

Britain immediately realized the Marshall Plan would be its "life-line." Even Soviet foreign minister V. M. Molotov (1890–1986) implored Soviet leader Joseph Stalin (1879–1953) to let him take a staff including Soviet economists to Paris on June 26 to at least explore ideas of the plan. Molotov knew the Soviet economy needed help. Begrudgingly, the ever-suspicious Stalin allowed Molotov to go.

By June 30, Molotov learned that the United States also saw Germany as a key participant in the plan. This enraged the Soviets, who had long lobbied for keeping defeated Germany a weak nation. Germany's invasion of the Soviet Union during World War II (1939–45) was still fresh in their minds. One of the Soviets' greatest postwar fears was that Germany would rebuild and again threaten the Soviet Union. Molotov returned to the Soviet Union with all hopes of Soviet participation destroyed. At this point, Stalin also firmly believed that the capitalist United States wanted to infiltrate the economies of Eastern Europe and eventually turn them to the capitalist system.

On July 7, Moscow ordered Eastern European countries—Albania, Bulgaria, Czechoslovakia, Finland, Hungary, Poland, Romania, and Yugoslavia—to not take part in the plan. All bowed to Moscow's wishes except Poland and Czechoslovakia. Stalin was furious and within a few days had slapped Czechoslovakia and Poland back into line. Stalin viewed the Marshall Plan as an aggressive escalation of the Cold War. He believed the United States wanted to strengthen the capitalist Western European nations and grab Eastern European economies as well. The Iron Curtain closed tighter over Eastern Europe.

On July 12, the Conference on European Economic Cooperation convened with sixteen Western European nations ready to make shopping lists of their individual wants and pull together a practical Marshall Plan. Washington had to stress that they wanted more than shopping lists. The nations also needed to devise long-term plans of cooperation such as eliminating trade barriers between each other. Finally on September 22, the Europeans had a proposal ready for Washington. They estimated $17 billion would be needed to successfully rebuild. (See the next excerpt for a continuation of the development of the Marshall Plan.)

Whatever happened to France and Italy? By late December 1947, the communists in France had lost favor with the French public. France was able to sustain its democratic government and would participate in the Marshall Plan. Defeating communists in Italy proved even more of a challenge. It took secret operations by the U.S. Central Intelligence Agency (CIA), which gathers and interprets the meaning of information on foreign activities as well as carries out secret foreign operations, and Pope Pius XII (1876–1958) to influence the electorate to defeat the communists in an election on April 18, 1948. Italy would also participate in the Marshall Plan.

A bombed-out Dresden, Germany, during World War II. The Soviets wanted Germany to remain weak after the war ended to limit chances of a rebuilt Germany threatening the Soviet Union. *Photograph by Fred Ramage. Reproduced by permission of Getty Images.*

Did you know ...

- Physicist J. Robert Oppenheimer (1904–1967), the father of the U.S. atomic bomb, also received an honorary degree at Harvard along with Marshall on June 5.

- Through well-placed Soviet spies, Molotov first learned that the United States and Britain also saw the Marshall Plan as a plan for the reconstruction of Germany. One of the most famous spy rings of the Cold War, consisting of four Brits, was responsible for snooping and sending a secret coded cable to Molotov on June 30. The men, called the Cambridge Spies, were Anthony F. Blunt (1907–1983), Guy Burgess (1910–1963), Donald Maclean (1913–1983), and Kim Philby (1911–1988).

- Czechoslovakia's misstep of first intending to participate in the Marshall Plan would ultimately lead to its takeover by communists in February 1948.

Consider the following …

- Later, after the Marshall Plan was in operation, debate raged as to whether the United States ever really wanted the Soviet Union and communist Eastern European countries to actually participate. What might have been the consequences of their participation?

- How do you think the Marshall Plan's aid should have been delivered? Through loans, outright gifts of money, or gifts of goods? Why?

- Marshall, in his speech, described a cycle of farmer–food-stuffs–city dweller–manufactured goods–farmer. Have class members explain this classic economic cycle and retell this cycle so that everyone understands. What had happened to the cycle in Europe immediately after World War II?

For More Information

Books

Cray, Ed. *General of the Army: George C. Marshall, Soldier and Statesman.* New York: Norton, 1990.

Donovan, Robert J. *The Second Victory: The Marshall Plan and the Postwar Revival of Europe.* New York: Madison Books, 1987.

Foreign Relations of the United States (FRUS), Volume III, 1947: The British Commonwealth; Europe. Washington, DC: U.S. Government Printing Office, 1972.

Hogan, Michael J. *The Marshall Plan: America, Britain, and the Reconstruction of Western Europe, 1947–1952.* New York: Cambridge University Press, 1987.

Stoler, Mark A. *George C. Marshall: Soldier-Statesman of the American Century.* Boston: Twayne Publishers, 1989.

Web Site

George C. Marshall European Center for Security Studies. http://www.marshallcenter.org (accessed on September 10, 2003).

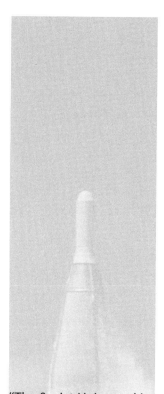

Harry S. Truman

Excerpt from "Special Message to the Congress on the Threat to the Freedom of Europe, March 17, 1948"

Published in *Public Papers of the Presidents of the United States: Harry S. Truman, January 1 to December 31, 1948*, published in 1964

"The Soviet Union and its satellites were invited to cooperate in the European recovery program. They rejected that invitation. More than that, they have declared their violent hostility to the program and are aggressively attempting to wreck it."

In July 1947, sixteen Western European nations that had chosen to participate in the U.S.-proposed European recovery plan known as the Marshall Plan met in Paris. After several months of discussion, on September 22, 1947, the nations had readied their proposal of immediate needs and long-term cooperation goals for Washington's review.

The U.S. Congress began to consider the $17 billion aid request. Using the logic of the Truman Doctrine, a program designed by President Harry S. Truman (1884–1972; served 1945–53) that sent aid to anticommunist forces in Turkey and Greece, the Truman administration argued that the Marshall Plan aid would help countries stop communist influence within their borders. Congress continued to debate, so in December, Truman managed to obtain an interim $600 million aid package approval from Congress for France, Italy, and Austria.

By January 1948, Truman reduced the original plan request down to $6.8 billion for a fifteen-month period. In February, he reduced it again to $5.3 billion to cover a twelve-month period.

EUROPE
During the Cold War

Eastern Europe
Western Europe

0 — 300 mi
0 — 300 km

Suddenly, several alarming events pushed Congress to pass the plan. First, in February, Czechoslovakia fell to a communist takeover that unseated the Western-supported government. This change represented the disappearance of the last democracy in Eastern Europe. Anticommunist feelings were running high in America and Western Europe. Fears increased about the political stability of Western Europe. Next, the newly established National Security Council (NSC) issued a report, NSC-20, concluding the goal of the Soviet Union was world domination. Another report, NSC-30, advocated the use of nuclear weapons as discouragement to further communist expansion. This represented a bold new approach for U.S. foreign policy.

Finally, on March 17, 1948, President Truman delivered a powerful speech to the joint session of Congress titled "Special Message to the Congress on the Threat to the Freedom of Europe." Truman described the "situation in Europe" as "critical." He charged that "one nation," meaning the So-

A map showing Eastern and Western European nations during the Cold War.
Reproduced by permission of the Gale Group.

viet Union, had refused to cooperate in establishing peace after World War II (1939–45). Further, that nation "and its agents have destroyed the independence and democratic character of a whole series of nations in Eastern and Central Europe." He called on Congress to act, to "face the threat to their liberty squarely and courageously."

Things to remember while reading the excerpt from the "Special Message to the Congress on the Threat to the Freedom of Europe":

- The amount of aid requested was massive. It was inevitable that, although time-consuming, Republicans and Democrats would battle in Congress over the expenditure for some months.

- The Marshall Plan addressed economic and political issues of Western Europe and was not intended to provide any military aid.

- By 1948, anticommunist feelings were running high in the United States. When Czechoslovakia fell in February 1948, U.S. military officials actually suggested that a Soviet invasion of Western Europe might happen at any time.

Excerpt from "Special Message to the Congress on the Threat to the Freedom of Europe, March 17, 1948"

Mr. President, Mr. Speaker, Members of the Congress:

I am here today to report to you on the critical nature of the situation in Europe, and to recommend action for your consideration.

Rapid changes are taking place in Europe which affect our foreign policy and our national security. There is an increasing threat to nations which are striving to maintain a form of government which grants freedom to its citizens. The United States is deeply concerned with the survival of freedom in those nations. It is of vital importance that we act now, in order to preserve the conditions under which we can achieve lasting peace based on freedom and justice.

The achievement of such a peace has been the great goal of this nation.

Almost 3 years have **elapsed** since the end of the greatest of all wars, but peace and stability have not returned to the world. We were well aware that the end of the fighting would not automatically settle the problems arising out of the war. The establishment of peace after the fighting is over has always been a difficult task. And even if all the Allies of World War II were united in their desire to establish a just and honorable peace, there would still be great difficulties in the way of achieving that peace.

But the situation in the world today is not primarily the result of natural difficulties which follow a great war. It is chiefly due to the fact that one nation [the Soviet Union] has not only refused to cooperate in the establishment of a just and honorable peace, but—even worse—has actively sought to prevent it.

The Congress is familiar with the course of events.

You know of the sincere and patient attempts of the democratic nations to find a secure basis for peace through negotiation and

President Harry S. Truman, reading at a press conference in the 1940s.
Reproduced by permission of AP/Wide World Photos.

Elapsed: Passed.

agreement. Conference after conference has been held in different parts of the world. We have tried to settle the questions arising out of the war on a basis which would permit the establishment of a just peace. You know the obstacles we have encountered, but the record stands as a monument to the good faith and integrity of the democratic nations of the world. The agreements we did obtain, imperfect though they were, could have furnished the basis for a just peace—if they had been kept.

But they were not kept.

They have been persistently ignored and violated by one nation.

The Congress is also familiar with the developments concerning the United Nations. Most of the countries of the world have joined together in the United Nations in an attempt to build a world order based on law and not on force. Most of the members support the United Nations earnestly and honestly, and seek to make it stronger and more effective.

One nation, however, has persistently obstructed the work of the United Nations by constant abuse of the **veto.** *That nation has vetoed 21 proposals for action in a little over 2 years.*

But that is not all. Since the close of **hostilities,** *the Soviet Union and its agents have destroyed the independence and democratic character of a whole series of nations in Eastern and Central Europe.*

It is this ruthless course of action, and the clear design to extend it to the remaining free nations of Europe, that have brought about the critical situation in Europe today.

The tragic death of the Republic of Czechoslovakia has sent a shock throughout the civilized world. Now pressure is being brought to bear on Finland, to the hazard of the entire Scandinavian peninsula. Greece is under direct military attack from rebels actively supported by her Communist dominated neighbors [Yugoslavia]. In Italy, a determined and aggressive effort is being made by a Communist minority to take control of that country. The methods vary, but the pattern is all too clear.

Faced with this growing menace, there have been encouraging signs that the free nations of Europe are drawing closer together for their economic well-being and for the common defense of their liberties.

In the economic field, the movement for mutual self-help to restore conditions essential to the preservation of free institutions is

Hostilities: World War II.

Veto: The power to legally block actions.

well under way. In Paris, the 16 nations which are cooperating in the European recovery program are meeting again to establish a joint organization to work for the economic restoration of Western Europe.

The United States has strongly supported the efforts of these nations to repair the devastation of war and restore a sound world economy. In presenting this program to the Congress last December, I emphasized the necessity for speedy action. Every event in Europe since that day has underlined the great urgency for the prompt adoption of this measure.

*The Soviet Union and its **satellites** were invited to cooperate in the European recovery program. They rejected that invitation. More than that, they have declared their violent hostility to the program and are aggressively attempting to wreck it.*

*They see in it a major obstacle to their designs to **subjugate** the free community of Europe. They do not want the United States to help Europe. They do not even want the 16 cooperative countries to help themselves....*

The door has never been closed, nor will it ever be closed, to the Soviet Union or to any other nation which genuinely cooperates in preserving the peace.

At the same time, we must not be confused about the central issue which confronts the world today.

The time has come when the free men and women of the world must face the threat to their liberty squarely and courageously.

The United States has a tremendous responsibility to act according to the measure of our power for good in the world. We have learned that we must earn the peace we seek just as we earned victory in the war, not by wishful thinking but by realistic effort.

At no time in our history has unity among our people been so vital as it is at the present time.

Unity of purpose, unity of effort, and unity of spirit are essential to accomplish the task before us.

Each of us here in this chamber today has a special responsibility. The world situation is too critical, and the responsibilities of this country are too vast, to permit any party struggles to weaken our influence for maintaining the peace.

Satellites: Nations politically dependent upon the Soviet Union.

Subjugate: Conquer.

What happened next ...

Congress approved $5.3 billion for the Marshall Plan on April 3, 1948. Within months, aid was headed to Europe. Only 20 percent was in loans because the United States did not want to burden Europe with debt. Some money grants were also sent without the need for countries to repay them. The bulk of the aid was in goods, food, fertilizers and tractors, and industrial equipment. The Fiat automobile manufacturer in Italy was rebuilt with assembly-line machinery sent from Detroit, Michigan, and Pittsburgh, Pennsylvania, which saved the Italian economy. Northern Greece needed mules for agriculture and received large and stubborn mules from Missouri. The plan provided more than $13 billion by 1952 to help maintain political and economic stability in the West. Passage of the plan essentially divided Europe economically into an East communist-dominated half and a West capitalist-supported half. Czechoslovakia ended up in the East, France and Italy in the West. The United States would continue to support a large foreign-aid program through the second half of the twentieth century.

Did you know ...

- Much of the Marshall Plan aid eventually returned to the American economy. As economies became healthy, Europeans bought America's finished goods and raw commodities. In addition, U.S. goods sent originally to help Europe were purchased by the U.S. government from American farmers and manufacturers.

- Between April 3, 1948, and June 30, 1952, Great Britain received the most aid at $3.2 billion. France was a close second at $2.7 billion. Tiny Iceland received the smallest amount of aid at $29 million.

- By the mid-1950s, Western European economies were far more robust than Eastern European economies.

Consider the following ...

- Why do you think the Soviets were so opposed to the rebuilding of West Germany? Why was the United States so determined to rebuild West Germany?

- If Western Europe had fallen under communist rule, predict how the future of the United States would have been affected.

- Before Congress passed the Marshall Plan, at the end of 1947, President Truman got Congress to agree to an interim $600 million package primarily for France, Italy, and Austria. Why were those particular countries chosen?

For More Information

Books

Ferrell, Robert. *Harry S. Truman: A Life.* Columbia: University of Missouri Press, 1994.

Offner, Arnold A. *Another Such Victory: President Truman and the Cold War, 1945–1953.* Stanford, CA: Stanford University Press, 2002.

Public Papers of the Presidents of the United States: Harry S. Truman, January 1 to December 31, 1948. Washington, DC: U.S. Government Printing Office, 1964.

Truman, Harry S. *Memoirs: Years of Trial and Hope 1946–1953.* London: Hodder and Stoughton, 1956.

Young, John. *Cold War Europe, 1945–1989: A Political History.* London: Edward Arnold, 1991.

Web Site

"Harry S. Truman." *The White House.* http://www.whitehouse.gov/history/presidents/ht33.html (accessed on September 10, 2003).

Communism Spreads

By April 1948, massive rebuilding aid via the Marshall Plan, a massive U.S. plan to promote Europe's economic recovery from the war, was headed to those Western European countries whose economies had been devastated by World War II (1939–45). Officially known as the European Recovery Program for Western Europe, the Marshall Plan was made available to all nations, though the communist regime rejected it. The United States feared that communist agitators, promising a better life, would overthrow the struggling democracies. (Agitators appeal to people's emotions to stir up public feeling over controversial issues.) Western Europe might fall just as Eastern Europe had fallen under the "Iron Curtain" (a term referring to the ruthless Soviet domination) of communism.

The excerpts that follow turn to another part of the world, China and Korea. In the 1930s, China's communist leader, Mao Zedong (1893–1976), and his forces, mostly consisting of peasants, were locked in a civil war with the noncommunist Nationalists under Chiang Kai-shek (1887–1975). There was a halt in the civil war as both fought the invading Japanese from 1937 to 1945, but the conflict was resumed at the end of World War II. The United States had sent some aid to the Nationalists, but by 1950, Mao's communists drove the Nationalists out of China to the island of Taiwan. The communists gained control of Mainland China. The U.S. government under the administration of President Harry S. Truman (1884–1972; served 1945–53) had clearly focused on Europe to the exclusion of China. It viewed China's fate as up to the Chinese people. In the United States, Chinese Nationalist supporters, known as the China Lobby, were outraged.

In the first excerpt, a 1949 article by journalist Isaac Don Levine (1892–1981) titled "Our First Line of Defense," Levine argues that the United States must defend against communist power wherever it is. He accused the U.S. State Department as having no "vision" for Asia. Overall, the fall of China was considered a grave, ominous loss for the free world. Under strong pressure from many sides, President Truman ordered the head of the Policy Planning Staff in the State Department, Paul H. Nitze (1907–), to thoroughly review U.S. foreign policy and its strategies worldwide. The result was the National Security Council (NSC) document number 68, known as NSC-68, which is excerpted here. Completed in April 1950, the strongly worded document called for a proactive foreign policy, one based on planning and action rather than on reaction to other countries' actions. Such a policy prepared the United States to build a healthy worldwide community capable of resisting communist influence. The document advised holding on to a tight policy of containment, a key U.S. Cold War policy to restrict the territorial growth of communist rule that was first put forth by Truman administration policy analyst George F. Kennan (1904–). NSC-68 also called for a massive increase in defense spending to further build up the military.

Just after the NSC-68 report was finished, in June 1950, the forces under the communist leader of North Korea, Kim Il Sung (1912–1994), attacked and quickly overran democratic South Korea. President Truman sent World War II legend General Douglas MacArthur (1880–1964) to Korea to command a temporary alliance of United Nations forces, predominately made up of U.S. forces. He was charged with halting and pushing communist forces out of South Korea. Not only did MacArthur accomplish this task, but he then spoke threateningly to China, even suggesting that the United States would use nuclear weapons. Talking out of turn, MacArthur was relieved of his command by President Truman and recalled to the United States. Still extremely popular with Americans, he was invited to speak before a joint session of the U.S. Congress. On April 19, 1951, he delivered his famous "Old Soldiers Never Die" speech, excerpted here. MacArthur's speech supported the importance of Asia as in Isaac Don Levine's article and the strong anticommunist philosophy in NSC-68.

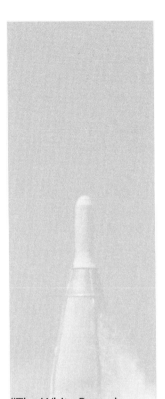

Isaac Don Levine

Excerpt from "Our First Line of Defense"
Originally published in *Plain Talk* magazine, September 1949

"The White Paper is a denial of the existence of a will to save Asia. The White Paper is at best a testimonial to spinelessness and a confession of guilty conduct in the past...."

The vast Chinese empire existed in the Far East for centuries. By the early 1890s, however, a more modern, European type of world encroached upon ancient China. By 1911, a revolution had ended the empire, but only economic and political instability resulted. As a consequence, civil war broke out in the 1930s. The Kuomintang, or Nationalists, led by Chiang Kai-shek (1887–1975) had ruled parts of China since the 1920s. The United States had recognized the Nationalist government since 1928. They were challenged by Mao Zedong (1893–1976) and his communist revolutionary forces. Mao, just like Soviet leader Joseph Stalin (1879–1953), strictly followed the philosophies of Karl Marx (1818–1883) and Vladimir I. Lenin (1870–1924) that had contributed to the birth of communism.

Mao's communist forces were largely peasants from China's agricultural areas. The civil war was interrupted in 1937 when the Japanese invaded China. The armies of both Chiang and Mao joined forces to stop Japanese aggression.

With the Japanese defeat and surrender in August 1945, the civil war resumed. In the United States, there was a large and influential group of Chinese Nationalist supporters, known as the China Lobby. They urged the United States to give strong backing to Chiang. Yet President Harry S. Truman (1884–1972; served 1945–53) was reluctant because of Chiang's growing reputation as a corrupt and oppressive leader. However, the fear of the spread of communism was beginning to sweep across America. Both everyday Americans and U.S. officials believed that any leader who openly labeled himself a communist, as Mao did, must be supported by Soviet leader Stalin. Under pressure, Truman sent a small amount of financial and military aid to the Nationalists.

President Truman sent General George C. Marshall (1880–1959) to China to attempt to work out a negotiated settlement between the Nationalists and communists. Marshall met with little success and by December 1946, he reported that a peaceful settlement was not likely. Soon the Nationalists were running out of money and military strength. During 1948, communist forces moved southward over China.

In January 1949, Chiang begged for military assistance from both the United States and the Soviet Union. Chiang knew that Stalin, perceiving Mao a threat to his own power, was not a strong supporter of Mao. Neither responded with aid, but the Soviets did implore Mao to halt his offensive and seek a settlement. By then, however, Mao's forces were unstoppable.

In August 1949, U.S. secretary of state Dean Acheson (1893–1971) wrote an analysis of the China situation. The report, called the White Paper, said that the fate of China lay with the Chinese themselves. The United States had done all it could and would do no more. Outraged, the China Lobby accused the U.S. State Department of overlooking the communist takeover of China.

In September 1949, journalist Isaac Don Levine published in the conservative U.S. magazine *Plain Talk* a widely read article, "Our First Line of Defense." Levine took strong issue with Acheson's perspective that the United States and other powers could not stop the takeover. He asserted that America's "first line of defense is wherever the communist power is." He accused the State Department of being misguided and of favoring Europe. His reference to "dollars and more dollars" was a direct reference to the Marshall Plan (see

Journalist Isaac Don Levine, shown here testifying before the House Un-American Activities Committee during the Alger Hiss hearings in 1948, criticized the Truman administration for its preference towards Europe over Asia. *Reproduced by permission of the Corbis Corporation.*

Chapter 2). Nothing like the Marshall Plan was available in Asia. He accused the United States of having no "vision" for China. The excerpt that follows is from Levine's original article in *Plain Talk*.

Meanwhile, in September, communist forces pushed the Nationalists off Mainland China. They fled to the Chinese island of Formosa, renamed Taiwan. There, Chiang established what he called the Republic of China (ROC). On October 1, 1949, Mao proclaimed communist rule over Mainland China and called it the People's Republic of China (PRC).

Things to remember while reading "Our First Line of Defense":

- Massive corruption among Chiang's closest loyalists and his Nationalist army had caused many Chinese to withdraw their support of Chiang.

- In the United States, the "loss" of China was considered a major blow, a huge victory for communism worldwide.

- Many in America held on to the so-called "China myth" that the United States had a centuries-old responsibility to protect China.

Excerpt from "Our First Line of Defense"

When Secretary of State [Dean] Acheson declared before the Senate Foreign Relations and Armed Services Committees that America's "first line of defense is still in Europe," he exposed the chaos which underlies our foreign policy....

With the **deluge** of the Second World War behind us, our first line of defense is wherever the Communist power is. That should be the keystone of any foreign policy.

It is arguable whether the people of the United States would go to war should there be a Soviet seizure of power, on the order of the Czechoslovak coup, in Finland or in Norway. But most **sober** observers would agree that a Communist coup in the Philippines, resulting in the establishment in Manila [the capital city of the Philippines] of a Soviet regime, would drive the American people into a war of national defense....

First and foremost is the question: Why the **White Paper** now?... The position of nationalist China at the beginning of August, on the eve of the release of the White Paper, was grave but not hopeless....

It is known that China's ambassador in Washington, Dr. Wellington Koo, had called at the White House weeks before the White Paper was issued and posed the following questions, in effect, before President [Harry] Truman:

"Why should the United States strike a finishing blow with its White Paper at the Nationalist forces while they are desperately struggling to hold the surging Communist armies? Was it the intent of the U.S. to speed the victory of the Communist elements? And was not the U.S. officially committed to a policy of containing the combating Soviet aggression and Communist expansion throughout the world?"

Deluge: Many responsibilities.

Sober: Serious.

White Paper: U.S. secretary of state Dean Acheson's written analysis of the China situation.

Our unsavory record of Teheran, Yalta, and Potsdam: Reference to some critics' contentions that the United States made too many concessions to the Soviets in post–World War II agreements during conferences held in these cities.

Rapacious despots: Greedy absolute rulers or tyrants.

Extenuation: Representation of an offense as less serious.

Red Army: Soviet army.

New arms program: Development of nuclear weapons.

Inducements: Persuasions.

Edifice: Large military structure.

Kremlin aggressors: Soviet government.

Colossus adrift: Lack of a consistent policy toward communism.

Buy precarious peace piecemeal: Try to bring about peace by responding to situations as they individually occur rather than by a broader response.

Dollars and more dollars: A reference to the money spent through the Marshall plan.

Initiative: Action.

How and why President Truman came to yield to the Far Eastern "experts" [officials] in the State department will undoubtedly make fascinating reading at some future date. But the step taken by Secretary Acheson has climaxed **our unsavory record of Teheran, Yalta, and Potsdam** with a leaf from the book of **rapacious despots.** There was far more justification for [Soviet leader Joseph] Stalin's last-minute attack on Japan and even more **extenuation** for [Italian leader Benito] Mussolini's stab in the back of France than there was for our using at this hour the dagger of the White Paper on sick China....

At best our present course of 'normalization' is calculated to achieve a stalemate, with Moscow in control of nearly half of Western Europe and most of Asia. Such a state of affairs condemns the world to chronic crisis, to economic and political fits, and puts a fatal burden upon America.

Instead of re-arming a crippled western Europe, let us disarm the **Red Army.** This can be achieved at a fraction of the cost of the **new arms program** by encouraging, through **inducements** to resettlement, the mass desertion of soldiers and able-bodied men from the Soviet zones which would undermine the Soviet **edifice** from within.

Let us boldly pick up the banner of Asian liberation and independence. With Japan extinct as a sea power and in our camp, we can wield a weapon against the Soviets in China which would make the **Kremlin aggressors** run to cover in no time. General [Douglas] MacArthur, moved from Tokyo to Formosa or Chungking, could turn the Japanese weapon to most effective use.

The White Paper is a denial of the existence of a will to save Asia. The White Paper is at best a testimonial to spinelessness and a confession of guilty conduct in the past.... It is one more alarming token of a **colossus adrift,** of an America guided abroad by men who would **buy precarious peace piecemeal** with **dollars and more dollars** rather than steer the world toward a stable peace with vision, with **initiative,** with courage, with honor.

What happened next ...

On October 2, 1949, the Soviets recognized Mao's PRC government. The United States, under continuing pressure from the China Lobby, recognized Chiang's Taiwan government, the ROC, as the official Chinese government.

In December, Mao traveled to Moscow for Stalin's seventieth birthday celebration. Mao deeply respected Stalin, but Stalin always perceived Mao as a threat. Nevertheless, Mao successfully negotiated the Sino-Soviet Treaty of Friendship, Alliance, and Mutual Assistance. (The term *Sino* means Chinese.) Mao and Stalin signed the historic treaty on February 14, 1950. Stalin in effect recognized China as part of the communist world and promised China $300 million in loans. In the years to come, however, the Soviets provided little of the promised aid, and Mao's China would become an adversary of the Soviet Union. Mao adopted a strong anti-U.S. policy and seized U.S. diplomatic property. Historians widely viewed this agreement as a new and second front of the Cold War.

In January 1950, President Truman refused to move against the PRC. He, no doubt partly influenced by events in China and the growing clash in Korea with communist forces, announced the development project to build a hydrogen bomb. The Soviets had just successfully detonated an atomic bomb in 1949. Truman ordered Paul H. Nitze (1907–), who had replaced George F. Kennan (1904–) as head of the Policy Planning Staff in the State Department, to review U.S. defense policies worldwide. The National Security Council (NSC) document NSC-68 resulted (see the next excerpt in this chapter).

Opposition to the handling of China by the U.S. State Department continued to run high. U.S. senator Joseph R. McCarthy (1909–1957) of Wisconsin, the vicious and leading U.S. anticommunist critic, went after State Department officials who he presumed to be the "experts" mentioned in Levine's article. Ultimately, the United States maintained ties with Nationalist Chinese on Taiwan. The United States had no diplomatic ties with Mao's communist China until 1972 when U.S. president Richard Nixon (1913–1994; served 1969–74) managed to open relations.

Did you know …

- Between 1945 and 1949, the United States gave Chiang $2 billion in military aid. Stalin had provided little aid or support to the Chinese communists.

- Mao used captured Japanese military equipment left behind from Japan's unsuccessful invasion of China to help defeat Chiang's army.

- The communist overrun of China was seen as another "domino" fall as communism was seemingly spreading over the world. Secretary of State Acheson had earlier warned of a domino effect, saying that if one or two countries fell to the communists, such as Greece and Turkey, then all of Western Europe, the Middle East, and even African nations could fall like dominos to the communists.

Consider the following …

- In light of the Truman Doctrine, which promised that the United States would help any nation threatened by an attempted communist takeover, do you agree with the U.S. policy to let China "fall"? Why or why not?

- Consider the Korean War (1950–53) and the Vietnam War (1954–75). Do you think Levine's statement, that "our first line of defense is wherever the Communist power is," contributed to U.S. intervention in those two areas?

For More Information

Books

Leffler, Melvyn P. *The Specter of Communism: The United States and the Origins of the Cold War, 1917–1953*. New York: Hill and Wang, 1994.

Levine, Isaac Don. *Plain Talk: An Anthology from the Leading Anti-Communist Magazine of the 40s*. New Rochelle, NY: Arlington House, 1976.

Miscamble, Wilson D. *George F. Kennan and the Making of American Foreign Policy, 1947–1950*. Princeton, NJ: Princeton University Press, 1992.

Paterson, Thomas G. *On Every Front: The Making of the Cold War*. New York: Norton, 1979.

Sircusa, Joseph M. *Into the Dark House: American Diplomacy and the Ideological Origins of the Cold War*. Claremont, CA: Regina Books, 1998.

Paul H. Nitze

Excerpt from "National Security Council Report on Soviet Intentions (NSC-68)"

Originally published in *Foreign Relations of the United States (FRUS)*, 1950, Volume I, National Security Affairs, Foreign Economic Policy, published in 1977

By 1950, a Red Scare was rampant in the United States. The Red Scare was a time in the 1950s when Americans were particularly fearful and wary of communists penetrating into U.S. society. World events of 1948 and 1949 caused great alarm and anxiety in America. These events included a communist takeover of Czechoslovakia, a Soviet blockade of Berlin, the communist victory in China, and the successful detonation of an atomic bomb by the Soviets on August 29, 1949.

U.S. president Harry S. Truman (1884–1972; served 1945–53), always a man of action, ordered Paul H. Nitze (1907–), director of policy planning at the U.S. State Department, to reevaluate U.S. foreign policies and strategic plans now that the Soviets had the atomic bomb. Nitze assembled a team of administrative officials from the State Department and the Defense Department to write a top-secret report to offer analysis of and recommendations for U.S. foreign policy. Known as National Security Council (NSC) document 68 (NSC-68), it was completed and presented to appropriate U.S. officials on April 7, 1950.

"It is quite clear from Soviet theory and practice that the Kremlin seeks to bring the free world under its dominion by the methods of the cold war. The preferred technique is to subject by infiltration and intimidation.... Those institutions of our society that touch most closely our material and moral strength are obviously the prime targets: labor unions, civic enterprises, schools, churches, and all media for influencing opinion."

In NSC-68, Nitze and the other authors painted a picture of the Soviet Union as overwhelmingly bent on taking over the world. The authors used many frightening words such as "fanatic," "mass destruction," "annihilation," "domination," and "mortally challenged." In the report, the authors set up a grave battle between the "idea of freedom" versus the "idea of slavery" under communistic control. The authors repeated many times that the Kremlin (the location of the Soviet government in Moscow) must be "frustrated" into "decay" by every means known to Cold War strategy. According to Nitze and his associates, the policy of "containment" demanded "maintenance of a strong military posture." Acknowledging that the country's "very independence as a nation may be at stake," the authors listed eleven imperative points in "a comprehensive and decisive program to win the peace and frustrate the Kremlin." Finally, the report warned the U.S. government and American people to remember that "the cold war is in fact a real war in which the survival of the free world is at stake."

The report rested partly on an old idea in the United States that when the nation was in trouble, usually acceptable limits (money for defense or espionage activities, for example) could not stand in the way of whatever leaders deemed necessary. The NSC-68 report also perpetuated the proactive diplomacy first started in the "Long Telegram" (see Chapter 1) sent by Truman administration policy analyst George F. Kennan (1904–). Stunned and amazed by the frightening, warlike tone, U.S. officials read and reread the very long report.

Things to remember while reading the "National Security Council Report on Soviet Intentions (NSC-68)":

- Nitze, the chief author of NSC-68, was known for his hawkish, or prowar, tendencies.

- Nitze replaced Kennan, original author of the containment policy, as director of the State Department's policy planning staff. Kennan intended for containment to be carried out by diplomatic means and was very opposed to the continuing U.S. nuclear development program and buildup of weapons.

- With fear of the Soviets running rampant in the United States, U.S. senator Joseph R. McCarthy (1909–1957) of Wisconsin made his dramatic announcement in February 1950 that the U.S. State Department was infiltrated with hundreds of employees who were communists. McCarthy added to the U.S. hysteria and made NSC-68 seem correct in its approach.

- In January 1950, Americans learned that Soviet spies had infiltrated to the heart of the U.S. atomic bomb development project, the Manhattan Project, in the mid-1940s. The spies had regularly funneled information to the Soviet atomic bomb project.

- All events combined, the American sense of security in the spring of 1950 was dramatically shaken. It seemed entirely possible that the Cold War could be lost right on American soil. It was believed that day-and-night vigilance was critical.

Paul H. Nitze, author of the top-secret NSC-68 report.
Reproduced by permission of AP/Wide World Photos.

Excerpt from "National Security Council Report on Soviet Intentions (NSC-68)"

*The Soviet Union ... is **animated** by a new **fanatic faith**, **antithetical** to our own, and seeks to impose its absolute authority over the rest of the world. Conflict has, therefore, become **endemic** and is waged, on the part of the Soviet Union, by violent or non-violent methods in accordance with the **dictates of expediency**. With the development of increasingly terrifying weapons of mass destruction, every individual faces the ever-present possibility of annihilation should the conflict enter the phase of total war....*

Animated: Motivated.

Fanatic faith: Communism.

Antithetical: Completely opposite.

Endemic: Restricted to a specific place.

Dictates of expediency: Anything needed to further the cause of communism.

The issues that face us are momentous, involving the fulfillment or destruction not only of this Republic [United States] but of civilization itself. They are issues which will not await our deliberations. With conscience and resolution this Government and the people it represents must now take new and fateful decisions....

*The **Kremlin** regards the United States as the only major threat to the achievement of its fundamental design. There is a basic conflict between the idea of freedom under a government of laws, and the idea of slavery under the grim **oligarchy** of the Kremlin....*

The idea of freedom is the most contagious idea in history.... The breadth of freedom cannot be tolerated in a society which has come under the domination of an individual or group of individuals with a will to absolute power....

*Thus unwillingly our free society finds itself mortally challenged by the Soviet system. No other value system is so wholly irreconcilable with ours, so **implacable** in its purpose to destroy ours, ... and no other has the support of a great and growing center of military power....*

*Practical and ideological considerations therefore both **impel** us to the conclusion that we have no choice but to demonstrate the superiority of the idea of freedom ... and to attempt to change the world situation by means short of war in such a way as to frustrate the Kremlin design and hasten the decay of the Soviet system....*

Our overall policy at the present time may be described as one designed to foster a world environment in which the American system can survive and flourish. It therefore rejects the concept of isolation and affirms the necessity of our positive participation in the world community.... [We must produce] *a policy of attempting to develop a healthy international community ...* [and] *the policy of "containing" the Soviet system....*

*As for the policy of "containment," it is one which seeks by all means short of war to (1) block further expansion of Soviet power; (2) expose the falsities of Soviet **pretensions**; (3) **induce a retraction** of the Kremlin's control and influence; and, (4) in general, so foster the seeds of destruction within the Soviet system that the Kremlin is brought at least to the point of modifying its behavior to conform to generally accepted international standards....*

In the concept of "containment," the maintenance of a strong military posture is deemed to be essential.

Kremlin: Soviet government.

Oligarchy: A government in which only a few persons hold all the power.

Implacable: Relentless.

Impel: Force.

Pretensions: Claims.

Induce a retraction: Cause a withdrawal.

At the same time, it is essential to the successful conduct of a policy of "containment" that we always leave open the possibility of negotiation with the U.S.S.R. [the Soviet Union]....

In "containment" it is desirable to exert pressure in a fashion which will avoid so far as possible directly challenging Soviet prestige, to keep open the possibility for the U.S.S.R. to retreat before pressure with a minimum loss of face....

We have failed to implement adequately ... aspects of "containment." In the face of obviously mounting Soviet military strength ours has declined relatively.... We now find ourselves at a diplomatic **impasse** with the Soviet Union, with the Kremlin growing bolder....

It is quite clear from Soviet theory and practice that the Kremlin seeks to bring the free world under its dominion by the methods of the cold war. The preferred technique is to subject by **infiltration** and **intimidation**.... Those institutions of our society that touch most closely our material and moral strength are obviously the prime targets: labor unions, civic enterprises, schools, churches, and all media for influencing opinion....

A program for rapidly building up strength and improving political and economic conditions will place heavy demands on our courage and intelligence; it will be costly; it will be dangerous. But half-measures will be more costly and more dangerous, for they will be inadequate to prevent and may actually invite war. Budgetary considerations will need to be subordinated to the stark fact that our very independence as a nation may be at stake....

A comprehensive and decisive program to win the peace and frustrate the Kremlin design ... would probably involve:

(1) The development of an adequate political and economic framework for the achievement of our long-range objectives.

(2) A substantial increase in expenditures for military purposes adequate to meet the requirements for the tasks listed in Section D-1 [a recommendation section].

(3) A substantial increase in military assistance programs, designed to foster cooperative efforts, which will adequately and efficiently meet the requirements of our allies for the tasks referred to in Section D-1-e.

(4) Some increase in economic assistance programs [for our allies] and recognition of the need to continue these programs until their purposes have been accomplished....

Impasse: A situation with no escape.

Infiltration: The act of secretly penetrating a group or an organization.

Intimidation: Threats meant to cause fear and influence decision-making.

*(6) Development of programs designed to build and maintain confidence among other peoples in our strength and resolution, and to wage **overt** psychological warfare calculated to encourage mass defections from Soviet allegiance and to frustrate the Kremlin design in other ways.*

*(7) Intensification of **affirmative** and timely measures and operations by **covert** means in the fields of economic warfare and political and psychological warfare with a view to **fomenting** and supporting unrest and revolt in selected strategic satellite countries.*

(8) Development of internal security and civilian defense programs.

*(9) Improvement and intensification of **intelligence activities**.*

*(10) Reduction of Federal **expenditures** for purposes other than defense and foreign assistance, if necessary by the **deferment** of certain desirable programs.*

Our position as the center of power in the free world places a heavy responsibility upon the United States for leadership....

Our national security demands that we achieve our objectives by the strategy of the cold war, building up our military strength in order that it may not have to be used....

The whole success of the proposed program hangs ultimately on recognition by this Government, the American people, and all free peoples, that the cold war is in fact a real war in which the survival of the free world is at stake.

Overt: Out in the open.

Affirmative: Positive.

Covert: Secret.

Fomenting: Causing.

Intelligence activities: Spying.

Expenditures: Spending.

Deferment: Delay.

What happened next ...

President Truman and the Republican-controlled Congress were not prepared to spend the billions of dollars requested to comply with the recommendations in NSC-68. The report was widely viewed as overblown, painting a picture of the Soviets on a determined march to world conquest. Afterall, it was only five years after the end of World War II (1939–45), in which the Soviets suffered massive damage. George F. Kennan, author of the "Long Telegram," believed that the Soviets had no intention of going to war with anyone at this time. However, Nitze's report was less interested in possible Soviet inten-

tions and more interested in what the Soviets were actually capable of militarily, especially now that they had atomic weapons. Nevertheless, NSC-68 was shelved, but not for long.

President Harry S. Truman meets with the National Security Council for a defense briefing.
Reproduced by permission of the Corbis Corporation.

The Soviets had paid attention in 1949 when Secretary of State Dean Acheson (1893–1971) said that the Southeast Asian country of Korea was outside the U.S. perimeter of defense. Coupled with the fact that the United States had not stood in the way of the communist takeover of China, the Soviets and the communist leader of North Korea, Kim Il Sung (1912–1994), expected no U.S. action when Kim's army launched a surprise military attack on democratic South Korea on June 25, 1950. The Soviets, as revealed in Soviet documents released in the 1990s, reasoned that if the United States was in Japan, then they needed to have Korea.

NSC-68 immediately came off the shelf. Truman decided that the United States must respond. Korea became the first hot spot in the Cold War, and it became a test of the United States' tougher policy on confronting communist expansion.

Did you know …

- The NSC-68 report called for military defense spending to go from a budget of less than $14 billion a year to $50 billion a year.

- As a result of the communist North Korean invasion of South Korea, the basic elements of NSC-68 were widely viewed as correct.

- The United States began a massive military buildup to counter any possible communist aggression.

Consider the following ...

- Recall Isaac Don Levine's words in the first excerpt of this chapter. In light of NSC-68 and the Korean invasion, do you think Levine's viewpoint of U.S. defense was justified?

- Imagine yourself as a young person in the summer of 1950. What would your assessment of Soviet intentions be?

For More Information

Books

Foreign Relations of the United States (FRUS), 1950, Volume I, National Security Affairs, Foreign Economic Policy. Washington, DC: U.S. Government Printing Office, 1977.

LaFeber, Walter. *America, Russia, and the Cold War, 1945–1996.* 8th ed. New York: McGraw-Hill, 1997.

Larson, Deborah W. *Anatomy of Mistrust: U.S.-Soviet Relations During the Cold War.* Ithaca, NY: Cornell University Press, 1997.

McCullough, David. *Truman.* New York: Simon and Schuster, 1992.

Talbott, Strobe. *The Master of the Game: Paul Nitze and the Nuclear Peace.* New York: Vintage Books, 1989.

Web Site

Truman Presidential Museum and Library. http://www.trumanlibrary.org (accessed on September 10, 2003).

Douglas MacArthur

Excerpt from "Old Soldiers Never Die; They Just Fade Away"
Speech, April 19, 1951
Published in *Congressional Record*, 1951

Before World War II (1939–45), Korea was a colony of Japan. With Japan's surrender ending World War II in August 1945, the Soviet Union and the United States divided Korea into two parts at the thirty-eighth parallel. The North was under Soviet communist influence; the South under the influence of the democratic United States. The North became the Democratic People's Republic of Korea under communist Kim Il Sung (1912–1994). The South became the Republic of Korea led by Syngman Rhee (1875–1965), who had lived in the United States for thirty years. In June 1949, both Soviet and U.S. forces pulled out of Korea. Military disturbances and skirmishes increased as both Kim and Rhee tried to claim leadership over the entire country.

On June 25, 1950, Kim launched a surprise military assault on South Korea, most likely with the knowledge and approval of Soviet leader Joseph Stalin (1879–1953). If the United States had a presence in Japan, the Soviets wanted Korea.

U.S. president Harry S. Truman (1884–1972; served 1945–53) immediately sought and got a United Nations (UN) resolution to assist South Korea. Eventually, sixteen nations

"When I joined the Army even before the turn of the century, it was the fulfillment of all my boyish hopes and dreams. The world has turned over many times since I took the oath on the plain at West Point, and the hopes and dreams have long since vanished. But I still remember the refrain of one of the most popular barrack ballads of that day which proclaimed most proudly that—'Old soldiers never die; they just fade away.'"

President Harry S. Truman and General Douglas MacArthur in 1950.

Reproduced by permission of AP/Wide World Photos.

would participate, but the United States was by far the major military contributor. On June 27, Truman authorized U.S. naval and air forces to move to Korea. On June 30, U.S. ground forces were sent. North Korea had already pushed down through South Korea. Truman made General Douglas MacArthur (1880–1964), who had been serving as Supreme Commander of the Allied Forces in Japan since the end of World War II, commander of all United Nations troops in Korea. General MacArthur brilliantly landed troops at Inchon behind North Korean lines, cutting the communist army in two. The North Koreans made a hasty retreat back to the thirty-eighth parallel. MacArthur led UN forces into North Korea and pushed them all the way to the China border. MacArthur did not take Chinese threats of invasion seriously, but China, with two to three hundred thousand troops, pushed MacArthur back to the thirty-eighth parallel. MacArthur insisted the United States should attack China, perhaps targeting specific areas with nuclear weapons. MacArthur said that the Soviets would not enter the conflict and the United States need not worry about them.

Appalled at MacArthur's severe demands, Truman fired MacArthur on April 11, 1951. It was a highly unpopular move with many Americans. When MacArthur arrived in San Francisco, half a million people turned out to meet him. MacArthur then proceeded across the country, greeted enthusiastically by thousands all along the way. He was invited to address a joint session of Congress.

MacArthur spoke to Congress on April 19, 1951. His main themes were anticommunism and the importance of Asia, a point journalist Isaac Don Levine (1892–1981) wrote in an article (see earlier excerpt) made in response to an analysis of the China situation, called the White Paper, written by U.S. secretary of state Dean Acheson (1893–1971), which suggested that the fate of China lay with the Chinese themselves. Several of MacArthur's statements became quite well known, especially, "In war, indeed, there can be no substitute for victory." This sentence seemed to smack at the policy of containment of communism. Apparently, MacArthur would rather see an all-out attack by the military instead of the maintenance of just a strong-enough presence to "contain" the enemy. Near the end of the speech, he quoted a line from an old ballad he had sung as a cadet at West Point: "Old soldiers never die; they just fade away."

Things to remember while reading the excerpt from the "Old Soldiers Never Die; They Just Fade Away" speech, April 19, 1951:

- General Douglas MacArthur, who commanded U.S. troops in the Pacific during World War II, was a larger-than-life, extremely popular war hero.

- President Harry Truman knew that the dismissal of MacArthur would likely cause a firestorm of protest in the United States.

- It was a very special occurrence for a U.S. general to address a joint session of Congress. The previous occasion was by General Dwight D. Eisenhower (1890–1969) at the end of World War II in 1945. The speech received maximum media coverage.

Excerpt from the "Old Soldiers Never Die; They Just Fade Away" speech, April 19, 1951

*Mr. President, Mr. Speaker, and distinguished Members of the Congress, I stand on this **rostrum** with a sense of deep humility and great pride—humility in the wake of those great American architects of our history who have stood here before me, pride in the reflection that this forum of legislative debate represents human liberty in the purest form yet devised. [Applause.] Here are centered the hopes, and aspirations, and faith of the entire human race.*

*I do not stand here as advocate for any **partisan** cause.... I trust, therefore, that you will do me the justice of receiving that which I have to say as solely expressing the considered viewpoint of a fellow American. I address you with neither **rancor** nor bitterness in the fading twilight of life with but one purpose in mind—to serve my country. [Applause.]*

*The issues are global and so interlocked that to consider the problems of one sector, **oblivious** to those of another, is but to court disaster for the whole.*

While Asia is commonly referred to as the gateway to Europe, it is no less true that Europe is the gateway to Asia, and the broad influence of the one cannot fail to have its impact upon the other.

There are those who claim our strength is inadequate to protect on both fronts—that we cannot divide our effort. I can think of no greater expression of defeatism. [Applause.] If a potential enemy can divide his strength on two fronts, it is for us to counter his effort.

The Communist threat is a global one. Its successful advance in our sector threatens the destruction of every other sector. You cannot appease or otherwise surrender to communism in Asia without simultaneously undermining our efforts to halt its advance in Europe.... [Applause.]

*Efforts have been made to distort my position. It has been said, in effect, that I am a **warmonger**. Nothing could be further from the truth. I know war as few other men now living know it, and nothing to me is more revolting. I have long advocated its complete abolition as its very destructiveness on both friend and foe has rendered it useless*

Rostrum: Podium.

Partisan: Strong support for a cause.

Rancor: Anger.

Oblivious: Blind to something or unknowing.

Warmonger: One who enthusiastically favors war.

as a means of settling international disputes. Indeed, on the second day of September 1945, just following the surrender of the Japanese Nation on the battleship Missouri, I formally cautioned as follows:

"Men since the beginning of time have sought peace. Various methods through the ages have been attempted to devise an international process to prevent or settle disputes between nations. From the very start, workable methods were found insofar as individual

General Douglas MacArthur (center, with glasses) was the most controversial U.S. military figure of the Cold War because of his strong anticommunist views.
Reproduced by permission of AP/Wide World Photos.

citizens were concerned, but the mechanics of an **instrumentality** of larger international scope have never been successful. Military alliances, balances of power, leagues of nations, all in turn failed, leaving the only path to be by way of the crucible of war. The utter destructiveness of war now blots out this alternative. We have had our last chance. If we will not devise some greater and more equitable system, **Armageddon** will be at our door. The problem basically is theological and involves a spiritual **recrudescence** and improvement of human character that will synchronize with our almost matchless advances in science, art, literature, and all material and cultural developments of the past 2,000 years. It must be of the spirit if we are to save the flesh." [Applause.]

But once war is forced upon us, there is no other alternative than to supply every available means to bring it to a swift end. War's very object is victory—not prolonged indecision. [Applause.] In war, indeed, there can be no substitute for victory. [Applause.]

There are some who for varying reasons would **appease** Red China. They are blind to history's clear lesson. For history teaches with unmistakable emphasis that appeasement but begets new and bloodier war. It points to no single instance where the end has justified that means—where appeasement has led to more than a sham peace. Like blackmail, it lays the basis for new and successively greater demands, until, as in blackmail, violence becomes the only other alternative. Why, my soldiers asked of me, surrender military advantages to an enemy in the field? I could not answer. [Applause.] Some may say to avoid spread of the conflict into an all-out war with China; others, to avoid Soviet intervention.... Like a cobra, any new enemy will more likely strike whenever it feels that the **relativity** in military or other potential is in its favor on a world-wide basis.

The tragedy of Korea is further heightened by the fact that as military action is confined to its territorial limits, it condemns that nation, which it is our purpose to save, to suffer the devastating impact of full naval and air bombardment, while the enemy's **sanctuaries** are fully protected from such attack and devastation. Of the nations of the world, Korea alone, up to now, is the sole one which has risked its all against communism. The magnificence of the courage and fortitude of the Korean people defies description. [Applause.] They have chosen to risk death rather than slavery. Their last words to me were "Don't scuttle the Pacific." [Applause.]

I have just left your fighting sons in Korea. They have met all tests there and I can report to you without reservation they are splendid in

Instrumentality: The ways to settle disputes.

Armageddon: Decisive last battle.

Recrudescence: Revival.

Appease: Placate.

Relativity: Loss of absolute will.

Sanctuaries: Hiding places.

every way. [Applause.] It was my constant effort to preserve them *and end this savage conflict honorably and with the least loss of time and a minimum sacrifice of life. Its growing bloodshed has caused me the deepest anguish, and anxiety. Those gallant men will remain often in my thoughts and in my prayers always. [Applause.]*

I am closing my 52 years of military service. [Applause.] When I joined the Army even before the turn of the century, it was the ful-

General Douglas MacArthur delivers a farewell address to Congress after being relieved of his command in Korea in 1951. *Reproduced by permission of the Corbis Corporation.*

fillment of all my boyish hopes and dreams. The world has turned over many times since I took the oath on the plain at West Point, and the hopes and dreams have long since vanished. But I still remember the refrain of one of the most popular barrack ballads of that day which proclaimed most proudly that—

"Old soldiers never die; they just fade away."

And like the old soldier of that ballad, I now close my military career and just fade away—an old soldier who tried to do his duty as God gave him the light to see that duty.

Good-bye.

What happened next ...

Popular protest at MacArthur's dismissal resulted in a U.S. Senate investigation. However, the investigation results did not help his cause. If MacArthur had moved on China, the results could have been devastating for the world. General Omar Bradley (1893–1981), who replaced MacArthur, said an all-out war with China would have been "The wrong war, wrong place, wrong time, wrong enemy." Nevertheless, conservatives believed MacArthur's aggression was just what was needed. Liberal thought was with President Truman—that an aging military man (MacArthur) had gotten out of hand and could have led the United States into a nuclear war if the Soviet Union had jumped in.

The Korean War dragged on until a cease-fire agreement was finally signed in June 1953. U.S. troops would remain in South Korea into the twenty-first century.

Did you know ...
- General MacArthur graduated first in his class at West Point in 1903.

- Fifty-four thousand Americans and 3.6 million Koreans were killed in the Korean War.

- One million Chinese were killed or wounded in the Korean War, including the son of Chinese communist leader Mao Zedong (1893–1976).

- An official peace treaty was never signed between North and South Korea, only a cease-fire agreement. Korea remained an area of controversy throughout the twentieth century and into the twenty-first.

Consider the following ...

- Do you think MacArthur would have caused a nuclear war to be unleashed? Why or why not?

- MacArthur delivered his speech eloquently and raised issues about war that still are debated at the beginning of the twenty-first century. Choose a point that interests you and describe how it would be received in various American groups, liberal and conservative, in the twenty-first century.

For More Information

Books

Blair, Clay. *The Forgotten War: America in Korea, 1950–1953*. New York: Time Books, 1987.

Congressional Record, 1951. Washington, DC: Government Printing Office, 1951.

MacArthur, Douglas. *Reminiscences*. New York: McGraw-Hill, 1964.

Manchester, William. *American Caesar: Douglas MacArthur, 1880–1964*. Boston: Little, Brown, 1978.

Peret, Geoffrey. *Old Soldiers Never Die: The Life of Douglas MacArthur*. New York: Random House, 1996.

Web Site

United States of America Korean War Commemoration. http://korea50.army.mil (accessed on September 10, 2003).

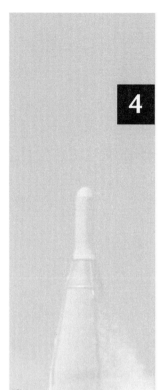

4

Those Who Strove for Peace

By 1952, both the democratic United States and the communist Soviet Union were locked in the Cold War (1945–91). The United States was ready to defend against communism anywhere in the world. With sixty member nations, the United Nations (UN), which formed in 1945 at the end of World War II (1939–45), struggled to become an important worldwide peacekeeping organization. Many critics said the UN was only a propaganda platform from which the communists could speak. Eleanor Roosevelt (1884–1962), wife of deceased U.S. president Franklin D. Roosevelt (1882–1945; served 1933–45) and herself a member of the U.S. delegation to the UN, spoke forcefully on behalf of the UN. The first excerpt here is "Mrs. Franklin D. Roosevelt's Address to the [1952] Democratic National Convention on the Importance of the United Nations." It is one of several speeches given in this general time period by Eleanor Roosevelt that were hailed worldwide. Even critics of the UN conceded that she made significant contributions to public thought on the future of the UN.

U.S. president Dwight D. Eisenhower (1890–1969; served 1953–61) made two famous speeches in 1953 that also nudged along the thought process about peace. The second excerpt that follows is "The Chance for Peace" address delivered before the American Society of Newspaper Editors on April 16, 1953. The third excerpt is the "Atoms for Peace" speech delivered before the General Assembly of the United Nations in New York City on December 8, 1953.

Amid an ever-escalating nuclear arms race between the two superpowers, Eisenhower nevertheless spoke eloquently in both speeches for the peace process. He advocated limiting the arms race and using nuclear power for the betterment of mankind, not its destruction. However, the fear and mutual distrust between the United States and the Soviet Union was too great. Eisenhower's thoughts were too far ahead of their time. It would be many decades before the steps he called for in the two speeches would be realized.

Eleanor Roosevelt

Excerpt from "Mrs. Franklin D. Roosevelt's Address to the Democratic National Convention on the Importance of the United Nations, Chicago, Illinois, July 23, 1952"

Reprinted in *A Treasury of Great America Speeches*, published in 1970

"In examining what the UN has done, and what it is striving to do, it must be remembered that peace, like freedom, is elusive, hard to come by, harder to keep. It cannot be put into a purse or a hip pocket and buttoned there to stay."

In Chicago, Illinois, on July 23, 1952, Eleanor Roosevelt (1884–1962), wife of the late U.S. president Franklin D. Roosevelt (1882–1945; served 1933–45), spoke to the Democratic National Convention concerning the United Nations (UN). Since President Roosevelt's death in 1945, Eleanor Roosevelt had continued to be an influential public figure. In this speech, she spoke to those in the Democratic Party not yet convinced of the worth of the UN. She was also speaking to those outside the party who considered the UN to be only a forum for communists to proclaim their party line.

The UN was born in 1945 when fifty member nations voted to accept a charter, or document establishing the organization. The UN was the second attempt to establish a worldwide peacekeeping organization in the twentieth century. The first attempt, known as the League of Nations, was formed after World War I (1914–18), but it proved ineffective. On December 10, 1948, the UN approved a Universal Declaration of Human Rights that Eleanor Roosevelt had helped to author. In June 1950, the Security Council of the UN approved a resolution to send

UN troops to Korea to halt communist North Korea's invasion of democratic South Korea.

In her speech, Eleanor Roosevelt first related that her husband had been determined to establish "another world organization to help us keep the peace of the world." She stated that the United Nations was "mankind's best hope" to promote peace. She reminded her audience that peace was "elusive, hard to come by, harder to keep." She affirmed that the United States could "no longer live apart from the rest of the world." Calling those who attack the United Nations "short-sighted," she stated that the United States, because of its "national strength," must provide a key leadership role for the democratic nations of the world. She spoke of the tragedy in Korea and of the many men still fighting there at the time. She also pointed out that Korea was the first "application," or use of combined forces from a number of nations, under the banner of the UN. (The UN had also helped to keep the peace in Iran, Greece, Palestine, Indonesia, Pakistan, and India.) Eleanor Roosevelt, while strongly affirming the need to halt the spread of communism, also noted that it was fortunate that the UN provided a place where the United States and communists could meet.

Since her husband died, Eleanor Roosevelt had, as an individual, carved a place for herself in foreign affairs. She had a strong, forceful character and obvious talent for persuasive public speaking. This speech was considered an example of her strength of expression. Even critics of the United Nations credited her with stimulating thought and debate on the important subject of the peacekeeping organization.

Things to remember while reading "Mrs. Franklin D. Roosevelt's Address to the Democratic National Convention on the Importance of the United Nations":

- Eleanor Roosevelt was a member of the U.S. delegation to the United Nations from 1945 to 1951.

- The UN was only seven years old and had many critics. It was still unclear if the UN could indeed survive as the world's forum for debate and compromise to keep peace.

Former first lady Eleanor Roosevelt speaks to the Democratic National Convention in 1952 about the worth of the United Nations. *Courtesy of the Library of Congress.*

League of Nations: An international organization created after World War I to peacefully resolve disputes between nations.

Excerpt from "Mrs. Franklin D. Roosevelt's Address to the Democratic National Convention on the Importance of the United Nations"

You are very kind to me and I am glad to have been asked to talk to you about the United Nations, about its past, about what it is doing today and more important, about its future.

I remember well, even though it seems a long time ago, hearing for the first time a statement and the reasons why, when the war ended, we must make another try to create another world organization to help us keep the peace of the world. This talk took place in my husband's study in the White House one evening during the bitter days of the last war when victory was not yet in sight.

*My husband, discussing what would happen after the war, turned to a friend and said in effect, "When this war is over and we have won it, as we will, we must apply the hard lessons learned in the war and in the failure of the **League of Nations** to the task of building a society of nations dedicated to enduring peace. There will be sacrifices and discouragements but we must not fail for we may never have another chance."*

There have been sacrifices and discouragements, triumphs and set-backs. The United Nations is attempting to convert this last chance, carrying mankind's best hope, into an effective instrument that will enable our children and our children's children to maintain peace in their time. The path upon which we have set our course is not an easy one. The trail is often difficult to find. We must make our maps as we go along but we travel in good company with men and women of good-will in the free countries of the world.

Without the United Nations our country would walk alone, ruled by fear, instead of confidence and hope. To weaken or hamstring the United Nations now, through lack of faith and lack of vision, would be to condemn ourselves to endless struggle for survival in a jungle world.

In examining what the UN has done, and what it is striving to do, it must be remembered that peace, like freedom, is elusive, hard to come by, harder to keep. It cannot be put into a purse or a hip pocket and buttoned there to stay. To achieve peace we must recognize the historic truth that we can no longer live apart from the rest of the world. We must also recognize the fact that peace, like freedom, is not won once and for all. It is fought for daily, in many small acts, and is the result of many individual efforts.

These are days of shrinking horizons, a "neighborhood of nations though unhappily all of us are not as yet good neighbors."

We should remember that the UN is not a cure-all. It is only an instrument capable of effective action when its members have a will to make it work. It cannot be any better than the individual nations are. You often ask what can I, as an individual, do to help the US, to help in the struggle for a peaceful world.

I answer—Make your own country the best possible country for all its citizens to live in and it will become a valuable member of the Neighborhood of Nations. This can only be done with home, community, representatives.

The UN is the machinery through which peace may be achieved and it is the responsibility of 60 nations and their delegations to make that machinery work. Yet you and I may carry the greatest responsibility because our national strength has given us opportunities for leadership among the nations of the free world.

Eleanor Roosevelt, reading the United Nations Bill of Rights. The document was formulated by the Economic and Social Council, which she led.
Reproduced by permission of the Corbis Corporation.

The UN is the only machinery for the furtherance of peace that exists today. There is a small articulate minority in this country which advocates changing our national symbol which is the eagle to that of the ostrich and withdrawing from the UN. This minority reminds me of a story of a short-sighted and selfish man who put green goggles on his cow and fed her sawdust. The cow became sick and died. I warn you against the short-sighted and selfish men who are trying to distort the vision of the American people. We must have eagle eyes. These men who lack vision are poor in hope. They turn their backs on the future and live in the past. They seek to weaken and destroy this world organization through their attacks on the UN. They are expressing a selfish, destructive approach which leads not to peace but to chaos and might eventually lead to World War Three....

*This brings us to the action taken by the UN which has brought sorrow into many American homes. The Communist attack on Korea and the brilliant fight put up by our armies is a matter of history. When the attack occurred we had two choices. We could meet it or let aggression triumph by **default** and thereby invite further piecemeal conquests all over the Globe. This inevitably would have led to World War Three just as the appeasement of Munich and seizure of Czechoslovakia led to World War Two, the most destructive war in history....*

We pray for a just and lasting peace in Korea for the sake of the people of that land and for our own men and those soldiers of the United Nations fighting with them. We cannot hurry this peace until the Communists agree to honest terms. If you ask the reason why our men are in Korea I think it was perhaps best summed up by an American flying Ace, Major James Jabara, who upon returning to his home in Wichita, Kansas, in an interview was asked what his feelings were while fighting in Korea. Major Jabara said, "I fought in Korea so I would not have to fight on Main Street in Wichita."

Korea was not only the first successful application of collective security on the part of the UN to stop aggression, without provoking general war, but it has stimulated a free world to build up its defenses. It has not been as quick in the achievement of results as it would have been if the UN had been fully organized to put down any aggression. It has been impossible to organize that machinery as yet because two nations, the US and the USSR [the Soviet Union] haven't been able to come to an agreement as to how this collective security within the UN may be organized. We think the fault lies with the USSR because she will not see that without a planned

Default: Inactivity.

method of disarmament and control of all weapons, adequately ver-
ified through inspection, we and many other nations in the world
cannot feel safe, but at least through the UN we can go on with ne-
gotiations and pray for a pure heart and clean hands which may
eventually bring us the confidence even of the Soviet Union and
lead us to the desired results.

In the UN we meet with the Communists and it is fortunate this
meeting place exists. We know we cannot relax our vigilance or stop
our efforts to control the spread of communism. Their attacks on us
in the UN have one great value—they keep us from forgetting our
*shortcomings or to become **apathetic** in our efforts to improve our*
democracy.

The UN has helped to keep the peace in many areas of the
world, notably in Iran and Greece and Palestine and Indonesia, and
Pakistan and India. These disputes might have spread into a gener-
al war and torn the free world apart and opened the way for Com-
munist expansion and another world war.

Eleanor Roosevelt, sitting with cadets at West Point military academy in 1951. After President Franklin D. Roosevelt's death in 1945, the former first lady continued to be an influential public figure. *Reproduced by permission of the Franklin Delano Roosevelt Library.*

Apathetic: Lacking emotion or desire.

Eleanor Roosevelt, speaking at the 1956 Democratic National Convention.
Reproduced by permission of Corbis Corporation.

Bi-partisan: Both Democratic and Republican.

While the UN came into being under the present Administration and President [Harry] Truman has been steadfast in his support of the organization, the UN would not be in existence today if it were not for strong **bi-partisan** support in the very beginning.

I beg you to keep an open mind, never to forget the interests of your own country but to remember your own country may be able *to make a contribution which is valuable in the area of human rights and freedoms in joining with other nations not merely in a declaration but in **covenants.***

I returned not long ago from parts of the world where our attitude on human rights and freedoms affects greatly our leadership.

Some of you will probably be thinking that once upon a time the old lady speaking to you now did a tremendous amount of traveling around the United States. In fact, you may remember a cartoon showing two men down in a coal mine, one man saying to the other: "Gosh, here comes Eleanor. Now what is she doing—traveling around the world just making more trouble?"...

I hope all our travels may serve the great common hope that through the United Nations peace may come to the world....

Covenants: Formal agreements.

What happened next ...

One year later, on July 27, 1953, the United Nations' forces signed a cease-fire agreement with North Korea, ending the Korean War. The UN survived its early critics to become the key organization for keeping world peace, security, and human rights. By the beginning of the twenty-first century, it had more than 160 member nations.

Eleanor Roosevelt remained an influential figure in international affairs. She received dignitaries from all over the world at her home, Val Kill, in Hyde Park, New York. Presidents of the United States also sought out her advice. She died in 1962.

Did you know ...

- Although the energetic Eleanor Roosevelt was sixty-seven years of age when she gave this address, she continued to write and to travel around the world pursuing human rights for oppressed people and worldwide peace.

- President Franklin D. Roosevelt served the country the longest of any U.S. president, from 1933 to 1945.

Throughout that time, Eleanor Roosevelt, as first lady, maintained a high public profile traveling throughout the United States, acting, in effect, as the eyes and ears of the president. President Roosevelt, confined to a wheelchair after contracting polio as a young adult, could not move about the country as easily.

Consider the following ...

- Eleanor Roosevelt quotes Korean veteran Major James Jabara (1923–1966) from Wichita, Kansas, as saying, "I fought in Korea so I would not have to fight on Main Street in Wichita." Explain what he meant.

- Research the United Nations, its structure, and the important dates in its history through 2000.

For More Information

Books

Bauer, Andrew, ed. *A Treasury of Great America Speeches.* New York: Hawthorne Books, 1970.

Cook, Blanche W. *Eleanor Roosevelt.* New York: Viking, 1992.

Glendon, Mary Ann. *A World Made New: Eleanor Roosevelt and the Universal Declaration of Human Rights.* New York: Random House, 2001.

Hilderbrand, Robert C. *Dumbarton Oaks: The Origins of the United Nations and the Search for Postwar Security.* Chapel Hill: University of North Carolina Press, 1990.

Pruden, Caroline. *Conditional Partners: Eisenhower, the United Nations, and the Search for a Permanent Peace.* Baton Rouge: Louisiana State University Press, 1998.

White, N. D. *Keeping the Peace: The United Nations and the Maintenance of International Peace and Security.* New York: St. Martin's Press, 1997.

Dwight D. Eisenhower

Excerpt from "The Chance for Peace" address delivered before the American Society of Newspaper Editors, April 16, 1953

Published in *Public Papers of the Presidents of the United States: Dwight D. Eisenhower*, Volume 1953

On April 16, 1953, U.S. president Dwight D. Eisenhower (1890–1969; served 1953–61) addressed the American Society of Newspaper Editors. He titled his address "The Chance for Peace," in response to statements made by the new premier of the Soviet Union, Georgy Malenkov (1902–1988). Soviet premier Joseph Stalin (1879–1953) had died in March and, with his death, his terror-filled dictatorship at last ended. Nikita Khrushchev (1894–1971) became the new Soviet Communist Party leader, the secretary general, a very powerful position.

Malenkov hoped to focus on Soviet internal issues and domestic economy and the well-being of the Soviet people. In strong contrast to Stalin's views that capitalism and communism could not peacefully coexist in the world and that war was inevitable, Malenkov declared peaceful solutions existed to solve the international Cold War problems. In early April, he had proposed talks to reduce military forces in Europe so he could concentrate more on Soviet issues. In response, President Eisenhower delivered his "Chance for Peace" speech.

During World War II (1939–45), Eisenhower had become a legend as a commanding general. Before being elect-

"Now a new leadership has assumed power in the Soviet Union. Its links to the past, however strong, cannot bind it completely. Its future is, in great part, its own to make. This new leadership confronts a free world aroused, as rarely in its history, by the will to stay free. This free world knows, out of the bitter wisdom of experience, that vigilance and sacrifice are the price of liberty."

ed to the U.S. presidency in November 1952, Eisenhower had served as a U.S. army general in World War II. In December 1943, President Franklin D. Roosevelt (1882–1945; served 1933–45) made Eisenhower supreme commander of Allied forces to lead a massive invasion across the English Channel at the Normandy shores of France. Eisenhower executed a brilliant plan and was able to keep the strong, diverse personalities of the other Allied commanders focused toward the common goal of pushing back the occupying Germans. After liberating France, Eisenhower was promoted to a five-star general in December 1944. He was victorious at the Battle of the Bulge in Belgium and began moving troops into Germany. In the final months of the war, Eisenhower decided to let Soviet troops march on and take Germany's capital city of Berlin. He hoped to foster goodwill with the Soviets in anticipation of postwar cooperation and to avoid some difficult fighting for his own troops.

Following the German surrender in May 1945, Eisenhower returned to a hero's ticker-tape parade in New York City and spoke to an enthusiastic joint session of Congress in Washington, D.C. President Roosevelt then sent him to Germany as head of the U.S.-occupied zone in Germany. There, he tried to cooperate with Stalin on postwar policies, but Stalin ignored key agreed-upon points such as allowing free elections in Eastern European countries. Shortly thereafter, in November, Eisenhower returned to Washington, D.C., to replace General George C. Marshall (1880–1959) as army chief of staff. Eisenhower retired in February 1948 as an extremely popular World War II general. He wrote the bestseller *Crusade in Europe* and served as president of Columbia University for two years. Then President Harry S. Truman (1884–1972; served 1945–53) talked him into commanding the Allied forces of the North Atlantic Treaty Organization (NATO). The organization was a newly formed military alliance between Western European countries and the United States and Canada.

The U.S. Republican Party leaders had been trying unsuccessfully to talk Eisenhower into running for political office for several years. They finally convinced him to run in the 1952 presidential election. Eisenhower chose Richard M. Nixon (1913–1994), a young U.S. representative from Califor-

nia with a strong anticommunist record, as his vice presidential running mate. Immensely popular with the public, Eisenhower won easily. The public had grown dismayed with President Truman, who had been unable to direct the Korean War (1950–53) to a successful end and had "allowed" a communist takeover of China in 1949. Also, in November 1952, the United States had detonated the world's first hydrogen bomb (H-bomb) on the Marshall Island of Eniwetok. The H-bomb exploded with the force of 10 million tons (9 million metric tons) of TNT—one thousand times more force than the atomic bomb dropped on Hiroshima, Japan, in August 1945. The world had become a more dangerous place.

Following Stalin's death and at Malenkov's overtures of a peaceful coexistence, President Eisenhower's words in "The Chance for Peace" were not directed only at those attending a newspaper editors' conference but to all Americans, to the Soviets, and to the world as a whole. First, he de-

U.S. president Dwight D. Eisenhower at the first press conference of his presidency in 1953.
Reproduced by permission of AP/Wide World Photos.

scribed "the vastly different vision of the future" that the democratic United States and the communist Soviet Union held. All in the name of protecting themselves from each other, both countries were spending vast sums of money for arms buildup. Eisenhower clearly, specifically, and with a great deal of feeling described how money for armaments, or military supplies, was taking away from "those who hunger and are not fed, those who are cold and are not clothed." He spoke of the new terrible superbombs. President Eisenhower recognized the new Soviet leadership and expressed a great deal of interest in discussing arms reduction.

Eisenhower, however, also made a number of difficult challenges to the Soviets. He called on the Soviets to consider their policies in divided Germany, to halt aggressive acts in Korea and Southeast Asia, to release thousands of prisoners of war it still held from World War II, and to allow Eastern European nations a "free choice of their own forms of government." He called on the Soviets to show how they were breaking with the past and entering a new phase of cooperation. After a listing of possible topics of discussion for armament reductions, he called for a "practical" system of inspection under the United Nations "to assure all armaments limitations that might be agreed to were properly carried out." He called on the Soviets to act, saying, "the hunger for peace is in the hearts of all peoples—those of Russia and of China no less than of our own country."

Things to remember while reading "The Chance for Peace":

- Between the two superpowers, the United States and the Soviet Union, was an overwhelming sense of mistrust. It was difficult to come to any agreements when each feared that the other's actions were calculated to weaken the other.

- One of Eisenhower's major presidential goals was to balance the federal budget, which would require reductions in military spending.

- The idea of inspection systems under the control of the United Nations that could guarantee the United States and the Soviet Union were complying with any arms agreements reached was a radical new idea. The inspections dubbed "Open Skies" called for both the Soviet Union and the United States to fly inspections over the other to alleviate fears of surprise attacks.

Excerpt from "The Chance for Peace"

In this Spring of 1953 the free world weighs one question above all others: the chance for a just peace for all peoples.

To weigh this chance is to summon instantly to mind another recent moment of great decision. It came with that yet more hopeful spring of 1945, bright with the promise of victory and of freedom. The hope of all just men in that moment too was a just and lasting peace.

The 8 years that have passed have seen that hope waver, grow dim, and almost die. And the shadow of fear again has darkly lengthened across the world....

In that spring of victory [1945] the soldiers of the Western Allies met the soldiers of Russia in the center of Europe. They were triumphant comrades in arms. Their peoples shared the joyous prospect of building, in honor of their dead, the only fitting monument—an age of just peace. All these war-weary peoples shared too this concrete, decent purpose: to guard vigilantly against the domination ever again of any part of the world by a single, unbridled aggressive power.

This common purpose lasted an instant and perished. The nations of the world divided to follow two distinct roads.

The United States and our valued friends, the other free nations, chose one road.

The leaders of the Soviet Union chose another....

*This way [the United States' way] was faithful to the spirit that inspired the United Nations: to prohibit **strife,** to relieve tensions, to banish fears. This way was to control and to reduce armaments. This was to allow all nations to devote their energies and resources to the great and good tasks of healing the war's wounds, of clothing and feeding and housing the needy, of perfecting a just political life, of enjoying the fruits of their own free toil.*

Strife: Conflict.

The Soviet government held a vastly different vision of the future.

In the world of its design, security was to be found, not in mutual trust and mutual aid but in force: huge armies, subversion, rule of neighbor nations. The goal was power superiority at all cost. Security was to be sought by denying it to all others.

The result has been tragic for the world and, for the Soviet Union, it has also been **ironic.**

The amassing of Soviet power alerted free nations to a new danger of aggression. It compelled them in self-defense to spend unprecedented money and energy for armaments. It forced them to develop weapons of war now capable of inflicting instant and terrible punishment upon any aggressor....

What can the world, or any nation in it, hope for if no turning is found on this dread road?

The worst to be feared and the best to be expected can be simply stated.

President Dwight D. Eisenhower, addressing the nation about the newly signed cease-fire agreement in Korea in July 1953.
Reproduced by permission of the Corbis Corporation.

The worst *is atomic war.*

The best *would be this: a life of* **perpetual** *fear and tension; a burden of arms draining the wealth and the labor of all peoples; a wasting of strength that defies the American system or the Soviet system or any system to achieve true abundance and happiness for the peoples of this earth.*

Every gun that is made, every warship launched, every rocket fired signifies, in the final sense, a theft from those who hunger and are not fed, those who are cold and are not clothed.

This world in arms is not spending money alone.

It is spending the sweat of its laborers, the genius of its scientists, the hopes of its children.

The cost of one modern heavy bomber is this: a modern brick school in more than 30 cities.

It is two electric power plants, each serving a town of 60,000 population.

Ironic: Opposite of what is expected.

Perpetual: Constant.

It is two fine, fully equipped hospitals.

It is some 50 miles of concrete highway.

We pay for a single fighter plane with half million bushels of wheat.

We pay for a single destroyer with new homes that could have housed more than 8,000 people.

This, I repeat, is the best way of life to be found on the road the world has been taking.

This is not a way of life at all, in any true sense. Under the cloud of the threatening war, it is humanity hanging from a cross of iron.

These plain and cruel truths define the peril and point the hope that come with this spring of 1953.

This is one of those times in the affairs of nations when the gravest choices must be made, if there is to be a turning toward a just and lasting peace.

It is a moment that calls upon the governments of the world to speak their intentions with simplicity and with honesty.

It calls upon them to answer the question that stirs the hearts of all sane men: is there no other way the world may live?

The world knows that an era ended with the death of Joseph Stalin. The extraordinary 30-year span of his rule saw the Soviet Empire expand to reach from the Baltic Sea to the Sea of Japan, finally to dominate 800 million souls.

The Soviet system shaped by Stalin and his predecessors was born of one World War. It survived with stubborn and often amazing courage a second World War. It has lived to threaten a third.

Now a new leadership has assumed power in the Soviet Union. Its links to the past, however strong, cannot bind it completely. Its future is, in great part, its own to make.

This new leadership confronts a free world aroused, as rarely in its history, by the will to stay free.

This free world knows, out of the bitter wisdom of experience, that vigilance and sacrifice are the price of liberty.

It knows that the defense of Western Europe imperatively demands the unity of purpose and action made possible by the

North Atlantic Treaty Organization, embracing a European Defense Community.

It knows that Western Germany deserves to be a free and equal partner in this community and that this, for Germany, is the only safe way to full, final unity.

It knows that aggression in Korea and in southeast Asia are threats to the whole free community to be met by united action.

This is the kind of free world which the new Soviet leadership confronts. It is a world that demands and expects the fullest respect of its rights and interests. It is a world that will always accord the same respect to all others.

So the new Soviet leadership now has a precious opportunity to awaken, with the rest of the world, to the point of peril reached and to help turn the tide of history.

Will it do this?

We do not yet know. Recent statements and gestures of Soviet leaders give some evidence that they may recognize this critical moment.

We welcome every honest act of peace.

We care nothing for mere rhetoric.

*We are only for sincerity of peaceful purpose attested by deeds. The opportunities for such deeds are many. The performance of a greater number of them waits upon no complex **protocol** but upon the simple will to do them. Even a few such clear and specific acts, such as the Soviet Union's signature upon an Austrian treaty or its release of thousands of prisoners still held from World War II, would be impressive signs of sincere intent. They would carry a power of persuasion not to be matched by any amount of **oratory**....*

With all who will work in good faith toward such a peace, we are ready, with renewed resolve, to strive to redeem the near-lost hopes of our day.

*The first great step along this way must be the conclusion of an honorable **armistice** in Korea.*

This means the immediate cessation of hostilities and the prompt initiation of political discussions leading to the holding of free elections in a united Korea.

North Atlantic Treaty Organization: A peacetime alliance of the United States and eleven other nations, and a key factor in the attempt to contain communism.

Protocol: Diplomatic rules and etiquette.

Oratory: Speech.

Armistice: Cease-fire.

It should mean, no less importantly, an end to the direct and indirect attacks upon the security of Indochina [a former federation of states in Southeast Asia, including Laos, Cambodia, and areas that became Vietnam] *and Malaya* [now part of Malaysia]. *For any armistice in Korea that merely released aggressive armies to attack elsewhere would be a fraud.*

We seek, throughout Asia as throughout the world, a peace that is true and total.

Out of this can grow a still wider task—the achieving of just political settlements for the other serious and specific issues between the free world and the Soviet Union.

None of these issues, great or small, is **insoluble**—*given only the will to respect the rights of all nations.*

Again we say: the United States is ready to assume its just part.

We are ready not only to press forward with the present plans for closer unity of the nations of Western Europe but also, upon that foundation, to strive to foster a broader European community, **conducive to** *the free movement of persons, of trade, and of ideas.*

This community would include a free and united Germany, with a government based upon free and secret ballot.

This free community and the full independence of the East European nations could mean the end of the present unnatural division of Europe.

As progress in all these areas strengthens world trust, we could proceed **concurrently** *with the next great work—the reduction of the burden of armaments now weighing upon the world. To this end we would welcome and enter into the most solemn agreements. These could properly include:*

1. The limitation, by absolute numbers or by an agreed international ratio, of the sizes of the military and security forces of all nations.

2. A commitment by all nations to set an agreed limit upon that proportion of total production of certain strategic materials to be devoted to military purposes [that is, to limited production of armaments].

3. International control of atomic energy to promote its use for peaceful purposes only and to insure the prohibition of atomic weapons.

Insoluble: Impossible to solve.

Conducive to: Allowing for.

Concurrently: Together.

4. A limitation or prohibition of other categories of weapons of great destructiveness [nuclear weapons].

5. The enforcement of all these agreed limitations and prohibitions by adequate safeguards, including a practical system of inspection under the United Nations....

This idea of a just and peaceful world is not new or strange to us. It inspired the people of the United States to initiate the European Recovery Program [the Marshall Plan] *in 1947. That program was prepared to treat, with like and equal concern, the needs of Eastern and Western Europe.*

We are prepared to reaffirm, with the most concrete evidence, our readiness to help build a world in which all peoples can be productive and prosperous.

This Government is ready to ask its people to join with all nations in devoting a substantial percentage of the savings achieved by disarmament to a fund for world aid and reconstruction. The purposes of this great work would be to help other peoples to develop the undeveloped areas of the world, to stimulate profitable and fair world trade, to assist all peoples to know the blessings of productive freedom.

The monuments to this new kind of war would be these: roads and schools, hospitals and homes, food and health.

We are ready, in short, to dedicate our strength to serving the needs, rather than the fears, of the world.

We are ready, by these and all such actions, to make of the United Nations an institution that can effectively guard the peace and security of all peoples.

I know of nothing I can add to make plainer the sincere purpose of the United States.

I know of no course, other than that marked by these and similar actions, that can be called the highway of peace.

I know of only one question upon which progress waits. It is this:

What is the Soviet Union ready to do?...

Is the new leadership of the Soviet Union prepared to use its decisive influence in the Communist world, including control of the flow of arms, to bring not merely an **expedient** *truce in Korea but genuine peace in Asia?*

Is it prepared to allow other nations, including those of Eastern Europe, the free choice of their own forms of government?

Expedient: Speedy.

President Dwight D. Eisenhower (behind desk), at a 1955 press conference. *Reproduced by permission of AP/Wide World Photos.*

*Is it prepared to act in concert with others upon serious disarmament proposals to be made firmly effective by **stringent** U.N. control and inspection?...*

If we strive but fail and the world remains armed against itself, it at least need be divided no longer in its clear knowledge of who has condemned humankind to this fate.

The purpose of the United States, in stating these proposals, is simple and clear.

Stringent: Strict.

These proposals spring, without ulterior purpose or political passion, from our calm conviction that the hunger for peace is in the hearts of all peoples—those of Russia and of China no less than of our own country.

What happened next ...

Only two days later, U.S. secretary of state John Foster Dulles (1888–1959) spoke at the same convention of newspaper editors. His words were harshly anticommunist, unlike Eisenhower's.

British prime minister Winston Churchill (1874–1965) had once again been elected prime minister of Great Britain in 1951. A few weeks after Eisenhower's speech, on May 11, Churchill proposed that the world leaders hold a summit meeting to relieve Cold War tensions. Dulles and West German chancellor Konrad Adenauer (1876–1967) argued against such a meeting. They charged that the Soviets were not sincere in peaceful coexistence but only trying to weaken the West. Furthermore, U.S. senator Joseph R. McCarthy (1909–1957) of Wisconsin had stirred up a strong fear of communists among Americans. Dulles successfully used this fear, arguing that Eisenhower's administration could not afford to appear weak in dealing with the communists. The idea of talks between Eisenhower, Malenkov, and Khrushchev faded.

In Korea, after difficult negotiations, a cease-fire agreement was signed in July 1953, bringing an end to hostilities. The new president had managed to bring an end to the stalemated Korean War in just six months (see Chapter 3).

Did you know ...

- When Eisenhower ran for president, his campaign slogan was simply "I Like Ike." On the one hand, his personable mannerisms brought a great deal of comfort to Americans. On the other hand, the Soviets considered Ike a direct threat. They reasoned that if Americans had elected a general, then they must be preparing for war.

- Eisenhower grew up in a strong Mennonite family. Mennonites were known for their extreme pacifism, or opposition to war. Eisenhower's mother was very distressed when he went to West Point. He went to West Point in part because the education was free.

- After the Korean cease-fire, Eisenhower would not lose another U.S. soldier to combat through the remainder of his presidency, an accomplishment of which he was immensely proud.

- It was President Eisenhower, working behind the scenes, together with army lawyer Joseph Welch (1890–1960), who finally brought an end to Senator McCarthy's radical anticommunist campaign in Congress.

Consider the following ...

- Review Eisenhower's list of the cost of single armaments in terms of practical needs of people. Construct a chart to better visualize this list.

- President Eisenhower used some strong imagery in his "Chance for Peace" speech. He described "humanity" as "hanging from a cross of iron." Analyze on several levels what point he was trying to convey. Think in terms of armaments and also of Winston Churchill's famous "Iron Curtain Speech," in which Churchill warned the still-disbelieving Americans that indeed the Soviets were occupying large territories in Eastern Europe with no intention of leaving.

- Although the speech did not result in a summit meeting between the leaders, consider what impact Eisenhower's list of possible arms control suggestions might have played in future negotiations. Was a seed possibly planted?

For More Information

Books

Ambrose, Stephen F. *Eisenhower*. New York: Simon and Schuster, 1983–1984.

Brendon, Piers. *Ike: His Life and Times*. New York: Harper & Row, 1986.

Burk, Robert F. *Dwight D. Eisenhower: Hero and Politician.* Boston: Twayne Publishers, 1986.

Divine, Robert A. *Eisenhower and the Cold War.* New York: Oxford University Press, 1981.

Public Papers of the Presidents of the United States: Dwight D. Eisenhower, Volume 1953. Washington, DC: U.S. Government Printing Office.

Web Site

The Dwight D. Eisenhower Library and Museum. http://www.eisenhower.utexas.edu (accessed on September 11, 2003).

Dwight D. Eisenhower

Excerpt from "Peaceful Uses of Atomic Energy" Speech before the General Assembly of the United Nations, New York City, December 8, 1953

Originally published in *Public Papers of the Presidents of the United States: Dwight D. Eisenhower*, **Volume 1953**

T he hopes expressed by U.S. president Dwight D. Eisenhower (1890–1969; served 1953–61) in April 1953 in his "Chance for Peace" speech were all but dashed on August 12, 1953. On that day, the Soviets answered the successful U.S. hydrogen bomb test on November 1, 1952, with their own detonation of a thermonuclear, or hydrogen, bomb. Although much smaller than the U.S. bomb, it meant that the Soviets were in the arms race for the deadliest weapons man had yet devised. Even more frightful, the Soviet H-bomb, unlike the enormous U.S. H-bomb, was small enough to be carried by a bomber aircraft.

On December 8, 1953, eight months after his "Chance for Peace" speech, Eisenhower went before the General Assembly of the United Nations in New York City to deliver his "Peaceful Uses of Atomic Energy" speech, more popularly known as the "Atoms for Peace" speech. Eisenhower, in clear, frightening language, described how both the United States and Soviet Union could annihilate each other with nuclear weapons. He proposed instead to turn the awesome atomic power into an instrument for peaceful power—to

"Experts would be mobilized to apply atomic energy to the needs of agriculture, medicine, and other peaceful activities. A special purpose would be to provide abundant electrical energy in the power-starved areas of the world. Thus the contributing powers would be dedicating some of their strength to serve the needs rather than the fears of mankind."

President Dwight D. Eisenhower, presenting his "Atoms for Peace" speech to the United Nations in 1953. *Reproduced by permission of the Corbis Corporation.*

"provide abundant electrical energy in the power-starved areas of the world." He called for international cooperation under the United Nations' control in setting up a nuclear material stockpile that "would be allocated to serve the peaceful pursuits of mankind."

Things to remember while reading "Peaceful Uses of Atomic Energy" speech:

- At the time of the speech, the nuclear technology already existed to build plants to produce nuclear power.

- Eisenhower's speech was forward-thinking and in contrast to the thinking of many U.S. military "hawks," or those eager to use the new technology to attack the Soviets.

- Nuclear bomb development programs were proceeding ahead at a rapid pace in both the United States and the Soviet Union.

Excerpt from
"Peaceful Uses of Atomic Energy" speech

*I feel **impelled** to speak today in a language that in a sense is new—one which I, who have spent so much of my life in the military profession, would have preferred never to use.*

That new language is the language of atomic warfare.

The atomic age has moved forward at such a pace that every citizen of the world should have some comprehension ... of the extent of this development of the utmost significance to every one of us. Clearly, if the peoples of the world are to conduct an intelligent search for peace, they must be armed with the significant facts of today's existence.

*My recital of atomic danger and power is necessarily stated in United States terms, for these are the only **incontrovertible** facts that I know. I need hardly point out to this Assembly, however, that this subject is global, not merely national in character.*

On July 15, 1945, the United States set off the world's first atomic explosion. Since that date in 1945, the United States of America has conducted 42 test explosions.

Atomic bombs today are more than 25 times as powerful as the weapons with which the atomic age dawned, while hydrogen weapons are in the ranges of millions of tons of TNT equivalent [that is, hydrogen weapons are equal to millions of tons of the conventional explosive, dynamite].

Today, the United States' stockpile of atomic weapons, which, of course, increases daily, exceeds by many times the explosive equivalent of the total of all bombs and all shells that came from every plane and every gun in every theater of war in all of the years of World War II.

A single air group, whether afloat or land-based, can now deliver to any reachable target a destructive cargo exceeding in power all the bombs that fell on Britain in all of World War II....

But the dread secret, and the fearful engines of atomic might, are not ours alone.

In the first place, the secret is possessed by our friends and allies, Great Britain and Canada, whose scientific genius made a

Impelled: Forced.

Incontrovertible: Indisputable.

tremendous contribution to our original discoveries, and the designs of atomic bombs.

The secret is also known by the Soviet Union.

The Soviet Union has informed us that, over recent years, it has devoted extensive resources to atomic weapons. During this period, the Soviet Union has exploded a series of atomic devices, including at least one involving thermo-nuclear reactions [a hydrogen bomb].

If at one time the United States possessed what might have been called a monopoly of atomic power, that monopoly ceased to exist several years ago. Therefore, although our earlier start has permitted us to accumulate what is today a great quantitative advantage [the United States had more nuclear weapons stockpiled than the Soviet Union did], *the atomic realities of today **comprehend** two facts of even greater significance.*

First, the knowledge now possessed by several nations will eventually be shared by others—possibly all others.

*Second, even a vast superiority in numbers of weapons, and a consequent capability of devastating **retaliation**, is no preventive, of itself, against the fearful material damage and toll of human lives that would be inflicted by surprise aggression.*

The free world, at least dimly aware of these facts, has naturally embarked on a large program of warning and defense systems. That program will be accelerated and expanded.

But let no one think that the expenditure of vast sums for weapons and systems of defense can guarantee absolute safety for the cities and citizens of any nation. The awful arithmetic of the atomic bomb does not permit of any such easy solution. Even against the most powerful defense, an aggressor in possession of the effective minimum number of atomic bombs for a surprise attack could probably place a sufficient number of his bombs on the chosen targets to cause hideous damage.

Should such an atomic attack be launched against the United States, our reactions would be swift and resolute. But for me to say that the defense capabilities of the United States are such that they could inflict terrible losses upon an aggressor—for me to say that the retaliation capabilities of the United States are so great that such an aggressor's land would be laid waste—all this, while fact, is not the true expression of the purpose and the hope of the United States.

Comprehend: Embrace.

Retaliation: Ability to strike back.

To pause there would be to confirm the hopeless finality of a belief that **two atomic colossi** are doomed … to eye each other indefinitely across a trembling world. To stop there would be to accept helplessly the probability of civilization destroyed—the **annihilation** of the irre-placeable heritage of mankind handed down to us generation from generation—and the condemnation of mankind to begin all over again the age-old struggle upward from savagery toward decency, and right, and justice.

Surely no sane member of the human race could discover victo-ry in such desolation. Could anyone wish his name to be coupled by history with such human **degradation** and destruction.…

My country wants to be constructive, not destructive. It wants agreements, not wars, among nations. It wants itself to live in free-dom, and in the confidence that the people of every other nation enjoy equally the right of choosing their own way of life.

So my country's purpose is to help us move out of the dark chamber of horrors into the light, to find a way by which the minds

President Dwight D. Eisenhower, being briefed by Lewis Strauss, chairman of the Atomic Energy Commission. *Reproduced by permission of the Corbis Corporation.*

Two atomic colossi: Two giants of atomic power: the United States and the Soviet Union.

Annihilation: Complete destruction.

Degradation: A lowering of the moral character.

of men, the hopes of men, the souls of men everywhere, can move forward toward peace and happiness and well being....

The United States, heeding the suggestion of the General Assembly of the United Nations, is instantly prepared to meet privately with such other countries [Great Britain, Canada, and France] *as may be "principally involved," to seek "an acceptable solution" to the atomic armaments race which overshadows not only the peace, but the very life, of the world.*

We shall carry into these private or diplomatic talks a new conception.

The United States would seek more than the mere reduction or elimination of atomic materials for military purposes.

*It is not enough to take this weapon out of the hands of the soldiers. It must be put into the hands of those who will know how to strip its **military casing** and adapt it to the arts of peace.*

*The United States knows that if the fearful trend of atomic military buildup can be reversed, this greatest of destructive forces can be developed into a great **boon**, for the benefit of all mankind.*

*The United States knows that peaceful power from atomic energy is no dream of the future. That capability, already proved, is here—now—today. Who can doubt, if the entire body of the world's scientists and engineers had adequate amounts of **fissionable material** with which to test and develop their ideas, that this capability would rapidly be transformed into universal, efficient, and economic usage.*

To hasten the day when fear of the atom will begin to disappear from the minds of people, and the governments of the East and West, there are certain steps that can be taken now.

I therefore make the following proposals:

*The Governments principally involved ... begin now and continue to make joint contributions from their stockpiles of normal uranium and fissionable materials to an International Atomic Energy Agency. We would expect that such an agency would be set up under the **aegis** of the United Nations....*

The Atomic Energy Agency could be made responsible for the impounding, storage, and protection of the contributed fissionable and other materials. The ingenuity of our scientists will provide special safe

Military casing: Exclusive military use.

Boon: Gift; here, a reference to the peaceful use of atomic energy.

Fissionable material: Chemical elements, such as uranium and plutonium, used in atomic weapons.

Aegis: Direction and control.

*conditions under which such a bank of fissionable material can be made essentially **immune to surprise seizure.***

The more important responsibility of this Atomic Energy Agency would be to devise methods whereby this fissionable material would be allocated to serve the peaceful pursuits of mankind. Experts would be mobilized to apply atomic energy to the needs of agriculture, medicine, and other peaceful activities. A special purpose would be to provide abundant electrical energy in the power-starved areas of the world. Thus the contributing powers would be dedicating some of their strength to serve the needs rather than the fears of mankind.

The United States would be more than willing—it would be proud to take up with others "principally involved" the development of plans whereby such peaceful use of atomic energy would be expedited.

What happened next ...

On January 12, 1954, before Soviet premier Georgy Malenkov (1902–1988) had responded to the "Atoms for Peace" speech, U.S. secretary of state John Foster Dulles (1888–1959) announced a new U.S. military strategy toward fighting communist expansion. He proclaimed that in response to any communist military aggression no matter if only small in scale, the United States would retaliate with a massive nuclear weapon response. Nuclear war seemed a drastic response to a localized hostile action. This strategy was designed to avoid war by threatening the ultimate nuclear war.

Nevertheless, Dulles contended that focusing on nuclear capability would prove much cheaper than maintaining the massive conventional air and ground forces called for in the National Security Council Report 68 (see Chapter 3). Eisenhower, for whom a sounder U.S. economy was a high priority, was interested that he could spend less on military defense by scaling down the large U.S. conventional forces and weapons while developing a much more powerful military. Eisenhower chose this path. As a result, he was able to cut the 1955 defense budget by 25 percent from the 1954 budget. Ground forces were re-

President Dwight D. Eisenhower, delivering the 1955 commencement address at Penn State University, promoted the use of atomic power for peaceful purposes.
Reproduced by permission of AP/Wide World Photos.

duced by 33 percent, and the air force would play a larger role. In keeping with the new policy, North Atlantic Treaty Organization (NATO) forces were supplied with small nuclear arms and the number of ground NATO divisions were cut by 75 percent.

By early 1955, Nikita Khrushchev (1894–1971) had won an ongoing power struggle since Stalin's death in 1953 with Malenkov and taken full reign of the Soviet government. He considered the new U.S. strategy as very aggressive and threatening to Soviet interests. He too was interested in strengthening the Soviet industrial and agricultural economy and spending less on large conventional armies and arms. Like Eisenhower and Dulles, he decided to concentrate on a buildup of nuclear weapons. When conflicts arose, both the Soviets and the Americans could threaten each other with nuclear war, pushing each other to the brink. The strength of both actually deterred either from starting a war. This strategy became known as brinkmanship.

Did you know ...

- Even with the peaceful words of "Atoms for Peace," mutual fear was still too great. The United States and the Soviet Union continued successfully to test hydrogen bombs. On March 1, 1954, the United States' "Bravo" tested at fifteen hundred times the power of the Hiroshima bomb. The Soviets perfected smaller H-bombs that were dropped from aircraft. Both nations stockpiled nuclear weapons.

- The B-52 bomber, the United States' first intercontinental jet bomber capable of delivering nuclear bombs to Soviet targets, became the backbone of U.S. air power.

- Although "Atoms for Peace" had called for arms limitations, serious talks on the matter did not occur until 1963, when the United States and the Soviets pushed each other to the brink over the island of Cuba, in a situation that came to be called the Cuban Missile Crisis (see Chapter 8).

Consider the following ...

- Is brinkmanship a valid strategy with which to avoid war? What might some pitfalls of brinkmanship be?

- Could there be a winner in a massive nuclear war?

- Find out what other countries in the mid-1950s possessed, or were developing, nuclear capabilities.

For More Information

Books

Brands, H. W., Jr. *Cold Warriors: Eisenhower's Generation and American Foreign Policy.* New York: Columbia University Press, 1988.

Eisenhower, Dwight D. *The White House Years.* Garden City, NY: Doubleday, 1963–65.

Marks, Frederick W., III. *Power and Peace: The Diplomacy of John Foster Dulles.* Westport, CT: Praeger, 1993.

Pach, Chester J., Jr., and Elmo Richardson. *The Presidency of Dwight D. Eisenhower.* Lawrence: University Press of Kansas, 1991.

Public Papers of the Presidents of the United States: Dwight D. Eisenhower, Volume 1953. Washington, DC: U.S. Government Printing Office.

Rhodes, Richard. *Dark Sun: The Making of the Hydrogen Bomb.* New York: Simon and Schuster, 1995.

Web Site

The Dwight D. Eisenhower Library and Museum. http://www.eisenhower.utexas.edu (accessed on September 11, 2003).

Homeland Insecurities | 5

Between 1947 and 1953, the United States experienced what was known as a Red Scare. The Red Scare was a period of time in the United States when Americans felt particularly threatened by communism. They feared that communism would gain a power base within the United States, and communists might eventually take over. This time period paralleled the early years of the Cold War, an intense battle of ideologies, or social and political ideas, between the democratic United States and communist Soviet Union. What appalled Americans most was that a few other Americans apparently were embracing the communist philosophy and carrying out subversive activities, or secret attempts from within, to undermine the U.S. government. Americans became obsessed with the fear and hatred of communism and subversive elements, both real and imagined, within their homeland. Without constant vigilance, the Cold War might be lost right on U.S. soil.

The chief anticommunist warriors were J. Edgar Hoover (1895–1972), director of the Federal Bureau of Investigation (FBI); members of the House Un-American Activities Committee (HUAC); and U.S. senator Joseph R. McCarthy

(1909–1957) of Wisconsin. The first excerpt here, "How to Fight Communism," comes from the June 9, 1947, issue of *Newsweek* magazine and was written by Hoover. In his article, Hoover described the threat of communists within the United States—who they were, what their mission was, where they lurked. He ended with a call to "uncover, expose, and spotlight their activities." The *Newsweek* article included a sidebar titled "Ten 'Don'ts' by Mr. Hoover." The list of "don'ts" was widely publicized to be studied and applied in combating communism on the home front.

The second excerpt is from the House Un-American Activities Committee (HUAC) public hearing in October 1947 of Hollywood filmmakers, actors, and screenplay writers. The HUAC was a committee of the U.S. House of Representatives charged with the investigation of subversive activities that posed a threat to the U.S. government. Two of the so-called friendly witnesses called were author and screenplay writer Ayn Rand (1905–1982) and actor and future U.S. president Ronald Reagan (1911–; served 1981–89). Rand, a native of Russia, testified about the real conditions in Russia as opposed to those put forth in the movie "Song of Russia." Reagan's testimony concerned the possible infiltration of the Screen Actors Guild with communists.

The third excerpt, "One Hundred Things You Should Know About Communism in the U.S.A.," is part of a series of booklets on the communist conspiracy published by the HUAC in 1948. This booklet contained one hundred questions and answers written for easy reading and clear-cut explanations for U.S. citizens.

The last excerpt is "Joseph McCarthy's Speech on Communists in the State Department," delivered on February 9, 1950. The speech kicked off McCarthy's anticommunist campaign. In the speech, he claimed that the United States was in an "all out battle" between communism and the American democratic way of life. During the speech, McCarthy held up a list on which he claimed to have written the names of several hundred U.S. State Department employees who were communists.

Hoover, HUAC, and McCarthy's repeated public statements, claims, and charges led to heightened apprehensions over communism in the United States. Americans were very susceptible to the dramatic, aggressive charges against suspected communist sympathizers.

J. Edgar Hoover

Excerpt from "How to Fight Communism"
Originally published in *Newsweek*, June 9, 1947

Published in *Newsweek* magazine's June 9, 1947, issue, "How to Fight Communism" by J. Edgar Hoover (1895–1972) attempted to educate Americans about communists in the United States and the threat they posed. Hoover was head of the U.S. Federal Bureau of Investigation (FBI).

Asked by President Franklin D. Roosevelt (1882–1945; served 1933–45) in the mid-1930s to monitor the activities of communists and other potential subversives within the United States, the focused and energetic Hoover undertook the mission. Hoover and his FBI agents became the chief domestic (within the United States) intelligence-gathering agency. They compiled information on the daily comings and goings of hundreds of individuals, always watching for those who might turn into enemies of democracy. Hoover kept lists of questionable individuals.

At the end of World War II (1939–45), the Cold War (1945–91) between the democratic United States and the communist Soviet Union began. The weapons of the Cold War immediately following the world war were chiefly words of propaganda and threats. Hoover developed close working

"Our best defense in the United States against the menace of Communism is our own American way of life. The American Communists cannot hope to reach their objective of destroying our form of government unless they first undermine and corrupt it, causing confusion and disrupting public confidence in the workings of democracy."

FBI director J. Edgar Hoover appears before the House Un-American Activities Committee in March 1947. *Reproduced by permission of the Corbis Corporation.*

relationships with conservative congressmen who helped maintain a considerable budget for the FBI. In 1946, Hoover launched a major propaganda campaign against communists using media such as radio programs, television, and magazine articles.

In this excerpt from "How to Fight Communism," Hoover stated that the best way to fight communism was to strengthen the American way of life. He said that America stood between free societies and a worldwide communist takeover. Hoover described two types of communists: those "out in the open" who spoke in "high sounding phrases" and the underground "communist conspirators." He stated that the communists were trying "to bring their total membership in the United States up to 100,000" but probably had one million sympathizers. He praised the press and the HUAC as doing outstanding jobs in educating Americans of the dangers and of exposing subversives. Lastly, Hoover stressed to Americans that they must work to "uncover, expose and spotlight" communists.

Things to remember while reading "How to Fight Communism":

- The campaign against communism dominated Hoover's life.

- The American public believed Hoover's FBI was the major government fighter and protector against threats made by communists against the U.S. homeland.

- Hoover freely used various tactics of surveillance, or spying, such as wiretaps (secretly listening to telephone conversations), break-ins, and the maintenance of extensive files on citizens never charged with any crimes. In the introduction to the *Newsweek* article, the magazine stated that "Hoover, who however controversial his views, is the one responsible Federal official most directly concerned with communists and communism."

Excerpt from "How to Fight Communism"

Our best defense in the United States against the menace of Communism is our own American way of life. The American Communists cannot hope to reach their objective of destroying our form of government unless they first undermine and corrupt it, causing confusion and disrupting public confidence in the workings of democracy.

Ours is the strongest democracy. We have more freedom and higher standards of living than any other people on earth. Yet our government—which has stood for almost two centuries as a beacon light amid world conflicts—is a central target of attack for the Red Fascists in the United States. It stands between them and world revolution....

Our surest weapon is truth. The Communists cannot endure the searching gaze of public observation. Their most effective work is carried on under a cloak of secrecy. Lies and deceit are their principal tools. No trick is too low for them. They are masters of the type of evasion advocated by that great god of Communism, [Vladimir] Lenin, who observed: "Revolutionaries who are unable to combine illegal forms of struggle with every form of legal struggle are very bad revolutionaries."

The first step in the fight to preserve the American way of life is the exposure of the true aims of Communism and then a contrast of them with our American way of life.

*There are two levels in the Communist organization. One level is "above ground" and its **espousers** are out in the open. They employ high-sounding, deceitful phrases.... The Communist brigades of swindlers and confidence men **extol** democracy but when they do they are speaking of Communism and not the American brand of democracy. They conceal their real designs by attaching themselves to **progressive causes**, to the cause of labor, social security and education.*

*The other level—the Communist underground—is composed of the disciplined brigades of Communist conspirators who drop their **dialectical** double talk behind locked doors. There the dangers of Communism become real....*

*The **preamble** of the Communist constitution also states that the party educates the working class "for its historic mission, the establishment of **socialism**." This "historic mission" is a revolution intended to overthrow our democratic government and substitute a Soviet of the United States.*

*The fact that the Communists teach the revolution by force and violence is well illustrated by statements of Communist **functionaries**. One instructor advised his class: "We must as workers learn to hate the capitalist class. We cannot fight unless we hate. We ... the **vanguard** of the working class must teach the worker ... to hate. It will mean the spilling of blood. We will have streets of blood as they had in Russia, the worker must be organized so that revolution when it comes must not be a failure."*

*The Communists are agreed that the revolution will not come until the **precipitation** of a "great crisis" such as a general strike, a war which could be turned into civil strife, or a great economic depression.*

Our cue is to make democracy work so that the Communists will never have their "great crisis."

The Communists have been specific in defining the meaning of party membership. The Daily Worker *[Communist Party newspaper]* quoted *[Joseph]* Stalin on the subject: "We have Lenin's thor-

Espousers: Supporters.

Extol: Praise.

Progressive causes: Social causes that better man's way of living.

Dialectical: Publicly discussed.

Preamble: Introduction.

Socialism: A system of society in which the community or government owns or controls industry and land.

Functionaries: Communist Party officials.

Vanguard: Leaders.

Precipitation: Occurrence.

oughly tried and tested formula defining a member of the party.... A member is one who accepts the program of the party, pays membership dues and works in one of its organizations."...

The Communists are now carrying a vigorous campaign to bring their total membership in the United States up to 100,000. This figure, however, does not reveal their actual strength. Conservatively, there are an estimated one million others who in one way or another aid the Communist party....

We cannot hope successfully to meet the Communist menace unless there is a wide knowledge and understanding of its aims and designs. This knowledge outlaws the party in the hearts and minds of good citizens.

But where can this information be secured?

The American press and radio are alert to the threat of Red Fascism and have done a splendid job of exposing the evil. We are moving in the right direction.

*I have also been encouraged to note that spokesmen generally are being **circumspect** in using the label of "Communist."... It is deceptive and **detrimental**, however, to pin the label of "Communist" on honest American liberals and progressives merely because of difference of opinion. Honesty and common decency demand that the clear-cut line of **demarcation** that exists between liberals and Communists be recognized. Despite the Communist technique of labeling themselves as progressives there is no more effective or determined foe of Communism than the millions of honest liberals and progressives.*

Newspapers, magazines, radio and scores of well-documented books on the subject of Communism are sources of authentic information which can provide patriotic citizens with the facts.

There is renewed interest in Congress as manifested in the Committee on Un-American Activities of the House of Representatives. As this committee fulfills its obligation of public disclosure of facts it is

J. Edgar Hoover addresses the National Crime Conference in 1934. Although Hoover was well known for his fight against communism, he achieved great success in combating all types of criminal activities. *Reproduced by permission of the Corbis Corporation.*

Circumspect: Discreet; cautious.

Detrimental: Harmful.

Demarcation: Difference or boundary.

An FBI poster, signed by
J. Edgar Hoover, warning
against sabotage and spies.
*Reproduced by permission of
the Corbis Corporation.*

WARNING
from the
FBI

The war against spies and saboteurs demands the aid of every American.

When you see evidence of sabotage, notify the Federal Bureau of Investigation at once.

When you suspect the presence of enemy agents, tell it to the FBI.

Beware of those who spread enemy propaganda! Don't repeat vicious rumors or vicious whispers.

Tell it to the FBI!

J. Edgar Hoover, *Director*
Federal Bureau of Investigation

The nearest Federal Bureau of Investigation office is listed on page one of your telephone directory.

*worthy of the support of loyal, patriotic Americans. This committee has for its purpose the exposure of un-American forces and as such its files contain **voluminous** information which, when used with **discretion**, provide an excellent source of information. The FBI, unlike this committee, must of necessity keep the contents of its files confidential.*

Citizens also should be alert to what is happening in their own circles. Do they have an intelligent, participating interest in the pro-

Voluminous: Much.

Discretion: Care.

grams of organizations to which they belong and of schools which their children attend? What kind of people do they elect to public office? Are there disloyal people on the public payrolls?

It is the right and responsibility of every citizen to insist on having public servants whose first loyalty is to the American way of life. One disloyal local, county, state or Federal employee can do irreparable harm by acts of disloyalty or by **indoctrinating** others with a **Marxian** philosophy.

Labor unions have always been a Communist target....

Communists in labor unions—like Communists everywhere—owe their first allegiance to the Communist party. They falsely claim that the ends of the party and of labor are the same....

In one union with nearly 100,000 members, 500 party members were able to control the union. Another union with 8,500 members sought to free itself from Communist control but failed despite the fact that there were less than 200 party members in the union....

Progressive American union members could quickly **divest** themselves of the Communist **barnacles** if they took as much interest in union affairs as the Communists do.

They should educate themselves to recognize the Communist party line so that they can identify the **"fellow travelers"** in their union. They should attend union meetings and take an unselfish interest in union elections. Above all, they should **scrutinize** the business affairs of the union to make certain that the union is using its resources for the welfare of its members and not for some "dressed-up" cause the Communists may be sponsoring.

Management can do more by looking out for the welfare of employees and getting closer to labor problems....

The party sometimes recruits members by misrepresentations. A **Negro** party member, for instance, pointed out at a Communist meeting that many Negroes, when recruited, thought they were joining a union instead of the Communist party. At this point the Negro was shouted down by party members.

Schools and colleges should be on the alert against Communist **infiltration**.... Parents should take a greater interest in school affairs and know what organizations attract their children. Communists recruit future members through the high-sounding youth

Indoctrinating: Teaching a belief or an idea.

Marxian: Pertaining to the ideas of German philosopher Karl Marx in the nineteenth century; later his ideas formed the basis for communism.

Divest: Rid.

Barnacles: Small sea creatures that attach themselves to other live or inanimate objects in the sea.

"Fellow travelers": What communists call each other.

Negro: African American.

Scrutinize: Carefully study.

Infiltration: The act of entering sneakily or gradually.

auxiliary, the American Youth for Democracy, formerly known as the Young Communist League.

The churches of America also are threatened by Communism.…

The churches of America should remember that the Communists' protestation of freedom of religion is a camouflage for their true thoughts. Lenin taught: "We must combat religion—this is the ABC of all materialism, and consequently Marxism." "Down with religion!" "Long live atheism!" "The **dissemination** of **atheist** views is our chief task."…

No organization worthy of its name has been immune from Communist attempts to infiltrate. The more respected the organization, the greater should be the vigilance.

Once organizations are captured by Communists, patriotic members have one of two alternatives: resign or organize to regain control. Their members would vote for officers who stand for the Constitution of the United States and not the **Communist Manifesto.**

If there were to be a slogan in the fight against Communism it should convey the thought: Uncover, expose, and spotlight their activities. Once this is done, the American people will do the rest— **quarantine** them from effectively weakening our country.

Auxiliary: An associated group.

Dissemination: Spread.

Atheist: Belief that there is no God.

Communist Manifesto: A document, written by German political philosophers Karl Marx and Friedrich Engels, that details the political ideology of communism.

Quarantine: Block.

What happened next …

In 1947, Hoover's FBI investigated the loyalty of the two to three million federal employees. Although only 212 people were fired for loyalty issues, Hoover uncovered alcoholics, homosexuals, and employees in a large amount of debt. It was believed those in debt might sell government secrets to the Soviets. Hoover was intent on exposing communists in labor unions and supplied the HUAC with incriminating information. He also developed a network of informers in Hollywood to report on activities there. Ronald Reagan (1911–), president of the Screen Actors Guild and future U.S. president, was one of Hoover's informants.

In 1950, Hoover's FBI was in charge of the investigation and arrests of the Atomic Spies, including Julius Rosenberg (1918–1953) and his wife, Ethel Rosenberg (1915–1953); Harry Gold (1910–1974); and David Greenglass (1922–). These Americans had passed secrets of the U.S. atomic bomb development program to the Soviets. In the 1960s, Hoover continued to build files. By then, the focus was on Vietnam War (1954–75) protesters and on civil rights activists, including Martin Luther King Jr. (1929–1968).

Did you know ...

- Hoover wrote a best-selling book, *Masters of Deceit,* in 1958 to educate the public about the threat of communism.

- By 1960, Hoover was one of the most powerful men in Washington, D.C.

- Hoover, a media hound, helped work on several television programs and Hollywood movies. For example, he collaborated on the popular *The FBI* television series that aired from 1965 to 1974.

- Hoover remained the director of the FBI until his death in 1972, a total of forty-eight years.

- In 1975 and 1976, a Senate investigative committee found Hoover had violated the civil liberties of many innocent Americans in his quest for subversives.

Consider the following ...

- Were the tactics used by J. Edgar Hoover justified to uncover communists in the 1940s and 1950s?

- What two types of communist operatives did Hoover describe?

- How many communist sympathizers were in the United States in 1947, according to Hoover? Analyze the reasons why people believed Hoover when he made this claim.

- List the institutions in U.S. society that Hoover said were vulnerable to infiltration by the communists.

For More Information

Books and Magazines

Hoover, J. Edgar. "How to Fight Communism." *Newsweek,* June 9, 1947.

Nash, Jay R. *A Critical Study of the Life and Times of J. Edgar Hoover and His FBI.* Chicago: Nelson-Hall, 1972.

Powers, Richard Gid. *Secrecy and Power: The Life of J. Edgar Hoover.* New York: Free Press, 1987.

Theoharis, Athan G., and John S. Cox. *The Boss: J. Edgar Hoover and the Great American Inquisition.* Philadelphia: Temple University Press, 1988.

Web Site

Federal Bureau of Investigation. http://www.fbi.gov (accessed on September 11, 2003).

Ayn Rand and Ronald Reagan

Excerpt from "Testimony from House Un-American Activities
Hollywood Hearings, October 1947"
Available at *CNN Interactive: Cold War* (Web site)

I n October 1947, to root out communist influence or propaganda either real or imagined in U.S. movies, the House Un-
American Activities Committee (HUAC) began investigating
the U.S. film industry in Hollywood, California. J. Edgar
Hoover (1895–1972), director of the Federal Bureau of Investigation (FBI), had already established a network of confidential
informers within the industry. Especially under investigation
by the HUAC were ten of Hollywood's producers, directors,
and screenplay writers. Aptly known as the Hollywood Ten,
they were summoned before the committee to explain their
politics and memberships or past memberships in organizations considered communist-leaning. Also called to testify
were twenty-four Hollywood witnesses. Two friendly witness
testimonies excerpted here were those of author and screenplay writer Ayn Rand (1905–1982) and actor Ronald Reagan
(1911–). Other famous Hollywood notables who testified were
actors Gary Cooper (1901–1961) and Robert Montgomery
(1904–1981) and producer Walt Disney (1901–1966).

In the first of the two testimonies, Rand answered
questions regarding a recent Hollywood film, *Song of Russia*,

"Try to imagine what it is like
if you are in constant terror
from morning till night and
at night you are waiting for
the doorbell to ring, where
you are afraid of anything
and everybody, living in a
country where human life is
nothing, less than nothing,
and you know it. You don't
know who or when is going
to do what to you because
you may have friends who
spy on you, where there is
no law and any rights of any
kind." —*Ayn Rand*

that the HUAC believed was produced as Soviet propaganda. Rand, who was born in Russia but left there to come to the United States for good in 1926, related how the Russian society pictured in *Song of Russia* was not the Russia she remembered. By 1947, Rand received national fame for her book *The Fountainhead.* She also had been writing screenplays for Hollywood producers for many years. Her testimony before the committee was riveting, as her talent to use words to create pictures was apparent. Near the end of the testimony, Rand commented that the Russians "try to live a human life, but you understand it is totally inhuman ... you are in constant terror from morning till night and at night you are waiting for the doorbell to ring, where you are afraid of anything and everybody, living in a country where human life is nothing, less than nothing, and you know it."

The second excerpted testimony comes from then-actor and president of the Screen Actors Guild, Ronald Reagan. Reagan had been active in the anticommunist movements in the late 1940s. This involvement sparked his interest in politics. The HUAC called Reagan to report to the best of his knowledge about members of the Screen Actors Guild who might have communist leanings.

Things to remember while reading the excerpt from "Testimony from House Un-American Activities Hollywood Hearings, October 1947":

- The HUAC's mission was to investigate any subversive activity that could lead to the overthrow of the U.S. government.

- The HUAC believed that several movies, such as the *Song of Russia,* glorified the communist system.

- The HUAC opened each questioning session with "Are you now or have you ever been a member of the Communist Party?" Any answer except "no" brought immediate suspicion.

Excerpt from "Testimony from House Un-American Activities Hollywood Hearings, October 1947"

Testimony by Ayn Rand before HUAC, October 20, 1947....

STRIPLING [Robert Stripling, Chief Investigator]: Would you give the committee a breakdown of your summary of the picture relating to either propaganda or an untruthful account or distorted account of conditions in Russia?

RAND: Yes. First of all I would like to define what we mean by propaganda. We have all been talking about it, but nobody—

STRIPLING: Could you talk into the microphone?

RAND: Can you hear me now? Nobody has stated just what they mean by propaganda. Now, I use the term to mean that communist propaganda is anything which gives a good impression of communism as a way of life. Anything that sells people the idea that life in Russia is good and that people are free and happy would be communist propaganda. Am I not correct? I mean, would that be a fair statement to make—that that would be communist propaganda?

Now, here is what the picture "Song of Russia" contains. It starts with an American conductor, played by Robert Taylor, giving a concert in America for Russian war relief. He starts playing the American national anthem and the national anthem dissolves into a Russian mob, with the sickle and hammer on a red flag very prominent above their heads. I am sorry, but that made me sick. That is something which I do not see how native Americans permit, and I am only a naturalized American. That was a terrible touch of propaganda. As a writer, I can tell you just exactly what it suggests to the people. It suggests literally and technically that it is quite all right for the American national anthem to dissolve into the Soviet....

*Then you see a Moscow restaurant that just never existed there. In my time, when I was in Russia, there was only one such restaurant, which was nowhere as luxurious as that and no one could enter it except **commissars** and **profiteers**. Certainly a girl from a village, who*

Commissars: Communist Party officials.

Profiteers: Sellers who make excessive profits taking advantage of people during a crisis.

*in the first place would never have been allowed to come voluntarily, without permission, to Moscow, could not afford to enter it, even if she worked 10 years.... From this restaurant they go on to this tour of Moscow. The streets are clean and prosperous-looking. There are no food lines anywhere. You see shots of the marble subway—the famous Russian subway out of which they make such **propaganda capital**. There is a marble statue of [Joseph] Stalin thrown in.*

There is a park where you see happy little children in white blouses running around.... They are not homeless children in rags, such as I have seen in Russia....

You see the manicured starlets driving tractors and the happy women who come from work singing. You see a peasant at home with a close-up of food for which anyone there would have been murdered. If anybody had such food in Russia in that time he couldn't remain alive, because he would have been torn apart by neighbors trying to get food....

That for a Communist Party member to have anything to do with religion means expulsion from the party. He is not allowed to enter a church or take part in any religious ceremony. For a private citizen, that is a non-party member, it was permitted, but it was so frowned upon that people had to keep it secret if they went to church....

I have never seen so much smiling in my life, except on the murals of the world's fair pavilion of the Soviets. If any one of you have seen it, you can appreciate it. It is one of the stock propaganda tricks of the communists, to show these people smiling....

MR. JOHN MCDOWELL: You paint a very dismal picture of Russia. You made a great point about the number of children who were unhappy. Doesn't anybody smile in Russia any more?

RAND: Well, if you ask me literally, pretty much no.

MCDOWELL: They don't smile?

RAND: Not quite that way, no. If they do, it is privately and accidentally. Certainly, it is not social. They don't smile in approval of their system.

MCDOWELL: Well, all they do is talk about food.

RAND: That is right.

MCDOWELL: That is a great change from the Russians I have always known, and I have known a lot of them. Don't they do things at all like Americans? Don't they walk across town to visit their mother-in-law or somebody?

Propaganda capital: Good propaganda.

*RAND: Look, it is very hard to explain. It is almost impossible to convey to a free people what it is like to live in a **totalitarian dictatorship.** I can tell you a lot of details. I can never completely convince you, because you are free. It is in a way good that you can't even conceive of what it is like. Certainly they have friends and mothers-in-law. They try to live a human life, but you understand it is totally inhuman. Try to imagine what it is like if you are in constant terror from morning till night and at night you are waiting for the doorbell to ring, where you are afraid of anything and everybody, living in a country where human life is nothing, less than nothing, and you know it. You don't know who or when is going to do what to you because you may have friends who spy on you, where there is no law and any rights of any kind....*

Testimony of Ronald Reagan before HUAC, October 23, 1947

*STRIPLING: As a member of the board of directors, as president of the Screen Actors Guild, and as an active member, have you at any time observed or noted within the organization a **clique** of ei-*

Totalitarian dictatorship: Country ruled by a central government that tolerates no difference of opinions.

Clique: A small exclusive group of people.

Ronald Reagan, testifying before the House Un-American Activities Committee in October 1947. *Reproduced by permission of AP/Wide World Photos.*

ther communists or **fascists** who were attempting to exert influence or pressure on the guild?

REAGAN: There has been a small group within the Screen Actors Guild which has consistently opposed the policy of the guild board and officers of the guild, as evidenced by the vote on various issues. That small clique referred to has been suspected of more or less following the tactics that we associate with the Communist Party.

STRIPLING: Would you refer to them as a disruptive influence within the guild?

REAGAN: I would say that at times they have attempted to be a disruptive influence.

STRIPLING: You have no knowledge yourself as to whether or not any of them are members of the Communist Party?

REAGAN: No, sir, I have no investigative force, or anything, and I do not know.

STRIPLING: Has it ever been reported to you that certain members of the guild were communists?

Fascists: Those who believe in a governmental system led by a dictator and marked by racism, militarism, and extreme support for one's nation.

REAGAN: Yes, sir, I have heard different discussions and some of them tagged as communists....

STRIPLING: Mr. Reagan, what is your feeling about what steps should be taken to rid the motion picture industry of any communist influences?

REAGAN: Well, sir, 99 percent of us are pretty well aware of what is going on, and I think, within the bounds of our democratic rights and never once stepping over the rights given us by democracy, we have done a pretty good job in our business of keeping those people's activities curtailed. After all, we must recognize them at present as a political party. On that basis we have exposed their lies when we came across them, we have opposed their propaganda, and I can certainly testify that in the case of the Screen Actors Guild we have been eminently successful in preventing them from, with their usual tactics, trying to run a majority of an organization with a well organized minority.

In opposing those people, the best thing to do is make democracy work. In the Screen Actors Guild we make it work by insuring everyone a vote and by keeping everyone informed. I believe that, as Thomas Jefferson put it, if all the American people know all of the facts they will never make a mistake. Whether the party should be outlawed, that is a matter for the government to decide. As a citizen, I would hesitate to see any political party outlawed on the basis of its political ideology. However, if it is proven that an organization is an agent of foreign power, or in any way not a legitimate political party—and I think the government is capable of proving that—then that is another matter. I happen to be very proud of the industry in which I work; I happen to be very proud of the way in which we conducted the fight. I do not believe the communists have ever at any time been able to use the motion picture screen as a sounding board for their philosophy or ideology.

CHAIRMAN: There is one thing that you said that interested me very much. That was the quotation from Jefferson. That is why this committee was created by the House of Representatives: to acquaint the American people with the facts. Once the American people are acquainted with the facts there is no question but that the American people will do the kind of job that they want done: that is, to make America just as pure as we can possibly make it. We want to thank you very much for coming here today.

REAGAN: Sir, I detest, I abhor their [communist] philosophy ... but at the same time I never as a citizen want to see our country *become urged, by either fear or resentment of this group, that we ever compromise with any of our democratic principles through that fear or resentment. I still think that democracy can do it.*

What happened next ...

Despite the "friendly" witnesses' willingness to testify, the Hollywood Ten refused to answer the HUAC's questions. Denouncing the questioning as an obvious violation of their constitutional rights, they took the Fifth Amendment's constitutional privilege of not responding to questions. As a result, all were convicted for contempt of court. Following an unsuccessful appeal to the U.S. Circuit Court of Appeals in 1948, eight served one year and two served six months in prison. Once released, they could get no work because other Hollywood producers had blacklisted them. Blacklisting refers to a practice of refusing work to those who were suspected of communist affiliation or communist sentiments.

Blacklisting spread throughout the radio industry and to the newly emerging television industry as well. Anyone found to have connections in any way to groups who might have supported subversive activities would be blacklisted. The communist paranoia was so rampant in American society that if it were discovered that a member of a group had ever had communist ties, real or imagined, then everyone in that group would be blacklisted. As for the HUAC and Hollywood, the message was clear—either cooperate with the HUAC or be blacklisted.

Did you know ...

- Ayn Rand, original name Alissa Zinooievna Rosenbaum, was born in St. Petersburg (later Petrograd), Russia, and educated at the University of Petrograd. There, she first watched American movies and was fascinated by the bright world projected on the screen. That world was in stark contrast to the dismal, dark atmosphere of Russia.

- Reagan would be elected the fortieth president of the United States in November 1980. It was in the later

1940s, under the communist scare in the United States, that Reagan's politics shifted from liberal leanings to very conservative.

- In October 1947, as the HUAC opened its investigation of Hollywood's film industry, fifty of Hollywood's most famous celebrities chartered a plane, named it the Star of the Red Sea (the term "red" refers to communists), and hopped across the country holding press conferences

Actor Humphrey Bogart (left) meets with investigators James Steadman, Robert E. Stripling, and Martin Dies during the HUAC's hearings on subversive activities.
Reproduced by permission of the Corbis Corporation.

where they touched down. They included Humphrey Bogart (1899–1957), Lauren Bacall (1924–), Ira Gershwin (1896–1983), Danny Kaye (1913–1987), and Frank Sinatra (1915–1998). They supported free expression in Hollywood films. Nevertheless, the HUAC was too powerful and Americans' fear of anything communist too great. Most of the fifty realized they were risking blacklisting and backtracked in their support of the Hollywood Ten. Realizing the trip had been a mistake, they quietly headed back to California as quickly as possible.

Consider the following …

- What symbolism used at the opening of the movie *Song of Russia* did Ayn Rand especially object to? What is her definition of propaganda?

- Although Reagan related that his Screen Actors Guild did probably have members that had Communist Party affiliations, what was his overall opinion of the Guild?

- At one point in Reagan's testimony, he ever so gently warned the HUAC not to go too far. Identify those words.

For More Information

Books

Barson, Michael, and Steven Heller. *Red Scared: The Commie Menace in Propaganda and Popular Culture.* San Francisco: Chronicle Books, 2001.

Branden, Barbara. *The Passion of Ayn Rand.* New York: Anchor Books, 1986.

Cohn, Roy. *McCarthy.* New York: New American Library, 1968.

Morris, Edmund. *Dutch: A Memoir of Ronald Reagan.* New York: Random House, 1999.

Sherrow, Victoria. *Joseph McCarthy and the Cold War.* Woodbridge, CT: Blackbirch Press, Inc., 1999.

Web Sites

CNN Interactive: Cold War http://www.cnn.com/SPECIALS/cold.war/ episodes/06/documents/huac (accessed on September 22, 2003).

"Hollywood Blacklist." *University of Pennsylvania, Department of English.* http://www.english.upenn.edu/~afilreis/50s/blacklist.html (accessed on September 12, 2003).

"Moderntimes Classic Film Pages." *House Un-American Activities Committee and Censorship Changes.* http://www.moderntimes.com/palace/huac.htm (accessed on September 12, 2003).

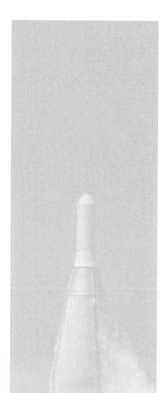

House Un-American Activities Committee (HUAC)

Excerpt from "One Hundred Things You Should Know About Communism in the U.S.A."

Reprinted from *Thirty Years of Treason: Excerpts From Hearings Before the House Committee on Un-American Activities, 1938–1968*, published in 1971

"[Question:] Why shouldn't I turn Communist? [Answer:] You know what the United States is like today. If you want it exactly the opposite, you should turn Communist. But before you do, remember you will lose your independence, your property, and your freedom of mind. You will gain only a risky membership in a conspiracy which is ruthless, godless, and crushing upon all except a very few at the top."

"**O**ne Hundred Things You Should Know About Communism in the U.S.A." was the first in a series of pamphlets put out by the House Un-American Activities Committee (HUAC) to educate the American public about communism in the United States. In May 1938, U.S. representative Martin Dies (1900–1972) of Texas managed to get his favorite House committee, HUAC, funded. It had been inactive since 1930. The HUAC was charged with investigation of subversive activities that posed a threat to the U.S. government.

With the HUAC revived, Dies claimed to have gathered knowledge that communists were in labor unions, government agencies, and African American groups. Without ever knowing why they were charged, many individuals lost their jobs. In 1940, Congress passed the Alien Registration Act, known as the Smith Act. The act made it illegal for an individual to be a member of any organization that supported a violent overthrow of the U.S. government, the Communist Party being its main target. Even as World War II (1939–45) raged through Europe and in the Pacific, the stubborn Dies kept the HUAC alive until 1944, when bad health

and constant criticism of his irresponsible charges caused him to step down.

Another Southern conservative congressman, John E. Rankin (1882–1960) of Mississippi, insisted that the HUAC be reestablished in 1945, this time as a permanent, standing House committee. The HUAC soon compiled a list of at least forty groups it labeled as intent on promoting communist ideas. Next, in October 1947, it opened an investigation of the Hollywood film industry (see previous excerpt).

America's apprehensions over communist influence in America snowballed in 1948 with a series of events. J. Edgar Hoover (1895–1972), director of the Federal Bureau of Investigation (FBI), likened communism to a disease spreading across America. Under the 1940 Smith Act, twelve leaders of the American Communist Party were tried and convicted. Elizabeth Bentley (1908–1963), an American-turned-Soviet spy, turned again and testified before the HUAC about a

Alger Hiss (seated at right) testifies before the House Un-American Activities Committee in November 1947. Hiss, a prominent U.S. State Department employee, was accused of turning over secrets to the Soviets in the late 1930s. *Reproduced by permission of AP/Wide World Photos.*

Washington-based spy ring of which she had been a member. Then, in August, Whittaker Chambers (1901–1961) broke the Alger Hiss case. Alger Hiss (1904–1996), a prominent U.S. State Department employee, was accused of turning over secrets to the Soviets in the late 1930s.

To educate the public, the HUAC began in 1948 a series of booklets that would help Americans identify and deal with communists. As reflected in their titles, the five booklets gave readers "one hundred things you should know about communism" as it pertained to the U.S.A., religion, education, labor, and government.

According to the HUAC, the booklets were intended "to help you know a Communist when you hear him speak and when you see him work."

Things to remember while reading "One Hundred Things You Should Know About Communism in the U.S.A.":

- The booklets were widely distributed across the country.

- Most Americans had no specific picture of what communism was, other than a looming threat.

- Although an honest attempt to educate, historians consider the booklets prime examples of U.S. propaganda.

Excerpt from "One Hundred Things You Should Know About Communism in the U.S.A."

*When a Communist heads the government of the United States—and that day will come just as surely as the sun rises—the government will not be a capitalist government but a Soviet government, and behind this government will stand the Red army to enforce the dictatorship of the **proletariat.***

Sworn statement of WILLIAM Z. FOSTER, Head of the Communist Party in the United States....

Proletariat: The working class of a society.

Every citizen owes himself and his family the truth about Communism because the world today is faced with a single choice: To go Communist or not to go Communist. Here are the facts.

1. What is Communism?

A system by which one small group seeks to rule the world.

2. Has any nation ever gone Communist in a free election?

No.

3. Then how do the Communists try to get control?

Legally or illegally, any way they can. Communism's first big victory was through bloody revolution. Every one since has been by military conquest, or internal corruption, or the threat of these.

CONSPIRACY is the basic method of Communism in countries it is trying to capture.

IRON FORCE is the basic method of Communism in countries it has already captured.

4. What would happen if Communism should come into power in this country?

Our capital would move from Washington to Moscow. Every man, woman, and child would come under Communist discipline.

5. Would I be better off than I am now?

No. And the next 17 answers show why.

6. Could I belong to a union?

Under Communism, all labor unions are run by the Government and the Communists run the Government. Unions couldn't help you get higher pay, shorter hours or better working conditions. They would only be used by the Communists to help keep you down.

More complete details are given in ONE HUNDRED THINGS YOU SHOULD KNOW ABOUT COMMUNISM AND LABOR.

7. Could I change my job?

No, you would work where you are told, at what you are told, for wages fixed by the Government.

8. Could I go to school?

You could go to the kind of school the Communists tell you to, AND NOWHERE ELSE. You could go as long as they let you AND NO LONGER.

You could read ONLY what the Communists let you; hear only what they let you, and as far as they could manage, you would KNOW only what they let you.

For details, see ONE HUNDRED THINGS YOU SHOULD KNOW ABOUT COMMUNISM AND EDUCATION.

9. Could I belong to the Elks, Rotary, or the American Legion?

No. William Z. Foster, the head of the Communists in the United States, says:

*Under the dictatorship all the capitalist parties—Republican, Democratic, Progressive, Socialist, etc.—will be **liquidated**, the Communist Party functioning alone as the Party of the **toiling** masses.*

*Likewise will be dissolved, all other organizations that are political props of the **bourgeois** rule, including chambers of commerce, employers' associations, Rotary Clubs, American Legion, YMCA, and such **fraternal orders** as the Masons, Odd Fellows, Elks, Knights of Columbus, etc.*

10. Could I own my own farm?

No. Under Communism, the land is the property of the Government, and the Government is run by the Communists.

You would farm the land under orders and you could not make any decisions as to when or where you would sell the produce of your work, or for how much.

11. Could I own my own home?

No. Under Communism, all real estate in the city as well as the country belongs to the government, which is in turn run by the Communists.

Your living quarters would be assigned to you, and you would pay rent as ordered.

12. What would happen to my insurance?

The Communists would take it over.

13. What would happen to my bank account?

*All above a small sum would be **confiscated**. The rest would be controlled for you.*

14. Could I leave any property to my family when I die?

No, because you wouldn't have any to leave.

Liquidated: Eliminated.

Toiling: Working.

Bourgeois: The wealthy, ruling class of a society.

Fraternal orders: Social groups formed for friendship and service.

Confiscated: Taken away.

15. Could I travel around the country as I please?

No. You would have to get police permission for every move you make, if you could get it.

16. Could I belong to a church?

In Russia, the Communists have for thirty years tried every way they could to destroy religion. Having failed that, they are now trying to USE religion from the inside and the same Party strategy is now operating in the United States of America. See ONE HUNDRED THINGS YOU SHOULD KNOW ABOUT COMMUNISM AND RELIGION.

17. Could I start up a business and hire people to work for me?

To do so would be a crime for which you would be severely punished.

*18. Could I teach what I please with "**academic freedom?**"*

You would teach only what the Communists authorize you to teach.

You would be asking for jail or death to try anything else.

19. Could I do scientific research free of governmental interference and restrictions?

Police and spies would watch your every move. You would be liquidated on the slightest suspicion of doing ANYTHING contrary to orders.

20. Could I have friends of my own choice as I do now?

No, except those approved by the Communists in charge of your life from cradle to grave.

21. Could I travel abroad or marry a foreigner?

No, except those approved by the Communists in charge of your life from cradle to grave.

22. Could I exchange letters with friends in other countries?

With the police reading your mail, you could try—once.

23. Could I vote the Communists out of control?

No. See ONE HUNDRED THINGS YOU SHOULD KNOW ABOUT COMMUNISM AND GOVERNMENT, showing the facts of Communist government in other countries and the facts of Communism at work within OUR OWN government.

Academic freedom: The ability to teach different ideas freely.

24. But doesn't Communism promise poor people a better life?

Communist politicians all over the world try in every way to break down nations as they are, hoping that in the confusion they will be able to seize control.

Promising more than you can deliver is an old trick in the history of the human race.

Compare Communism's promises with Communism's performances in countries where it has come to power.

25. What are some differences between Communist promise and Communist performance?

When it is agitating for power, Communism promises more money for less work and security against war and poverty. In practice, it has not delivered any of this, anywhere in the world.

26. But don't the Communists promise an end to racial and religious intolerance?

Yes, but in practice they have murdered millions for being religious and for belonging to a particular class. Your race would be no help to you under Communism. Your beliefs could get you killed.

27. Why shouldn't I turn Communist?

You know what the United States is like today. If you want it exactly the opposite, you should turn Communist. But before you do, remember you will lose your independence, your property, and your freedom of mind. You will gain only a risky membership in a conspiracy which is ruthless, godless, and crushing upon all except a very few at the top.

28. How many Communists are there in the world?

There are 20,000,000 Communists, more or less, in a world of 2,295,125,000. In other words, about one person in 115 is a Communist, on a world basis.

29. How many people are now ruled by Communism?

About 200,000,000 directly; 200,000,000 more indirectly, and an additional 250,000,000 are under daily Communist pressure to surrender.

30. Which countries are Communist controlled or governed?

Albania, Bulgaria, Czechoslovakia, Estonia, Hungary, Latvia, Lithuania, Poland, Romania, Russia, Yugoslavia. Important regions of Austria, Germany, China, Korea, Mongolia and Manchuria. Communism is concentrating now on immediate capture of Afghanistan, France, Greece, Latin America, Iran and Palestine. It has plans to seize every other country including the United States.

31. How many Communists are there in the United States?

There are approximately 80,000 out of a population of 145,340,000 people. J. Edgar Hoover has testified that "in 1917 when the Communists overthrew the Russian Government there was one Communist for every 2,277 persons in Russia. In the United States today there is one Communist for every 1,814 persons in the country."

32. Why aren't there more?

Because the Communist Party does not rely upon actual Party membership for its strength. J. Edgar Hoover testified: "What is important is the claim of the Communists themselves that for every Party member there are ten others ready, willing, and able to do the Party's work. Herein lies the greatest menace of Communism. For these are the people who **infiltrate** and corrupt various spheres of American life. So rather than the size of the Communist party the way to weigh its true importance is by testing its influence, its ability to infiltrate."

33. How are they organized?

Primarily around something they call a political party, behind which they operate a carefully trained force of spies, revolutionaries, and conspirators. The basic fact to remember is that Communism is a world revolutionary movement and Communists are disciplined agents, operating under a plan of war.

34. Where are their headquarters in the United States, and who is in charge?

Headquarters are at 35 East Twelfth Street, New York City. William Z. Foster, of 1040 Melton Avenue, New York City, has the title of "Chairman of the Communist Party of the United States," but Foster is actually just a **figurehead** under control of foreign operatives unseen by and unknown to rank and file Communists.

35. What is the emblem of the Communist Party in the United States?

The hammer and sickle.

Infiltrate: Go into.

Figurehead: A person who appears to be the head of a group but is not really.

36. What is the emblem of the Communist Party in the Soviet Union?

The hammer and sickle. It is also the official emblem of the Soviet Government.

37. What is the flag of the Communist Party in the United States?

The red flag, the same as that of all Communist Parties of the world.

38. What is the official song of the Communist Party of the United States?

The Internationale. Here is the Chorus: 'Tis the final conflict, Let each stand in his place; The International Soviet shall be the human race.

39. Do the Communists pledge allegiance to the flag of the United States?

The present head of the Communists in the United States had testified under oath that they DO NOT.

40. What is the Communist Party set-up?

At the bottom level are "shop and street units" composed of three or more Communists in a single factory, office, or neighborhood. Next is the section which includes all units in a given area of a city. Then come districts, composed of one or more States. At the top is the national organization, composed of a national committee and a number of commissions.

In the appendix of this pamphlet you will find listed the officers and address for each district of the Communist Party in the United States.

41. Who can become a member of the Communist Party of the United States?

Anybody over 17 years of age who can convince the Party that his first loyalty will be to the Soviet Union and that he is able to do the party's work as a Soviet agent. He must be an active member of a Party unit. He must obey ALL Party decisions. He must read the Party literature. He must pay dues regularly.

42. How do you go about joining the Party?

You must know some member in good standing who will vouch for you to his Party unit. Your acceptance still depends on the verdict of party officials that you WILL AND CAN obey orders.

43. Can you be a secret member?

All Communists are secret members until authorized by the Party to reveal their connection. Party membership records are kept in code. Communists have a real name and a "Party name."

44. Are meetings public like those of ordinary political parties?

No, meetings are secret and at secret addresses. Records are all secret and in code. Public demonstrations are held at regular periods.

45. What dues do you have to pay?

They are adjusted according to income. They may range from as low as 2 cents a week to $15 a week with special assessments in addition.

46. What do you have to promise?

To carry out Communist Party orders promptly. To submit without question to Party decisions and discipline. To work for "The triumph of Soviet power in the United States."

47. After you join, what do you have to do?

You have to obey the party in all things. It may tell you to change your home, your job, your husband, or wife. It may order you to lie, steal, rob, or to go out into the street and fight. It claims the power to tell you what to think and what to do every day of your life. When you become a Communist, you become a revolutionary agent under a discipline more strict than the United States Army, Navy, Marines, or Air Force have ever known.

48. Why do people become Communists then?

Basically, because they seek power and recognize the opportunities that Communism offers the unscrupulous. But no matter why a particular person becomes a Communist, every member of the Party must be regarded the same way, as one seeking to overthrow the Government of the United States.

49. What kind of people become Communists?

The real center of power in Communism is within the professional classes. Of course, a few poor people respond to the Communist claim that it is a "working class movement." But taken as a whole the Party depends for its strength on the support it gets from teachers, preachers, actors, writers, union officials, doctors, lawyers, editors, businessmen, and even from millionaires.

50. Can you quit being a Communist when you want to?

The Communists regard themselves as being in a state of actual war against life as the majority of Americans want it. Therefore, party members who quit or fail to obey orders are looked on as traitors to the "class war" and they may expect to suffer accordingly when and as the Party gets around to them.

51. How does the Communist Party of the United States work, day by day?

The Communist Party of the United States works inside the law and the Constitution, and outside the law and the Constitution with intent to get control any way it can.

52. What are some types of Communist activities within the law?

Working their way into key positions in the schools, the churches, the labor unions, and farm organizations. Inserting Communist propaganda into art, literature, and entertainment. Nominating or seeking control of candidates for public office. The immediate objective of the Communist Party is to confuse and divide the majority so that in a time of chaos they can seize control.

53. What are some types of Communist activities outside the law?

Spying, sabotage, passport fraud, perjury, counterfeiting, rioting, disloyalty in the Army, Navy and Air Force.

54. What are some official newspapers or magazines of the Communist Party?

Daily and Sunday Worker, *50 East Thirteenth Street, New York City;* Morning Friheit, *50 East Thirteenth Street, New York City;* Daily Peoples World, *590 Folsom Street, San Francisco, Calif.;* Masses and Mainstream, *832 Broadway, New York City;* Political Affairs, *832 Broadway, New York City. There are also numerous foreign language publications.*

55. Does the party also publish books and pamphlets?

Yes, thousands of them, through such official publishing houses as: International Publishers, 381 Fourth Street, New York City; Workers Library Publishers, 832 Broadway, New York City; New Century Publishers, 832 Broadway, New York City.

56. Does the party have public speakers and press agents?

Hundreds of them, paid and unpaid, public and secret, hired and volunteered, intentional and unintentional. Publicity seeking is one of the Party's principal "legal" occupations, intended to confuse people on all important issues of the day.

57. How does the Party get the money for all this?

At first it received money from Moscow but now it raises millions of dollars here in the United States through dues, **foundations**, **endowments**, special drives, and appeals.

58. Do only Communists carry out Communist work?

No. The party uses what it calls "Fellow Travelers" and "Front Organizations" in some of its most effective work.

59. What is a fellow traveler?

One who sympathizes with the party's aims and serves the party's purposes in one or more respects without actually holding a Party card.

60. Is he important in the Communist movement?

Vital. The fellow traveler is the HOOK with which the Party reaches out for funds and respectability and the WEDGE that it drives between people who try to move against it.

61. What is a Communist front?

An organization created or captured by the Communists to do the Party's work in special fields. The front organization is Communism's greatest weapon in this country today and takes it places it could never go otherwise—among people who would never willingly act as Party agents. It is usually found hiding among groups devoted to idealistic activities. Here are 10 examples out of hundreds of Communist fronts which have been exposed:

- 1. American Committee for Protection of Foreign Born.

- 2. American Slav Congress.

- 3. American Youth for Democracy.

- 4. Civil Rights Congress.

- 5. Congress of American Women.

- 6. Council for Pan-American Democracy.

- 7. International Workers Order.

- 8. National Committee to Win the Peace.

Foundations: Organizations that provide funds for activities.

Endowments: Gifts of money.

- *9. People's Institute of Applied Religion.*
- *10. League of American Writers.*

62. How can a Communist be identified?

It is easy. Ask him to name ten things wrong with the United States. Then ask him to name two things wrong with Russia. His answers will show him up even to a child. Communists will denounce the President of the United States but they will never denounce Stalin.

63. How can a fellow traveler be identified?

Apply the same test as above and watch him defend Communists and Communism.

64. How can a Communist front be identified?

If you are ever in doubt, write the House Committee on Un-American Activities, Room 226, House Office Building, Washington 25, D.C.

65. What do Communists call those who criticize them?

"Red baiters," "witch hunters," "Fascists." These are just three out of a tremendous stock of abusive labels Communists attempt to **smear** *on anybody who challenges them.*

66. How do they smear labor opposition?

As "scabs," "finks," "company stooges," and "labor spies."

67. How do they smear public officials?

As "reactionaries," "Wall Street tools," "Hitlerites," and "imperialists."

68. What is their favorite escape when challenged on a point of fact?

To accuse you of "dragging in a red herring," a distortion of an old folk saying that originally described the way to throw hounds off the track of a hot trail.

69. What is the difference in fact between a Communist and a Fascist?

None worth noticing.

70. How do Communists get control of organizations in which the majority are not Communists?

They work. Others won't.

Smear: Defame; malign.

They come early and stay late. Others don't.

They know how to run a meeting. Others don't.

They demand the floor. Others won't.

They do not hesitate to use physical violence or ANY form of persecution. They stay organized and prepared in advance of each meeting. The thing to remember is that Communists are trained agents under rigid discipline, but they can always be defeated by the facts.

71. When was the Communist party of the United States organized and where?

September 1919, at Chicago.

72. Has it always been called by its present name?

No. Here are the recorded, official name changes:

1919—Communist Party of America, and the Communist Labor Party of America.

1921—The above parties merged into the United Communist Party of America.

1922—The Communist Party of America and the Workers Party of America.

1925—The above merged into one organization known as Workers (Communist) Party of America.

1928—Communist Party of the United States.

1944—Communist Political Association.

1945 to present—Communist Party of the United States of America.

73. Why has it changed its name so often?

To serve Moscow and evade the law of the United States.

74. Why isn't the Communist Party a political party just like the Democratic and Republican parties?

Because it takes orders from Moscow.

75. Are the Communists agents of a foreign power?

Yes. The sworn testimony of several former members of the Communist Party who have spent years in being trained in Commu-

nist work, partly in Moscow, gives evidence to this. Official Commu-nist publications in the files of the committee also bear out this fact.

76. Where can a Communist be found in everyday American life?

Look for him in your school, your labor union, your church, or your civic club. Communists themselves say that they can be found "on almost any conceivable battlefront for the human mind."

77. What States have barred the Communist Party from the ballot?

Alabama, Arkansas, California, Delaware, Illinois, Indiana, Kansas, Ohio, Oklahoma, Oregon, Pennsylvania, Tennessee, Texas, Wisconsin, and Wyoming.

78. How does Communism expect to get power over the United States if it cannot win elections?

The Communists only compete for votes to cover their fifth-col-umn work behind a cloak of legality. They expect to get power by ANY means, just so they get it. The examples of Poland, Czechoslo-vakia, and other countries in Europe show just how many methods Communism applies. In each country different details—in all the same results.

79. Why don't Communists over here go to Russia if they like that system so much?

They are on duty here to take over this country. They couldn't go to Russia even if they wanted to, except on orders from Moscow.

80. Which Communists get such orders?

High Party officials and special agents who are to be trained in spying, sabotage, and detailed planning for capture of this country.

81. Where are they trained in Moscow?

The Lenin Institute, a college in revolution which teaches how to capture railroads, ships, radio stations, banks, telephone ex-changes, newspapers, waterworks, power plants, and such things.

82. Does Stalin let American Communists in to see him?

Yes. Earl Browder and William Z. Foster, the two heads of the Party for the last 20 years, have both admitted under oath that they conferred with Stalin. The records show that Browder, for instance, made 15 known trips to Moscow, several with false passports.

83. Are American Communists used in the Soviet Secret Service?

Yes, here are the names of a few such agents proved on the public records: Harry Gold, Julia Wadleigh, Nicholas Dozenberg, George Mink, Philip Aronberg, Charles Dirba, Pascal Cosgrove, J. Mindel, Alexander Trachtenberg, Julia Stuart Poyntz, Jack Johnstone, Charles Krumbein, and Albert Feirabend.

84. What central organization controls all the Communist Parties of the world?

An organization originally set up in Moscow by the Government of Russia, and known as the "Communist International" called Comintern for short. It has since changed its name to "Communist Information Bureau" and is known as the Cominform.

85. Who is the most important Communist in the United States today?

The Cominform representative.

86. Why is he here?

To see that American Communists follow the orders of the Soviet-directed Cominform in all things.

87. Do they?

Yes.

88. Has any representative of this central organization ever been caught?

*Yes. For example, over a period of 12 years one Gerhart Eisler, alias Brown, alias Edwards, alias Berger, did such work, making regular trips between the United States and Europe. On February 6, 1947, his activities were exposed by the House Committee on Un-American Activities and he has since been convicted in court of **perjury** and **contempt** of Congress.*

89. What is the best way to combat Communism?

Detection, exposure, and prosecution.

90. Are these being done?

Millions of dollars have been spent by the Federal Bureau of Investigation, Army and Navy Intelligence, and other executive agencies to detect and keep track of Communists since the Party's organization in this country a generation ago. Exposure in a systematic way began with the formation of the House Committee on Un-

Perjury: Making a false statement under oath.

Contempt: In disobedience.

American Activities, March 26, 1938. Prosecution of Communists, as such, has never taken place in this country, as yet.

91. Have any Communists been prosecuted on other grounds?

*Yes. For violations of such laws as those governing passports, immigration, perjury, criminal **syndicism**, and contempt.*

92. Is this enough?

No. The House of Representatives maintains this Committee on Un-American Activities to study the problems of Communism and all other subversive movements and recommend new laws if it feels they are needed.

93. Has the Committee made any such recommendations?

Yes. On September 22, 1950, H.R. 9490 was passed by both the House and the Senate, and became Public Law 8 3l, eighty-first Congress, second session, "the Internal Security Act of 1950."

94. What does this law do?

The main points are: To expose Communists and their fronts by requiring them to register publicly with the Attorney General and plainly label all their propaganda as their own.

*To forbid Communists passports or Government jobs. To make it illegal for ANYBODY to try to set up in this country a **totalitarian dictatorship** having ANY connection with a foreign power. To prevent Communists and members of other totalitarian parties from entering the United States.*

95. What is Communism's greatest strength?

Its secret appeal to the lust for power. Some people have a natural urge to dominate others in all things. Communism invites them to try. The money, hard work, conspiracy, and violence that go into Communism, add up to a powerful force moving in a straight line toward control of the world.

96. What is Communism's greatest weakness?

The very things that give it strength. For just as some people have a natural lust to dominate everybody else, so do most people have a natural determination to be free. Communism can dominate only by force. Communism can be stopped by driving every Communist out of the place where he can capture power.

97. What is treason?

Syndicism: An organized crime group.

Totalitarian dictatorship: A government ruled by one party, in this case the Communist Party.

*Our Constitution says that "Treason against the United States, shall consist only in levying War against them, or in adhering to their Enemies, giving them Aid and Comfort. No Person shall be convicted of Treason unless on the Testimony of two Witnesses to the same **overt** Act, or on Confession in open Court."*

98. Are the Communists committing treason today?

The Soviet Union has launched what has been called a "cold war" on the United States. Therefore, Communists are engaged in what might be called "COLD WAR TREASON." If our war with Communism should ever change from "cold" to "hot" we can expect the Communists of the United States to fight against the flag of this country openly.

99. What should I do about all this?

Know the facts. Stay on the alert. Work as hard against the Communists as they work against you.

100. Where can I get information about Communism regularly?

Write the House Committee on Un-American Activities, Room 226, Old House Office Building, Washington, D.C.

Overt: Open; not secret.

What happened next ...

In 1949, the National Education Association, which represented public school teachers, declared communists "unfit" to teach in schools. Many universities also agreed that communists could not be professors. Many state governments required loyalty oaths that made employees swear they were not part of any communist organization. If they refused on the grounds that loyalty oaths violated an individual's liberties, then they could lose their job. Jackie Robinson (1919–1972), the first black Major League baseball player, testified before the HUAC about civil rights groups and communists. Then in 1950, U.S. senator Joseph R. McCarthy (1909–1957) of Wisconsin began his infamous four-year witch-hunt of accusing Americans of being communists, or traitors to their countries.

Did you know ...

- The HUAC hoped the one hundred question-answer format of the booklets would help anyone who got in a debate with a communist sympathizer to "destroy his arguments completely."

- In three short years, from the end of World War II in August 1945 to the publication of this booklet, the democratic United States and the communist Soviet Union had gone from being allies to being enemies.

- In 1969, the HUAC was renamed the Internal Security Committee. Six years later, in 1975, the committee was abolished and its responsibilities were given to the House Judiciary Committee.

Consider the following ...

- Seek out the HUAC's answer to "Could I go to school?" How is your schooling currently different from what it would be under communism, according to this pamphlet?

- In question number 30 of the excerpt, locate countries already listed under communist on a map. Draw an iron curtain.

- What is meant by a communist "front" organization?

For More Information

Books

Beck, Carl. *Contempt of Congress: A Study of the Prosecutions Initiated by the Committee on Un-American Activities, 1945–1957.* New York: Da Capo Press, 1974.

Bentley, Eric, ed. *Thirty Years of Treason: Excerpts from Hearings Before the House Committee on Un-American Activities, 1938–1968.* New York: Viking Press, 1971.

Carr, Robert K. *The House Committee on Un-American Activities, 1945–1950.* New York: Octagon Books, 1979.

Donner, Frank J. *The Un-Americans.* New York: Ballantine Books, 1961.

Kahn, Gordon. *Hollywood on Trial: The Story of the 10 Who Were Indicted.* New York: Boni & Gaer, 1948.

Joseph R. McCarthy

Excerpt from "Speech on Communists in the U.S. State Department Made Before the Women's Republican Club in Wheeling, West Virginia, February 1950"
Available at CNN Interactive: Cold War (Web site)

"Ladies and gentlemen, can there be anyone here tonight who is so blind as to say that the war is not on? Can there be anyone who fails to realize that the communist world has said, 'The time is now'— that this is the time for the showdown between the democratic Christian world and the communist atheistic world? Unless we face this fact, we shall pay the price that must be paid by those who wait too long."

U.S. senator Joseph R. McCarthy (1908–1957) of Wisconsin influenced the Cold War (1945–91) as much as or more than any other single American. He took the extreme concerns about communism and homeland security that citizens had and created a national hysteria. His name permanently entered the U.S. vocabulary with the term "McCarthyism," which came to mean "challenging a person's individual character with lies and mean-spirited suggestions." In early 1950, McCarthy was an ineffective Republican senator from Wisconsin. Worried about his chances for reelection in 1952, he decided to grab headlines by warning of disloyalty at the highest ranks of U.S. government in the State Department.

On February 9, 1950, McCarthy addressed the Ohio County Women's Republican Club in Wheeling, West Virginia. In the Wheeling speech, McCarthy played on the Cold War and Red Scare fears (fear of a communist takeover) by asserting that the communist world, particularly the Soviet Union, was in a showdown with the democratic nations led by the United States. McCarthy dramatically held up a list that he claimed contained names of U.S. State Department

employees who supposedly were known members of or influenced by the Communist Party. McCarthy refused to reveal his sources or give all but a few names on the list. Some time later, it was discovered that the list he held up was his laundry list. Nevertheless, he had caught America's attention and became an instant celebrity.

With the speech, he had crowned himself the leading U.S. anticommunist, the exposer of communists. The American people and press listened intently. McCarthy appeared on the covers of *Time* and *Newsweek* magazines. McCarthy had hit upon a potent issue that he would pound on for the next four years. The following excerpt from "Speech on Communists in the U.S. State Department" warned Americans of a threat from within.

Things to remember while reading "Speech on Communists in the U.S. State Department":

- Between 1947 and the end of 1949, McCarthy had developed a reputation in the U.S. Senate as a troublemaker.

He had made many enemies with arrogant, rude, inconsistent behavior.

- Nevertheless, McCarthy was a smooth energetic speaker and had a brilliant knack for grabbing news headlines at just the right time.

- Americans were already very fearful that the communists were indeed intent on taking over the United States.

Excerpt from "Speech on Communists in the U.S. State Department"

Ladies and Gentlemen: ...

*Five years after a world war has been won, men's hearts should anticipate a long peace, and men's minds should be free from the heavy weight that comes with war. But this is not such a period—for this is not a period of peace. This is a time of the Cold War. This is a time when all the world is split into two vast, increasingly hostile armed camps—a time of a **great armaments** race. Today we can almost physically hear the mutterings and rumblings of an invigorated god of war. You can see it, feel it, and hear it all the way from the hills of Indochina, from the shores of Formosa [the island of Taiwan] right over into the very heart of Europe itself....*

*Today we are engaged in a final, all-out battle between communistic **atheism** and Christianity. The modern champions of communism have selected this as the time. And, ladies and gentlemen, the chips are down—they are truly down....*

Ladies and gentlemen, can there be anyone here tonight who is so blind as to say that the war is not on? Can there be anyone who fails to realize that the communist world has said, "The time is now"—that this is the time for the showdown between the democratic Christian world and the communist atheistic world? Unless we face this fact, we shall pay the price that must be paid by those who wait too long.

Six years ago, at the time of the first conference to map out peace—Dumbarton Oaks [site of an estate used for conferences in the Washington, D.C., area]—there was within the Soviet orbit 180

Atheism: A belief that there is no God.

million people. Lined up on the anti-totalitarian side [against Communist Party rule] *there were in the world at that time roughly 1.625 billion people. Today, only six years later, there are 800 million people under the absolute domination of Soviet Russia—an increase of over 400 percent. On our side, the figure has shrunk to around 500 million. In other words, in less than six years the odds have changed from 9 to 1 in our favor to 8 to 5 against us. This indicates the swiftness of the tempo of communist victories and Amer-*

A political cartoon shows U.S. senator Joseph McCarthy hunting for communists in Secretary of State John Foster Dulles's desk. *Illustration by Reg Manning. Courtesy of the Library of Congress.*

Tempo: Pace; rate of speed.

ican defeats in the Cold War. As one of our outstanding historical figures once said, "When a great democracy is destroyed, it will not be because of enemies from without but rather because of enemies from within." The truth of this statement is becoming terrifyingly clear as we see this country each day losing on every front.

At war's end we were physically the strongest nation on Earth and, at least potentially, the most powerful intellectually and morally. Ours could have been the honor of being a **beacon** in the desert of destruction, a shining, living proof that civilization was not yet ready to destroy itself. Unfortunately, we have failed miserably and tragically to arise to the opportunity.

The reason why we find ourselves in a position of **impotency** is not because our only powerful, potential enemy has sent men to invade our shores, but rather because of the traitorous actions of those who have been treated so well by this nation. It has not been the less fortunate or members of minority groups who have been selling this nation out, but rather those who have had all the benefits that the wealthiest nation on earth has had to offer—the finest homes, the finest college education, and the finest jobs in government we can give.

This is glaringly true in the State Department. There the bright young men who are born with **silver spoons in their mouths** are the ones who have been worst....

In my opinion the State Department, which is one of the most important government departments, is thoroughly **infested** with communists.

I have in my hand 57 cases of individuals who would appear to be either card-carrying members or certainly loyal to the Communist Party, but who nevertheless are still helping to shape our foreign policy.

One thing to remember in discussing the communists in our government is that we are not dealing with spies who get 30 pieces of silver to steal the blueprints of new weapons. We are dealing with a far more sinister type of activity because it permits the enemy to guide and shape our policy....

I know that you are saying to yourself, "Well, why doesn't the Congress do something about it?" Actually, ladies and gentlemen, one of the important reasons for the **graft**, the corruption, the dishonesty, the disloyalty, the treason in high government positions—

Beacon: A source of light or inspiration.

Impotency: Weakness.

Silver spoons in their mouths: Wealth.

Infested: Overrun by something unwanted in large numbers.

Graft: Dishonest use of a person's position.

one of the most important reasons why this continues—is a lack of moral uprising on the part of the 140 million American people. In the light of history, however, this is not hard to explain.

*It is the result of an emotional hangover and a temporary moral **lapse** which follows every war. It is the apathy to evil which people who have been subjected to the tremendous evils of war feel. As the people of the world see mass murder, the destruction of defenseless and innocent people, and all of the crime and lack of morals which go with war, they become numb and **apathetic.** It has always been thus after war. However, the morals of our people have not been destroyed. They still exist. This cloak of numbness and apathy has only needed a spark to rekindle them. Happily, this spark has finally been supplied....*

[The existence of communists] *has lighted the spark which is resulting in a moral uprising and will end only when the whole sorry mess of twisted warped thinkers are swept from the national scene so that we may have a new birth of national honesty and decency in government.*

Lapse: Small slip.

Apathetic: Emotionless.

What happened next ...

The House Un-American Activities Committee (HUAC) eagerly investigated all those persons on whom McCarthy cast suspicion. Not only did he attack lower-level government officials, but he also reached to the highest levels with his charges. He attacked Secretary of Defense George C. Marshall (1880–1959), Secretary of State Dean Acheson (1893–1971), and even Presidents Harry S. Truman (1884–1972; served 1945–53) and Dwight D. Eisenhower (1890–1969; served 1953–61). Republican leadership knew the outrageousness of McCarthy's charges but also knew it was political suicide to try to stop him. The public listened to him. He was reelected as senator of Wisconsin in 1952.

When Eisenhower was inaugurated as president of the United States in 1953, he tried to reel in McCarthy by assigning him to an unimportant committee called the Government Operations Committee. Instead, McCarthy within that committee created the Permanent Subcommittee on In-

U.S. senator Joseph R. McCarthy of Wisconsin points to a map titled "Communist party organization of the U.S.A. Feb. 9, 1950," during HUAC testimony June 9, 1954, in Washington, D.C.
Reproduced by permission of the Corbis Corporation.

vestigations and appointed himself chairman. The subcommittee became the McCarthy Committee that continued its probing and destruction of individuals, organizations, and even libraries. Finally, by 1954, the public had caught on. Criticism of McCarthyism mounted. When McCarthy began to attack the U.S. Army, he had pushed too far. President Eisenhower, working behind the scenes, and Army attorney Joseph N. Welch (1890–1960) brought McCarthy's long tirade of unjustified attacks to an end. The Senate voted to censure McCarthy, meaning they regarded his behavior from 1950 to 1954 as dishonorable.

Did you know ...

- McCarthy's strategy was to attack then avoid. He attacked by casting doubt on an individual's political loyalties. Though never producing any evidence, he nonetheless forced the individual to publicly defend his or her name.

- By early 1951, much of the American public, mesmerized by McCarthyism, really did not care if his charges were true or not.

- Simply being named by McCarthy as a possible subversive was often career-ending.

- For decades, the McCarthy hearings adversely affected U.S. diplomatic efforts toward the communist countries of the Soviet Union, Eastern Europe, and China.

Consider the following ...

- Some called McCarthy a patriot; others accused him of vicious, irresponsible charges that ruined people's lives. Take a side and defend that stance.

- For decades, Americans struggled to comprehend how a person in the high-profile position of U.S. senator could discredit and trample the constitutionally protected liberties of so many people. What conditions in America allowed this to happen?

- In the twenty-first century, when someone accuses another of McCarthyism, of what are they accusing the person?

For More Information

Books

Herman, Arthur. *Joseph McCarthy: Reexamining the Life and Legacy of America's Most Hated Senator.* New York: Free Press, 2000.

Oshinsky, David M. *A Conspiracy So Immense: The World of Joe McCarthy.* Free Press, 1983.

Schrecker, Ellen. *Many Are the Crimes: McCarthyism in America.* Boston: Little, Brown, 1998.

Sherrow, Victoria. *Joseph McCarthy and the Cold War.* Woodbridge, CT: Blackbirch Press, 1999.

Web Sites

CNN Interactive: Cold War. http://www.cnn.com/SPECIALS/cold.war/episodes/06/documents/mccarthy (accessed on September 22, 2003).

Webcorp. *Senator Joe McCarthy—A Multimedia Celebration.* http://www.webcorp.com/mccarthy/mccarthypage.htm (accessed on September 15, 2003).

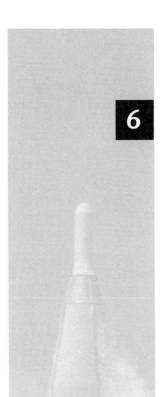

6 The Colorful Khrushchev

Nikita Khrushchev (1894–1971) was twenty-three years of age during the Bolshevik (Communist) Revolution in Russia in 1917. In the 1920s, Khrushchev was able to attend educational institutions established by the Communist Party to instruct young people in basic education and communist doctrine. A bright student and natural leader, Khrushchev began his rise in the Communist Party. By 1935, he held one of the top positions in the party: First Secretary of the Moscow city party. That same year, he was elected to the Soviet Central Committee, the organization that oversaw all the important administrative duties of the Communist Party. By 1939, he became a full member of the Politburo, the policy-making group of the Central Committee.

Khrushchev served in the Soviet army during World War II (1939–45) and rose to the rank of lieutenant general. Following World War II, Khrushchev was back in his native Ukraine in southern Russia, both as leader of the Ukraine Communist Party and as overseer of rebuilding the Ukraine's postwar economy. By the late 1940s, he had returned to Moscow and was one of the inner circle of Soviet leader Joseph

Stalin (1879–1953). He regularly dined with Stalin but managed to escape Stalin's regular purges of Soviet leaders. Stalin died in March 1953. A power struggle ensued between Khrushchev and Stalin's successor, Georgy Malenkov (1902–1988). By 1955, Khrushchev was firmly in power.

Khrushchev became the most colorful leader in Soviet history. Although he had come from a poor peasant background and had struggled to gain an education, he had learned rapidly from experience. He attacked all tasks with energy, enthusiasm, and directness. His mannerisms were boisterous, often rude, independent, and unconventional. Underneath the show was a warm, good-natured man who genuinely cared for the Soviet people and was more interested in the land and agriculture than in military weapons. With his rise to power, the terror tactics of Stalin's thirty-year dictatorship ended.

Soviet premier Nikita Khrushchev. *Courtesy of the Library of Congress.*

In the first excerpt here, the "Crimes of Stalin Speech," Khrushchev dared to reveal the murderous trail and paranoid life and activities of Stalin. The several-hour speech was met by shock, amazement, and thunderous applause. The second excerpt, from an article in *American Heritage*, by Sergei Khrushchev (1935–), is a firsthand look at Khrushchev's years in power, 1953 until 1964, through the eyes of his son. Sergei, as talented in the use of words as his father, shows a very human and practical Khrushchev carefully balancing the security of his country through the Cold War (1945–91). The final excerpt is from "Peace and Progress Must Triumph in Our Time," in which Nikita Khrushchev reported to the people of Moscow on his trip to the United States. The Soviets were very curious about what Americans were like, and Khrushchev related his impressions. In the address, he also called repeatedly for peaceful coexistence between the superpowers and for armament-reduction discussions.

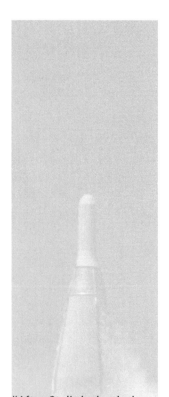

Nikita Khrushchev

Excerpt from "Crimes of Stalin Speech"
Published in *A Treasury of the World's Great Speeches*, published in 1954

"After Stalin's death the Central Committee of the Party began to implement a policy of explaining concisely and consistently that it is impermissible ... to elevate one person, to transform him into a superman possessing supernaturalistic characteristics akin to those of a god. Such a man supposedly knows everything, thinks for everyone, can do anything, is infallible in his behavior."

On the night of February 24, 1956, during the Twentieth Congress of the Communist Party being held at the Kremlin, Soviet leader Nikita Khrushchev (1894–1971) ordered a select group of delegates to a secret meeting under tight security. The Kremlin was a centuries-old fort in Moscow that was used as the headquarters of the Communist Party. As the delegates approached the doors of the room where the unscheduled night meeting was to occur, they were apprehensive. Some, no doubt remembering the Stalin purges, were quietly terrified. What would befall them in the next hour was completely unknown.

The gathering of the Twentieth Congress had been going on for ten days, since February 14. The last day would be Saturday, February 25. The number of delegates with voting rights in attendance was 1,355, with 81 more delegates there as advisors. The conference session had covered all aspects of Soviet society from economy, agriculture, and health, to the problems of unemployment of youth. There were a few subtle changes from previous Congresses. Noticeably absent was the picture of former Soviet leader Joseph

Stalin (1879–1953) in the main hall. In addition, Khrushchev, First Secretary of the Central Committee of the Communist Party, addressing a general meeting, had delivered a seven-hour report with hardly a mention of Stalin.

Unknown to those entering the secret Friday night meeting was that there was little to fear. Gone were the days when Stalin would simply look into a man's eyes and, depending on what he thought he read in those eyes, the man's life would continue or be shortly ended. A new day had dawned in the Soviet Union. No longer were all problems, perceived problems, or controversies settled by torture and murder as they had been under Stalin. When Stalin died, so did the terror. Nikita Khrushchev spoke to the delegates gathered on Friday night as no Soviet official had dared to speak for three decades. In a several-hour speech, he carefully explained the years of rule by Stalin and pointed out the flaws and crimes of the communist past. The speech became known as Khrushchev's "Crimes of Stalin Speech."

Things to remember while reading "Crimes of Stalin Speech":

- For thirty years, most of the delegates at the conference had been terrified of Stalin. A secret meeting could have easily meant the announcement of their death sentences.

- Stalin's legacy as a dictator was the Great Terror. The Terror involved execution or exile of millions of both opponents and supporters of the Communist Party.

- The Twentieth Congress was the first all-Party member conference since Stalin's death in 1953.

Excerpt from "Crimes of Stalin Speech"

Comrades! [fellow communists, friends]…

After [Joseph] *Stalin's death the **Central Committee** of the Party began to implement a policy of explaining concisely and consistently*

Central Committee: Key administrative body.

that it is **impermissible** and foreign to the spirit of Marxism-Leninism [the founding theory of communism] *to elevate one person, to transform him into a superman possessing* **supernaturalistic** *characteristics akin to those of a god. Such a man supposedly knows everything, thinks for everyone, can do anything, is* **infallible** *in his behavior.*

Such a belief about a man, and specifically about Stalin, was cultivated among us for many years....

In December 1922, in a letter to the Party Congress, Vladimir Ilyich [Lenin] *wrote: "After taking over the position of Secretary General* [head of the Communist Party and consequently of the Soviet Union as well], *Comrade Stalin accumulated in his hands immeasurable power and I am not certain whether he will be able to use this power with the required care.... Stalin is excessively rude, and this defect, which can be freely tolerated in our midst and in contacts among us Communists, becomes a defect which cannot be tolerated in one holding the position of the Secretary General. Because of this, I propose that the comrades consider the method by which Stalin would be removed from this position and by which another man would be selected for it, a man who, above all, would differ from Stalin in only one direction, namely, greater tolerance, greater loyalty, greater kindness and a more considerate attitude toward the comrades, a less* **capricious** *temper, etc."...*

Some years later, when **socialism** *in our country was fundamentally constructed, when the exploiting classes were generally* **liquidated**, *when the Soviet social structure had radically changed, when the social basis for political movements and groups hostile to the Party had violently* **contracted**, *when the ideological opponents* [opposition to communism] *of the Party were long since defeated politically—then the repression against them began.*

It was precisely during this period [1935 to 1938] *that the practice of* **mass repression** *through the government was born, first against the enemies of Leninism ... and subsequently also against many honest Communists, against those Party* **cadres** *who had borne the heavy load of the civil war* [the Bolshevik Revolution of 1918] *and the first and most difficult years of industrialization and* **collectivization.**

Stalin originated the concept "enemy of the people." This term ... made possible the usage of the most cruel repression ... against anyone who in any way disagreed with Stalin, against those who were only suspected of hostile intent, against those who had bad reputations.

Impermissable: Not allowable.

Supernaturalistic: Something beyond natural laws, such as characteristics of a god.

Infallible: Never making a mistake.

Capricious: Irrationally impulsive or unpredictable.

Socialism: A system of society in which the community or government owns or controls industry and land.

Liquidated: Gotten rid of.

Contracted: Decreased.

Mass repression: Keeping the whole population under strict control.

Cadres: Experienced military personnel.

Collectivization: Centralized control of production by the state.

This concept, *"enemy of the people,"* actually eliminated the possibility of any kind of ideological fight or the making of one's views known on this or that issue, even those of a practical character. In the main, and in actuality, the only proof of guilt used ... was the "confession" of the accused himself, and, as subsequent probing proved, "confessions" were acquired through physical pressures [torture] against the accused.

This led to ... the fact that many entirely innocent victims, who in the past had defended the Party line [communist ideals], *became victims....*

It was determined that of the one hundred thirty-nine members and candidates of the Party's Central Committee who were elected at the Seventeenth Congress, ninety-eight persons, i.e., 70 percent, were arrested and shot [mostly 1937 to 1938]. [***Indignation** in the hall.*]

Facts prove that many abuses were made on Stalin's orders.... He could look at a man and say: "Why are your eyes so shifty today?" or, "Why do you turn so much today and avoid looking me

Information card on Joseph Stalin, from the files of the St. Petersburg Tsarist police, around 1913.
Reproduced by permission of the Corbis Corporation.

Indignation: Strong displeasure in something considered unworthy.

directly in the eyes?" This sickly suspiciousness created in him a general distrust, even toward **eminent** party workers whom he had known for years. Everywhere and in everything he saw "enemies," "two-faces," and "spies."

Possessing unlimited power, he indulged in great willfulness and choked a person morally and physically [destroyed the person]. A situation was created where one could not express one's own will....

Comrades, let us reach for some other facts. The Soviet Union is justly considered as a model of a multinational State because we have in practice assured the equality and friendship of all nations which live in our great Fatherland.

All the more monstrous are the acts whose **initiator** was Stalin and which are rude violations of the basic Leninist principles of the nationality policy [communism] of the Soviet State. We refer to the mass deportations from their native places of whole nations,... this **deportation** action was not dictated by any military considerations....

I recall the days when the conflict between the Soviet Union and Yugoslavia began to be blown up artificially. Once, when I came from Kiev to Moscow, I was invited to visit Stalin, who, pointing to a copy of a letter sent to [Yugoslavian leader Josip] Tito, asked me, "Have you read this?"

Not waiting for my reply he answered, "I will shake my little finger and there will be no more Tito. He will fall."

We have paid dearly for this "shaking of the little finger." This statement reflects Stalin's **mania** for greatness, but he acted just that way: "I will shake my little finger—and there will be no Kossior"; "I will shake my little finger again and Postyshev and Chubar will be no more"; "I will shake my little finger once more—and Voznesensky, Kuznetsov [all Soviets that disappeared] and many others will disappear."

But this did not happen to Tito. No matter how much or little Stalin shook, not only his little finger but everything else that he could shake, Tito did not fall....

The question arises why [Lavrenty] Beria [head of the Soviet secret police, Stalin's main enforcer], who had liquidated tens of thousands of Party and Soviet workers, was not unmasked during Stalin's life? He was not unmasked earlier because he had very skillfully played on Stalin's weaknesses; feeding him with suspicion, he assisted Stalin in everything and acted with his support....

Eminent: High in rank.

Initiator: A person who begins or introduces.

Deportation: Sending undesirable people out of a country.

Mania: Excessive desire.

Stalin's reluctance to consider **life's realities** and the fact that he was not aware of the real state of affairs in the provinces can be illustrated by his direction of agriculture. All those who interested themselves even a little in the national situation saw the difficult situation in agriculture, but Stalin never even noted it. Did we tell Stalin about this? Yes, we told him, but he did not support us. Why? Because Stalin never traveled anywhere, did not meet city and kolkhoz [collective farm] workers; he did not know the actual situation in the provinces. He knew the country and agriculture only from films. And these films had dressed up and beautified the existing situation in agriculture. Many films so pictured kolkhoz life that the tables were bending from the weight of turkeys and geese. Evidently Stalin thought it was actually so....

Comrades! The Twentieth Congress of the Communist Party of the Soviet Union has manifested with a new strength the unshakable unity of our Party, its **cohesiveness** around the Central Committee, its resolute will to accomplish the great task of building communism. [Tumultuous applause.] And the fact that we present in all their **ramifications** the basic problems of overcoming the **cult of the individual** which is alien to Marxism-Leninism, as well as the problem of liquidating its burdensome consequences [righting the wrongs done under Stalin], is an evidence of the great moral and political strength of our party. [Prolonged applause.]

We are absolutely certain that our Party, armed with the historical resolutions of the Twentieth Congress, will lead the Soviet people along the Leninist path to new successes, to new victories. [Tumultuous, prolonged applause.]

Long live the victorious banner of our Party—Leninism. [Tumultuous, prolonged applause ending in ovation. All rise.]

Joseph Stalin, the brutal and absolute leader of the communist Soviet Union from 1929 until his death in 1953. *Reproduced by permission of Getty Images.*

Life's realities: Real-life conditions.

Cohesiveness: Sticking tightly.

Ramifications: Results of an action.

Cult of the individual: Glorification of an individual as if the individual were superhuman.

What happened next ...

The relief in the hall was overwhelming. Astonished at Khrushchev's words, the delegates broke out in thunderous, sustained applause. Copies of the speech were released to party leaders. Following the epic speech, special Communist Party meetings were held throughout the Soviet Union to carry forward Khrushchev's message. The U.S. Central Intelligence Agency (CIA) managed to get a copy of the speech out of Moscow. On June 4, 1956, a translated copy was released to the press by the U.S. State Department.

The Communist government in China under Mao Zedong (1893–1976) highly disapproved of Khrushchev's speech. To the Chinese, it broke from traditional communist doctrine. The speech also caused shock in Eastern European countries. Unintentionally, it fostered a mood of rebellion against communist rule, especially against hard-line Stalin supporters. The rebellious mood in Hungary broke into open revolt on November 1956. Khrushchev felt compelled to crush the revolt, killing soldiers and civilians alike. With his actions in Hungary, the prestige he had gained within the international community was lost.

Nevertheless, Khrushchev indeed went down a different path from Stalin. Rather than secluding himself in the Kremlin, he traveled widely across the Soviet Union and to foreign countries, including Great Britain and the United States.

Did you know ...

- Khrushchev, to survive the purges of Stalin, worked with Stalin as a close advisor in the 1930s and 1940s. In a January 1937 speech, he said, "Stalin is hope; ... Stalin is our banner! Stalin is our will! Stalin is our victory!"

- It was not surprising to many who knew the flamboyant, independent-thinking Khrushchev that he could deliver such a risky, revolutionary speech.

- The "Crimes of Stalin Speech" is considered Khrushchev's most dramatic moment in his colorful history as leader of the Soviet Union.

Consider the following ...

- According to Khrushchev, Stalin was out of touch with "life's realities," or the real conditions facing Soviet citizens. Why?

- Khrushchev spoke of "overcoming the cult of the individual." Explain what a "cult of the individual" is and why it is dangerous. Can you think of any European leaders during World War II who enjoyed "cult of the individual" status?

- If Stalin "shook his little finger" at you, what would happen?

For More Information

Books

Antonov-Ovseyenko, Anton. *The Time of Stalin: Portrait of a Tyranny.* New York: Harper & Row, 1980.

Conquest, Robert. *Stalin: Breaker of Nations.* New York: Viking, 1991.

Djilas, Milovan. *Conversations with Stalin.* London: Penguin, 1962.

Lewis, Jonathan, and Phillip Whitehead. *Stalin: A Time for Judgement.* New York: Pantheon Books, 1990.

Peterson, Houston. *A Treasury of the World's Great Speeches.* New York: Simon & Schuster, 1954.

Tucker, Robert C. *Stalin in Power: The Revolution from Above, 1928–1941.* New York: W. W. Norton, 1990.

Zubok, Vladislav M., and Constantine Pleshakov. *Inside the Kremlin's Cold War: From Stalin to Khrushchev.* Cambridge, MA: Harvard University Press, 1996.

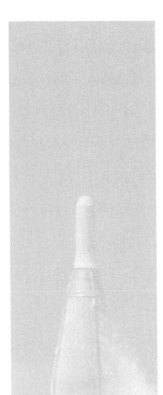

Sergei Khrushchev

Excerpt from "The Looking Glass"
Published in *American Heritage*, October 1999

"To restrain the West from a possible attack on the Soviet Union, Father decided to ... bluff.... He [said] 'We are producing missiles like sausages.' When I asked him how he could say that, since the Soviet Union had no more than half a dozen intercontinental missiles, Father [said], 'The main thing is that Americans think we have enough for a powerful strike in response.'"

Sergei Khrushchev (1935–) is the only child of Soviet leader Nikita Khrushchev (1894–1971) and his second wife, schoolteacher Nina Petrovna Khrushchev (1900–1984). In 1999, Sergei was living in the United States and was a senior fellow at the Thomas J. Watson, Jr., Center for International Studies at Brown University in Providence, Rhode Island. Sergei and his wife, Valentina Golenko, became American citizens in 1999. However, most of their adult life had been spent in the Soviet Union.

In this excerpt titled "The Looking Glass," from the October 1999 issue of *American Heritage, and the Creation of a Superpower*, Sergei Khrushchev gives a fascinating recounting of the Cold War years during which his father led the Soviet Union. Of course what makes his account riveting is that the American reader feels they are peeking inside a far-off, still little-understood country that once was greatly feared.

The excerpt begins about the time of the death of Joseph Stalin (1879–1953) in March 1953. Stalin had ruthlessly ruled over the Soviet Union for three decades. It was also the time when retired World War II (1939–45) army general and

American hero Dwight D. Eisenhower (1890–1969) became president of the United States. Sergei continues with the Geneva Conference of 1955, his father's domestic concerns, his dealings with the Soviet military, and his decisions on how to best answer the military might of the United States. Next, he explains how Eisenhower and his father began to dialogue with each other, speaks of the Cuban Missile Crisis, and lastly takes a moment to philosophically analyze the Cold War.

Things to remember while reading "The Looking Glass":

- During the entire Cold War (1945–91), Sergei related that he and his fellow Soviets feared that "our great national enemy," the United States, would destroy them if they made "the slightest false step or showed the least weakness." He believed that the people of the United States had the same fear of the Soviet Union. "For Americans, of course, the Soviet Union was the Evil Empire," but for Soviets the United States was the Evil Empire.

- Between Geneva in 1955 and meeting with President Eisenhower in 1959, Sergei related how his father and Eisenhower learned for the first time that the superpowers could actually talk to each other. That understanding set a basis that continued until the end of the Cold War.

Sergei Khrushchev, son of Nikita Khrushchev and author of *Nikita Khrushchev and the Creation of a Superpower*. Reproduced by permission of the Corbis Corporation.

Excerpt from "The Looking Glass"

When the Cold War began, people my age were in school, and when it ended, we were increasingly thinking about our pensions.

Our whole lives were spent amid the fear that our great national enemy would strike a fatal blow if we made the slightest false step or showed the least weakness. Who "we" were and who the enemy was depended on which country we considered our own, the Soviet Union or the United States.

*Virtually my entire life has been spent in Russia. When, already past maturity, I came to the United States, I was surprised by how much our fears and our determination to defend our ideals and our countries had coincided. For Americans, of course, the Soviet Union was the Evil Empire. Readers will be surprised and even **indignant** to learn that to us—or at least for most of my compatriots—the United States was the Evil Empire. Each side came very close to seizing the other by the throat in a fit of **righteous** indignation and, in defense of its ideals, using force to make it admit it was wrong (always a hopeless approach). Thanks to the statesmanlike and human wisdom of the leaders of both countries—and a certain amount of luck—we succeeded in avoiding such a "resolution" [a "hot" war, probably a nuclear war] of the ideological quarrel. The Cold War expired by itself, and we, having survived, can now look back, evaluate our recent past, and even joke about it.*

But at the time of Joseph Stalin's death in 1953, everything seemed to be heading toward a real war, a nuclear war. Today, when many secrets are secrets no longer, we know that at the beginning of the 1950s, Stalin ordered an accelerated buildup not only of the Soviet Union's armed forces but of those of his Warsaw Pact allies [a military alliance among Eastern European countries under Soviet domination] *as well, in order to be fully mobilized and ready for an armed clash by 1954 or 1955. By March 1953 the number of Soviet military personnel had reached 5,394,038, an insupportable burden for the economy of a country in peacetime. However, this gigantic army could have done little in case of a conflict, since the strategic air force of the United States, whose bases surrounded the Soviet Union, could have destroyed whatever it chose. Stalin did not possess a weapon capable of responding with a comparable **retaliatory strike** on American territory. He knew this and was deathly afraid of war, but at the same time he considered it **inevitable**. Motivated by fear, he ordered that ten thousand tactical IL–28 bombers with a range of about fifteen hundred miles be produced and stationed at airfields built on the Arctic Ocean ice, closer to U.S. territory. Soviet generals were fully aware that this was an impractical plan, but they did not dare*

Indignant: Strongly displeased.

Righteous: Morally right or justified.

Retaliatory strike: Return of weapons fire.

Inevitable: Unavoidable.

contradict Stalin. Preparations to implement it ended only with his death.

Another crazy scheme, similarly born out of fear, was actually carried out. An army of one hundred thousand men was stationed in tents on the Chukotsk tundra and charged with resisting an invasion from Alaska. It was assumed that the Americans would cross the Bering Strait on the ice. However, where they could go from there, surrounded by swamps, permafrost, and the **taiga,** has always remained a mystery to me. From Chukotka it is a good eight thousand miles to Moscow and at least twenty-five hundred miles to relatively inhabited regions of Siberia.

Anti-aircraft batteries were ranged like a fence around Moscow. Beside them lay open crates of gleaming shells ready to be fired. The sudden German air attack in June 1941 was continuing to dominate the Kremlin's thinking, just as Pearl Harbor lived on in Washington's.

I finished school and began studying at the Electric Power Institute in September 1952. I wanted to become an engineer in the field of automated control. We schoolboys and students were inclined to be militant, even aggressive: "Just let them poke their noses in here and we'll show them a thing or two." Sitting at our school desks, we, like our leaders in the Kremlin, felt sure that war was not far off. When America elected Gen. Dwight D. Eisenhower, a hero of the Second World War, as President in November 1952, we had no doubt what it meant: "The U.S.A. has decided to fight. Otherwise, why would they need a general as President?"

After living through the horrors of German bombings, we were not frightened by the atomic bomb. We **flaunted** our courage. During civil defense classes we were told to cover ourselves with something white, preferably a sheet, in the event of a nuclear blast, to reduce the radiation impact (I don't know how effective that would have been). A joke immediately went the rounds: "If an atomic bomb explodes, cover yourself with a sheet and crawl to the cemetery, but without hurrying. Why without hurrying? So as not to cause panic."

Then **Providence** intervened. On March 5, 1953, Stalin died. My father, who soon became the head of the new Soviet leadership, knew from personal experience what war was like. He had traveled the country's roads for four years during World War II, retreating from the western borders to Stalingrad and then advancing from Stalingrad to Kiev. From his first months in power he tried to discov-

Taiga: Vast subarctic evergreen forests.

Flaunted: Displayed for special attention.

Providence: Divine guidance; the idea of the guiding hand of God.

er whether the Americans were irrevocably bent on war or whether it was possible to reach agreement with them. Interestingly enough, the White House was thinking along more or less the same lines.

*In April 1953 President Eisenhower took the first step, delivering a rather **conciliatory** speech [the "Chance for Peace Speech;" see Chapter 4, second excerpt] at the National Press Club, in Washington. The next day it was published in full in Pravda [the Soviet Communist Party newspaper], an unprecedented event in those times. Probably this was the turning point from war to peace, and the beginning of dialogue. But it was only the beginning. Both parties had to learn to understand each other. Living on either side of the **iron curtain**, we knew nothing about each other. Diplomats and intelligence agents supplied their leaders with information, of course, but that was not enough to gain an understanding of the other side. We had to look into each other's eyes.*

*The first time that my father and President Eisenhower met was in Geneva in 1955, at the Four-Power Summit Conference. The most important thing that happened in Geneva was that Khrushchev and Eisenhower got to know each other, made their first contacts, and held their first talks. The first step is the most difficult. The process of getting acquainted was not without its curious moments. During one of the breaks between sessions, Eisenhower introduced Father to his assistant Nelson Rockefeller. Father inquired, "Is he that Rockefeller?" As Father told me when he returned to Moscow, his curiosity was very much aroused when he was told that this was indeed that Rockefeller. A multimillionaire, but looking no different from anyone else, not in top hat and tails but modestly dressed, moreover serving in a **subordinate** position. Continuing his account, Father said that he was dying to touch a real multi-millionaire, but he didn't know how that would be taken. He didn't hesitate for long, though, but spread his arms and embraced Rockefeller somewhere around the waist. (Rockefeller was a head and a half taller than Father.) At first Rockefeller was taken aback, but after a moment he responded in kind. I'm describing this to give the reader a sense of what the atmosphere was like in those years. It is hard for us now to imagine how distant we were from each other and how little we understood each other. Such episodes were more valuable than any routine session of negotiations, which were as yet essentially unproductive.*

The first misunderstandings also arose in Geneva, and some of them had far-reaching consequences. Eisenhower presented his

Conciliatory: Friendly and full of good will.

Iron curtain: Symbolic boundary between the bloc of Soviet-dominated communist countries in Eastern Europe and democratic Western Europe.

Subordinate: Less important.

Open Skies plan, which would allow each side to fly over the territories of the opposing group of countries in order to prevent a surprise attack. Father rejected such a plan outright. Not that he was against the idea itself. But if the American President feared a Soviet attack, Father was afraid of something quite different: that in the process of flying over our country, the Americans would discover our most important secret—how much weaker we were than they—and that discovery might prompt the United States to carry out a preventive strike. In subsequent years Father continued to oppose inspections for the same reason.

In Geneva initial judgments and opinions were formed on both sides. Father came to the conclusion that he could do business with Eisenhower, who had also experienced the recent war firsthand and would not seek a new one. But a long and difficult path lay ahead before mutual understanding could be reached, and the time had not yet come for an agreement. In order to be taken seriously, you had to become powerful, since peace on earth can only be achieved through strength—or from a position of strength, as people put it then.

Father had a special enthusiasm for corn. He thought it could help supply feed for livestock and thereby raise meat consumption in our country to American levels. It was thought that when this was achieved, true communism would come to the U.S.S.R. Father very much wanted to have a look, however **fleeting**, at what life would be like under communism—in other words, when Russians lived no worse than Americans, than those Americans who had dreamed of destroying communism.

Father believed that the system that gave people the best living standards would win.

After agriculture, Father's main concern was housing construction. By the time he came to power, this problem had become acute. Soviet citizens did not live in their own houses or apartments, as people in the United States and Europe did. In Russia several generations of a family—grandparents, their children and grandchildren, ten or more people—might be cooped up in one room of 150 square feet. They slept on the floor. In the morning long lines formed for the only toilet at the end of a hall with doors to a dozen similarly overpopulated rooms. It is hard to describe in words what it's like to stand in such a line; it has to be experienced.

Father was determined to resolve this problem, and he initiated the mass construction of apartment buildings. They were put to-

Fleeting: Quickly passing.

gether from concrete panels manufactured quickly on factory conveyor belts, like cars. The houses, like cars, looked exactly alike. Housing construction and agriculture required money, a great deal of money, and we had to economize on everything else.

During those years Father strictly prohibited the construction of administrative buildings, luxury homes for the leadership, and even theaters. All such money was channeled into building inexpensive housing, which was free for its new occupants. Even the Ministry of Defense had to line up for money. However, only a madman or traitor could neglect the country's security during the Cold War. Defense demanded its share of government spending. Because resources were inadequate, some way had to be found to manage, and that required major decisions. The most important decision was how to combine strengthening the country's security with reducing military spending.

Military professionals demanded that the Soviet army, air force, and navy be given equipment precisely **symmetrical to** that of the U.S. military. But that would take all the nation's financial resources, leaving nothing in the budget to build housing and provide people with normal lives. Father chose a different path. He tried to make the admirals and generals understand that the United States was much wealthier than we were and that if we competed with the Americans on that basis, we would spend our resources in vain and bring the country to ruin and even then not reach **parity**. The military insisted. Father angrily exclaimed, "You'll leave the country stark naked!"

Father finally decided to make use of his power and authority. He thought that we ourselves could determine the necessary minimum to ensure the country's security and ruthlessly eliminate the rest....

In 1956 only one type of ballistic missile was being built, the R-5M, with a nuclear warhead of seven kilotons. The U.S.S.R. had a total of 426 nuclear warheads. That year the United States had an overall nuclear superiority 10.8 times greater.

To restrain the West from a possible attack on the Soviet Union, Father decided to resort to bluff and intimidation....

It was in those years that he used the famous phrase "We are producing missiles like sausages." When I asked him how he could say that, since the Soviet Union had no more than half a dozen intercontinental missiles, Father only laughed: "We're not planning to start a war, so it doesn't matter how many missiles are deployed.

Symmetrical to: The same as.

Parity: An equal amount.

The main thing is that Americans think we have enough for a powerful strike in response. So they'll be wary of attacking us."

Such statements by Father were in fact received with enthusiasm on the other side of the ocean, since they made it easier for the American military to receive additional funds, and so the missile race was born and gained strength, bringing President John F. Kennedy to the White House. The race, which never existed, or rather in which only America took part, was the United States' internal competition to see who could grab more funds from the budget. Insofar as there was a real race, the United States always led. For example, only beginning in 1967 were large numbers of the UR-100 (SS-11) light ballistic missile deployed in the Soviet Union, five years later than the analogous American Minuteman I. The CIA must have known this, but the myth of Soviet missile superiority was useful, or seemed to be useful, not so much to Father as to the American **military industrial complex.**

President Eisenhower understood this very well. He and Father held meetings at Camp David in September of 1959. As they were taking a walk one day, Eisenhower brought up the subject of relations with the military and asked Father how he coped with his generals. Father reacted cautiously. He was not prepared to discuss such a subject with the American President.

"Then I'll start," said Eisenhower, smiling. "My military leaders come to me several times a year and ask for additional **appropriations** for new types of weapons. When I reply that the budget has been approved and printed and there's no place to find the money, they begin frightening me by saying that the Soviet Union is already developing such 'toys' and I'll be responsible if the United States is defeated in a future war. Naturally I have to give them the money."

Father replied that he was often subjected to such pressure from his own military-industrial complex.

"Maybe we should make a secret agreement between us to curb our military," proposed the President.

"That would be good," responded Father. "But the time has not yet come."

The time for confidential relations between Soviet and American leaders had truly not yet come, but, by 1959, a great deal had changed since 1955. Eisenhower and Father had learned to talk with each other, and the first signs of mutual confidence had ap-

Military industrial complex:
A politically powerful alliance of the military services and of the industry that provides materials to the military.

Appropriations:
Government funds provided for a specific purpose.

peared. A foundation was built for all of Father's future negotiations with Kennedy, Leonid Brezhnev's with a whole series of American Presidents, and Mikhail Gorbachev's with Ronald Reagan. In 1959 there was no longer talk of an inevitable and imminent war. Leaders of the two countries were working out the conditions for peaceful coexistence on our planet.

Another significant fact: Both sides began to feel the need for direct contact. In other words, they started to trust each other and to believe in the possibility and productivity of a dialogue devoted to preventing a nuclear war.

I shall only note here that for the first time in the history of the Cold War a secret personal correspondence between two leaders, and not mutual threats and propaganda escapades, was the main instrument for resolving the Cuban Missile Crisis. This is an extraordinarily important indication that both the president of the United States and the head of the Soviet government understood that though they may have been determined to defend their own principles and values, which were not compatible, it was only through dialogue that they could achieve their common goal of preserving life on earth.

In November 1963 John F. Kennedy died, and a year later, on October 1964, my father was removed from power. The leaders who replaced Father hurried to "correct his mistakes" by giving a new impetus to the arms race and producing tens of thousands of tactical nuclear weapons. By 1989 the Soviet army had seven thousand nuclear cannon. The Cold War was prolonged by twenty years and did not end until the start of the 1990s, with the dissolution of the Soviet Union.

What was the Cold War? Could it have been avoided? Was it a product of the ill will of politicians or was it historically inevitable? Probably the latter. For thousands of years peoples have resolved their conflicts by armed clashes. There was good reason for Karl von Clausewitz to write that war is a continuation of politics by other means. With the invention of nuclear weapons, politicians suddenly realized that war would no longer lead to victory, that both sides would lose. But they didn't know how to behave differently. So they behaved the same way, but without going to war. War without war was called "cold war." A very accurate definition. And at the beginning of this process, at the dawn of the Cold War, when a great deal was still unsettled and all the destructive consequences of the use of nuclear weapons were not apparent, it would have been very easy to yield to temptation and drift into a real war. I consider it a great achievement, a heroic deed, if you will, of the world leaders of those years, primarily American Presidents Dwight D. Eisenhower and John F. Kennedy and my Father, the chairman of the U.S.S.R. Council of Ministers, Nikita Khrushchev, that they showed the wisdom to pass safely over the reefs of a hot war and preserve the life of humankind. Thus the Cold War was a kind of transitional period from a disconnected world that used weapons as its main instrument for resolving world conflicts to some kind of different state of being—to a new world order, if you like.

What happened next ...

Sergei Khrushchev's book came out amidst the end of the Cold War. The Soviet Union broke apart in 1991 under Mikhail Gorbachev (1931–). In his book, Sergei Khrushchev looked to the future but recalled the recent past and predicted "humankind" would continue to depend "on the wisdom of the political leaders in power."

Sergei Khrushchev's message: "The Cold War has now passed into history. But the transition is far from complete. We stand at the beginning of a new phase of the transitional period and again face a real danger of new (so far limited, nonnuclear) armed conflicts. And God forbid that my Father's prophecy—that as soon as a nonnuclear war seriously affects the interests of the world's great powers, it will inevitably grow into a nuclear conflict—should come to pass. Again, just as forty years ago, our fate, the fate of the world and of humankind, depends on the wisdom of the political leaders in power."

Did you know ...

- Nikita Khrushchev was just as interested in agriculture, especially raising corn, as he was in armaments. This was due to his background in farming.

- Khrushchev decided to deal with America's vast military might by figuring out the "necessary minimums" of military armaments and equipment to ensure the Soviets' security, then to "bluff and intimidate" the Western powers into believing the Soviets had vastly more military capability than it really did.

- Nikita Khrushchev never had any intention of starting a nuclear war with the United States.

Consider the following ...

- Search out and list what surprised you about the Soviet Union. Read this excerpt to a grandparent and see what surprises them.

- Analyze and explain this quote from the excerpt: "War is a continuation of politics by other means. With the invention of nuclear weapons, politicians suddenly realized that war would no longer lead to victory, that both sides would lose. But they didn't know how to behave differently. So they behaved the same way, but without going to war. War without war was called 'cold war.' A very accurate definition."

- What were the important outcomes, including misunderstandings, of the 1955 Geneva, Four-Power Summit Conference?

- What were the two main domestic concerns of Nikita Khrushchev?

- Sergei Khrushchev offered a brief suggestion as to why the Cold War did not end after the Cuban Missile Crisis. What did he suggest?

For More Information

Books

Khrushchev, Nikita S. *Khrushchev Remembers*. Boston: Little, Brown, 1970.

Khrushchev, Nikita S. *Khrushchev Remembers: The Glasnost Tapes*. Boston: Little, Brown, 1990.

Khrushchev, Nikita S. *Khrushchev Remembers: The Last Testament*. Boston: Little, Brown, 1974.

Khrushchev, Sergei. *Nikita Khrushchev and the Creation of a Superpower*. University Park: Pennsylvania State University Press, 2000.

Nikita Khrushchev

Excerpt from "Peace and Progress Must Triumph in Our Time"
Originally published in *Soviet Booklets*

In September 1959, Nikita Khrushchev (1894–1971), accompanied by his wife, Nina Petrovina Khrushchev (1900–1984), visited the United States for the first time at the invitation of U.S. president Dwight D. Eisenhower (1890–1969; served 1953–61). On his return home, he reported on his trip to the people of Moscow at the packed Sports Palace of Lenin Stadium. His address, delivered on September 28, 1959, cleverly intertwined a call for peaceful coexistence of the world's nations, a travelogue-like accounting of each U.S. city he visited, and a call for disarmament discussions between the superpowers.

At each stop, Khrushchev perceptively related to his Moscovites how he was received. The trip began in Washington, D.C., where President Eisenhower greeted him with a welcome suitable for the leader of "our great country." Khrushchev was annoyed, however, at Vice President Richard M. Nixon (1913–1994), who had just delivered a speech before the Association of Dentists that indicated that he did not want the Cold War (1945–91) to end. Khrushchev moved onward to New York City, where he addressed the United Nations. Khrushchev reported that he was tightly guarded as he proceeded to Los An-

"A great deal would perish in [a nuclear] war. It would be too late to discuss what peaceful co-existence means when such frightful means of destruction as atom and hydrogen bombs, and ballistic rockets which are practically impossible to intercept and are capable of delivering nuclear warheads to any part of the globe, go into action. To disregard this is to shut one's eyes and ears and bury one's head like the ostrich does when in danger."

Soviet premier Nikita Khrushchev (right) walks with U.S. vice president Richard Nixon in Moscow, 1959. *Reproduced by permission of the Corbis Corporation.*

geles, California. Because of security concerns, he was not allowed to visit Disneyland, which he had very much wanted to do. Also he kept hearing speeches quoting him as saying the Soviets would "bury the capitalists." He said the quote was taken out of context, and to him it seemed that U.S. speech makers were "using the communist bogey to frighten people [Americans] who have only a vague notion of what communism is." Khrushchev complained of the too-tight security and the mean-spirited speeches while in Los Angeles.

The next morning, Khrushchev traveled to the "big and beautiful city" of San Francisco, and "everything had indeed changed." He was "unhandcuffed" (he could go out among crowds of people) and heard no more divisive speeches. He was warmly greeted there and spoke to the Longshoremen's Union. Soon he was off to Iowa, where he met his friend, farmer and businessman Roswell Garst (1898–1977), toured cornfields, and met with other farmers. It was then on to the industrial city of Pittsburgh, Pennsylvania, where he chatted not only with workers but also with businessmen and intellectuals. Lastly, he returned to Washington, D.C., for his meetings with Eisenhower.

The following excerpt is taken from the portions of the speech that dealt with the very serious points of peaceful coexistence and disarmament. Khrushchev related that in the twentieth century, humans should no longer live like beasts ready to destroy each other. Instead, he believed that nations must meet to resolve problems and begin to live peacefully side by side in "peaceful co-existence." He insisted that those who did not earnestly seek a peaceful coexistence were only intensifying the Cold War. Khrushchev next told the Soviet audience that indeed there were those in the United States who were against relieving Cold War tensions, and then he proceeded to thoroughly scold them. Khrushchev turned to the end of his trip—three days at Camp David, the U.S. presidential retreat 70 miles (113 kilometers) from Washington. It was during this time that Khrushchev and Eisenhower began to actually develop a dialogue of mutual confidence.

Things to remember while reading "Peace and Progress Must Triumph in Our Time":

- Although he felt warmly greeted by many people, Khrushchev also related that there were hostile and grim American faces in the crowd. The Cold War was, after all, still in a highly tense period.

- Despite tensions, Khrushchev was eager to relate that he wanted to "thaw the ice and normalize international relations."

- Relating his travels gave his curious audience a picture of America on a human level. It gave a human face to the need for peaceful coexistence.

Excerpt from "Peace and Progress Must Triumph in Our Time"

On his Visit to the United States to a meeting of Moscow People at the Sports Palace of the Lenin Stadium September 28, 1959.

The most farsighted statesmen of a number of countries have come to realize the need to make some kind of efforts to end the cold war, to do away with the tension which has developed in international relations, to clear the atmosphere and create more or less normal relations among states. Then the nations would be able to live and look to the future without fear.

*The 20th century is a century of the greatest flourishing of human thought and genius.... Must we, in this period of the flourishing of human genius, which is penetrating the secrets of nature and harnessing its mighty forces, put up with **primitive relations** being maintained like those that existed between people when man was still a beast?...*

Our times can and should become a time of the fulfillment of great ideals, a time of peace and progress.

The Soviet government has long been aware of this. Precisely for this reason we have repeatedly proposed to the great powers that a meeting between heads of government be arranged so as to exchange views on urgent international problems. When we made these proposals we were expressing our belief in man's reason. We believed that, given a wise approach, the proponents of various political views, countries with differing social systems, would be able to find a common language so as to resolve correctly and in the interests of consolidating peace the present-day problems that cause concern to all mankind.

*In our age of great technical progress, in conditions when there are states with different social systems, international problems cannot be resolved successfully in any other way than on principles of **peaceful co-existence**. There is no other way.*

*Those people who say they do not understand what peaceful co-existence is and are fearful of it, contribute, willingly or unwillingly, to the further intensification of the cold war, which will certainly extend if we do not interfere and stop it. It will reach a **pitch** where a spark might at any moment set off a world **conflagration**.*

Primitive relations: Continuing hostilities.

Peaceful co-existence: Maintaining international relations without hostilities.

Pitch: Tense level.

Conflagration: A large, destructive fire; here, meaning resulting from nuclear war.

Corn, Khrushchev, and Roswell Garst

Nikita Khrushchev saw Soviet production of corn as a means of raising the level of food production toward levels in America. Corn would supply feed for livestock and thereby raise meat production as well.

In 1955, about the same time as the end of the Geneva Conference, the KGB, the Soviet intelligence agency, placed a newspaper editorial from an Iowa paper, the *Des Moines Register,* on Khrushchev's desk. The article called on the superpowers to compete on the farm fields, a "corn race" instead of an "arms race." Immediately, Khrushchev sent the best Soviet agricultural scientists to Iowa to see the latest advances in corn production. Then the Soviet delegation invited American farmers to the Soviet Union. The Cold War was at its height, and only one Iowa farmer dared to take up the offer. He was Roswell Garst. Garst would subsequently make many visits to the Soviet Union, as he and

Khrushchev got along famously. Garst traveled to southern Russian cornfields to advise and supervise planting techniques. Khrushchev remarked, "This American capitalist cares more about our harvests than Soviet collective farmers do."

In his book *Nikita Khrushchev and the Creation of a Superpower,* Sergei Khrushchev, Nikita's son, related that on a trip to Iowa in the 1990s, the governor of Iowa quipped that when he had gone to the Soviet Union, the Russians he encountered exclaimed, "Iowa! The most famous American state! Nikita Khrushchev brought corn from there to the Soviet Union." It seemed the Iowa governor never ran into anyone in a foreign country that had ever even heard of Iowa. Sergei also related he believed the friendship between Garst and his father was no less fruitful than many months of negotiations of veteran diplomats in easing tensions between the two countries.

A great deal would perish in such a war. It would be too late to discuss what peaceful co-existence means when such frightful means of destruction as atom and hydrogen bombs, and ballistic rockets which are practically impossible to intercept and are capable of delivering nuclear warheads to any part of the globe, go into action. To disregard this is to shut one's eyes and ears and bury one's head like the ostrich does when in danger.

But if we, the people, imitate this ostrich and hide our heads in the sand, then, I ask you: What is the use of having this head if it is unable to avert the threat to its very life?

No, we must display human reason and confidence in this reason, confidence in the possibility of reaching agreement with states-

men of different countries, and mobilize the people by joint efforts to avert the war danger. It is necessary to have the will-power and courage to go against those who persist in continuing the cold war. It is necessary to bar the road to it, to thaw the ice and normalize international relations....

We also met with hostile and grim American faces....

What am I saying this for? Is it because I want to cool the relations between the Soviet Union and the United States? No, I am speaking about this because you ought to know the truth and so that you may see, not only the side that is pleasant to us, but also the other, backstage, side which should not be concealed. There are forces in America which are acting against us, against the easing of tension and for the continuation of the cold war.

*To disregard that would mean showing weakness in the struggle against those evil forces, against those evil spirits. No, they must be exposed; they must be shown to the world and publicly whipped; they must be subjected to the torments of **Hades.** Let those who want to continue the cold war fume. No ordinary people anywhere in the world, no sensible person will support them....*

*I jokingly said to Mr. [U.N. ambassador John Cabot] Lodge that if I, a representative of the working class, of the Communist Party of the Soviet Union, and he, a representative of the capitalist world, were by chance cast away on a desert island we would probably find a common language and ensure peaceful co-existence there. Why, then, cannot the states with differing social systems ensure co-existence? Our states are also, so to speak, on an island— after all, with the present-day means of communication, which have brought the continents so close together, our planet really resembles a small island, and we should realize this. Having understood the need for co-existence, we should pursue a peaceful policy, live in friendship, not **brandish** weapons but destroy them.*

Comrades, on September 25 we again met the United States President at the White House and left together with him by helicopter for his country residence, which is called Camp David. We stayed there on September 25, 26 and 27....

It should be taken into account, however, that with the President we could not, of course, clear out at one go all the cold war rubble that has piled up during many years. It will take time to clear out this rubbish, and not only clear it out but destroy it. Things dividing us are still too fresh in the memory. Sometimes it is

Hades: An underworld inhabited by desperate souls in Greek mythology.

Brandish: Display threateningly.

difficult for certain statesmen to give up the old positions, the old views and formulas.

But I will tell you with all frankness, dear comrades, that I got the impression from the talks and discussions on concrete questions with the United States President that he sincerely wishes to end the state of cold war, to create normal relations between our two countries, to promote the improvement of relations among all states. Peace is indivisible now and it cannot be ensured by the efforts of two or three countries alone. So we must strive for peace in such a way that all the nations, all the countries are drawn into this struggle.

We exchanged views with the United States President on questions of disarmament. He said that the United States government was studying our proposal and that the United States, just as we did, wanted complete disarmament under proper control [some sort of inspection program to ensure compliance]....

I want to tell you, dear comrades, that I do not doubt the President's readiness to exert his will and efforts to reach agreement between our two countries, to create friendly relations between our two nations and to solve urgent problems in the interests of strengthening peace.

At the same time I got the impression that there are forces in America which are not working in the same direction as the President. Those forces are in favor of continuing the cold war and in favor of the arms race. I would not be in a hurry to say whether those forces are large or small, influential or not influential, whether the forces supporting the President—and he is backed by the absolute majority of the American people—can win....

For our part we shall do everything we can to turn the barometer's hand away from "stormy," and even from "changeable," towards "fine"....

In our actions we rely on reason, on truth, on the support of all the people. Moreover, we rely on our great potential.

And let it be known to those who want to continue the cold war so as to turn it sooner or later into a shooting war, that in our times only a madman can start a war, and he himself will perish in its flames....

Dear Comrades Muscovites, we are boundlessly happy to return home, to see the faces of the Soviet people which are so dear to our hearts.

Long live the great Soviet people, who are successfully building communism under the leadership of the glorious Leninist party!

Long live Soviet-American friendship!

Long live friendship among all the peoples of the world!

What happened next ...

When Khrushchev left Camp David, the two super-power leaders' relationship seemed to be on a much stronger footing. The improved relations were referred to as the Spirit of Camp David. Although no agreements were concluded, Khrushchev and Eisenhower conferred on such topics as the high cost of developing and producing military "toys" to be sure they are ready for a future war. They commiserated on the power of the military leaders demanding more and more funds for more and more weapons. According to Sergei Khrushchev (see previous excerpt in this chapter), the first signs of mutual confidence appeared. They agreed to meet again in Europe in May 1960.

The improving relations chilled, however, just before the next scheduled meeting. On May 1, an American U-2 spy plane was shot down by a Soviet antiaircraft missile. The pilot was captured alive. Eisenhower refused to apologize, and Khrushchev refused to participate in the summit in protest. It also resulted in cancellation of the U.S. president's visit to the Soviet Union that had been widely heralded. The two would not meet again. Nevertheless, a foundation for future negotiations now existed.

Did you know ...

- Khrushchev's trip to the United States was followed intently by the Soviet public. The general feeling was pride that he was reaching out to the Americans.

- Khrushchev saw the trip as a starting point for ending the Cold War.

- Just before his arrival, a significant portion of the U.S. press had published statements, editorials, and articles that had a very anti-Khrushchev tone. Khrushchev considered this a "propaganda campaign against my visit."

Consider the following ...

- Relate Khrushchev's following symbolism of an ostrich to the Cold War: "But if we, the people, imitate this ostrich and hide our heads in the sand, then, I ask you: What is the use of having this head if it is unable to avert the threat to its very life?"

- What did Khrushchev and Eisenhower learn during their Camp David meeting?

- According to Sergei Khrushchev, with what does the ultimate fate of humankind "rest"?

For More Information

Books

Crankshaw, Edward. *Khrushchev: A Career.* New York: Viking, 1966.

Dockrill, Michael. *The Cold War, 1945–1963.* London: Macmillan, 1988.

Frankland, Mark. *Khrushchev.* New York: Stein and Day, 1979.

Khrushchev, Sergei. *Nikita Khrushchev: Creation of a Superpower.* University Park: Pennsylvania State University Press, 2000.

Linden, Carl A. *Khrushchev and the Soviet Leadership.* Baltimore: Johns Hopkins University Press, 1990.

Soviet Booklets. London: March Publicity Press, Ltd.

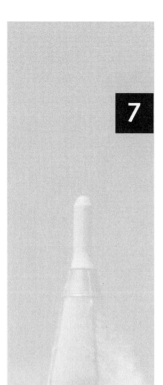

7 Endangered Berlin

By 1947, the Cold War (1945–91) clearly was the most threatening issue dominating international affairs. The Cold War was not fought on battlefields with large armies. Instead, it evolved into a battle of ideologies, or social and political ideas, between the communist Soviet Union and the democratic, capitalistic Western nations led by the United States. Communism is a system of government in which the nation's leaders are selected by a single political party that controls almost all aspects of society. Private ownership of property is eliminated and government directs all economic production. The goods produced and accumulated wealth are, in theory, shared relatively equally by all. At the epicenter of the Cold War were Germany and its capital city, Berlin.

World War II (1939–45) had come to an end in Europe on May 7, 1945, when Germany surrendered to the Allies in Reims, France. The Big Four allies were the United States, Great Britain, France, and the Soviet Union. Immediately, Germany was divided into four zones. Each zone was occupied by troops from one of the Big Four powers. The American, British, and French zones, under democratic influence, were soon collectively known as West Germany. The Soviet zone, under communist influence, was known as East Germany.

Berlin was located 110 miles (177 kilometers) deep within the Soviet zone. Nevertheless, Berlin was also divided into four sectors. The U.S., British, and French sectors became known as West Berlin. The Soviet sector was known as East Berlin. The three Western powers expected the Soviets to grant free access to West Berlin through road, rail, water, and air routes from West Germany across and over East Germany into West Berlin.

An actual peace treaty between the four powers concerning the future of Germany did not materialize despite extensive negotiations. The biggest dispute was reunification of Germany. Because of the damage Germany did to the Soviet Union in World War II, the Soviets were bitterly opposed to a reunified Germany, which they assumed would again pose a threat to the Soviet Union. The United States and Britain both agreed that a reunited, rebuilt Germany would hopefully stand in the way of further westward spread of communism. France detested the idea of a strong reunited Germany but nevertheless sided with the United States and Britain.

Relations between the Western powers and the Soviets continued to worsen, and no settlement could be reached. In response, the Soviets began to harass those using transportation routes into West Berlin. Democratic West Berlin, deep in Soviet-controlled East Germany, was a very sore thorn in the Soviets' side. The harassment soon escalated into a full blockade in June 1948 of all land and water routes into West Berlin, effectively blocking it from receiving supplies from West Germany. However, the United States, Britain, and to a lesser extent France organized an airlift of supplies into the stranded portion of the city. The airlift was an amazing success: By the spring of 1949, 8,000 tons (about 7,250 metric tons) of vital supplies arrived each day at West Berlin airports. On May 12, 1949, the Soviets halted the blockade and reopened highway, train, and water routes through East Germany into Berlin. Relations between the Western powers and the Soviets, however, remained frigid.

Through the 1950s, West Germany's economy regrouped and flourished. East Germany made progress but lagged far behind the West. More and more East Germans

Children cheer as a U.S. cargo plane with supplies for West Berlin flies overhead during the Soviet blockade of 1948–49.
Reproduced by permission of the Corbis Corporation.

finished their education in East Germany but then left for jobs in the free and capitalist West Germany. It is estimated that roughly three million East Germans left for the West during the 1950s. Those leaving were skilled industrial craftsmen, farmers, scientists, engineers, doctors, lawyers, and teachers. This was a brain and labor drain that struggling East Germany could not afford.

The refugees' escape route was through Berlin. Soon after taking power, East German leader Walter Ulbricht (1893–1973) had closed the entire 900-mile (1,448-kilometer) border between East and West Germany, making travel between the two impossible. But the four sectors in Berlin remained wide open, with many East Berliners making the daily commute to West Berlin for work and shopping. East Germans wishing to leave for the West simply made their way to East Berlin. Some, over a few weeks or months, discreetly took a few belongings at a time into West Berlin.

When ready, East Germans then simply registered at a refugee assembly camp in the Western sector. Most were sent on into West Germany, where jobs were plentiful.

The migration from east to west was devastating to the East German economy. Ulbricht complained loud and long to the Soviets and demanded that Soviet leader Nikita Khrushchev (1894–1971) do something to stop the population loss. Ulbricht demanded the Soviet army be used to invade West Berlin, rid it of Western influence, and unite Berlin under his control. This would close the last route out and stop the population drain. However, Khrushchev knew the Western powers had drawn a "line in the sand" at Berlin as evidenced by the Berlin airlift of 1948 and 1949. Nevertheless, he reinitiated a crisis state in Berlin in November 1958 by demanding that the United States proceed with work on a German peace treaty. If they did not, Khrushchev would deal directly with East Germany and turn over to the East Germans control over all transportation routes into West Berlin. The United States rejected Khrushchev's demands.

The first excerpt is the "Radio and Television Report to the American People on the Berlin Crisis, July 25, 1961," from U.S. president John F. Kennedy (1917–1963; served 1961–63). Kennedy had just returned from his first and only meeting with Khrushchev and reported on the grave Berlin situation. The second excerpt, "Khrushchev's Secret Speech on the Berlin Crisis, August 1961," is the Soviet leader's reaction to Kennedy's speech on July 25 (the first excerpt). Khrushchev spoke to a small group of top leaders of the Communist Party in the Soviet Union and to leaders of the Socialist (Communist) parties in Eastern European countries, including Walter Ulbricht of East Germany.

By August 13, 1961, the infamous Berlin Wall would be in place dividing East Berlin from West Berlin. The wall remained until November 1989. In June 1963, President Kennedy traveled to a divided Berlin and delivered his stirring speech, commonly known as the "I am a Berliner" speech. The third excerpt is from this speech. He addressed this speech to thousands of West Berliners gathered at Rudolph Wild Platz, West Berlin, on June 26, 1963.

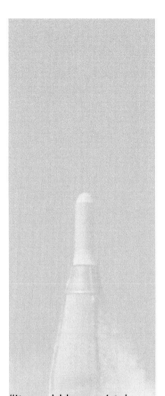

John F. Kennedy

Excerpt from "Radio and Television Report to the American People on the Berlin Crisis, July 25, 1961"

Published in *Public Papers of the Presidents of the United States: John F. Kennedy, 1961*

"It would be a mistake for others to look upon Berlin, because of its location, as a tempting target. The United States is there; the United Kingdom and France are there; the pledge of NATO is there—and the people of Berlin are there. It is as secure, in that sense, as the rest of us—for we cannot separate its safety from our own."

On November 27, 1958, Soviet premier Nikita Khrushchev (1894–1971), irritated that a German peace treaty had yet to be agreed on, threw Berlin into another crisis when he sent a letter to Western powers. The letter gave them six months to make substantial progress on a German peace treaty. If the Western powers did not accomplish this, Khrushchev would make a separate treaty with East Germany on May 27, 1959. In this treaty, all transportation routes into West Berlin would be turned over to East German control. The East Germans would then presumably do all they could to force out the Western powers and make West Berlin a part of East Germany. Khrushchev also demanded withdrawal of Western troops from Berlin.

The Soviets and East German leader Walter Ulbricht (1893–1973) were pleased with Khrushchev's tough stand. The peace treaty they sought would permanently divide Germany and recognize both East and West Germany as independent nations. East Germany would provide the communist buffer between the West and the Soviet Union. The United States instead wanted Germany reunited into one country.

U.S. president Dwight D. Eisenhower (1890–1969; served 1953–61) and the Western allies rejected Khrushchev's demands and collectively held their breath. The Western allies would not pull out of Berlin, nor could they come to terms on a peace treaty to the liking of the Soviets. They believed Khrushchev would not actually go to war—which could risk turning into a nuclear war—over Berlin. They guessed right. Khrushchev backed down from his six-month ultimatum. May 27, 1959, passed without incident.

John F. Kennedy (1919–1963; served 1961–63) was elected U.S. president in November 1960 and took office on January 20, 1961. During the previous year-and-a-half, tough negotiations over Berlin had continued. The increasingly bold Ulbricht demanded economic assistance from the Soviets as thousands of East German workers and professionals continued to leave for West Germany. His excessive demands strained the Soviet Union's economy. He also relentlessly implored Khrushchev to halt the population drain by taking over West Berlin. In this atmosphere, the new U.S. president met with Khrushchev in June 1961 in Vienna, Austria.

In Vienna, both Khrushchev and Kennedy held a tight line—neither budged on their stands on Germany and Berlin. The young Kennedy was clearly taken aback by Khrushchev's behavior. The Soviet leader talked too loudly, spoke rudely, and generally created quite an uproar. Kennedy had been warned but never expected the level of intimidation coming from Khrushchev. Unwavering but shaken, Kennedy returned to the United States. He addressed the American people over radio and television on July 25, 1961, concerning his talks about Berlin with Khrushchev.

Things to remember while reading the excerpt from "Radio and Television Report to the American People on the Berlin Crisis, July 25, 1961":

- West Berlin had become a symbol or "outpost" of the free world within a communist-dominated area. Western powers had drawn the line to stop the spread of communism at Berlin in 1948 with the Berlin airlift. They would not leave West Berlin.

- Both the United States and the Soviet Union possessed stockpiles of nuclear weapons. Should a dispute ever push the powers to war, the Soviets could destroy West Germany, England, and France in a matter of minutes. Soviet missiles could reach the United States just as U.S. missiles were reaching the Soviet Union.

- Khrushchev was under intense pressure from Soviet leaders at home and East German leader Ulbricht to rid Berlin of Westerners and to halt the exodus of East Germans through Berlin to the West.

Excerpt from "Radio and Television Report to the American People on the Berlin Crisis, July 25, 1961"

Good evening:

U.S. president John F. Kennedy wipes his brow before speaking to the nation about the Berlin Crisis on July 25, 1961. *Reproduced by permission of the Corbis Corporation.*

*Seven weeks ago tonight I returned from Europe to report on my meeting with Premier [Nikita] Khrushchev and the others. His grim warnings about the future of the world ... [and] Berlin, his subsequent speeches and threats which he and his agents have launched, and the increase in the Soviet military budget that he has announced, have all prompted a series of decisions by the Administration and a series of consultations with the members of the **NATO** organization....*

The immediate threat to free men is in West Berlin. But that isolated outpost is not an isolated problem. The threat is worldwide. Our effort must be equally wide and strong.... We face a challenge in Berlin, but there is also a challenge in southeast Asia, where the borders are less guarded, the enemy harder to find, and the dangers of communism less apparent to those who have so little. We face a challenge ... indeed wherever else the freedom of human beings is at stake.

*Let me remind you that the fortunes of war and diplomacy left the free people of West Berlin, in 1945, 110 miles behind the **Iron Curtain.**...*

NATO: North Atlantic Treaty Organization, a peacetime alliance of the United States and eleven other nations.

Iron Curtain: Symbolic boundary between the bloc of Soviet-dominated communist countries in Eastern Europe and democratic Western Europe.

Thus, our presence in West Berlin, and our access thereto, cannot be ended by any act of the Soviet government. The NATO **shield** was long ago extended to cover West Berlin—and we have given our word that an attack upon that city will be regarded as an attack upon us all.

For West Berlin—lying exposed 110 miles inside East Germany, surrounded by Soviet troops and close to Soviet supply lines, has many roles. It is more than a showcase of liberty, a symbol, an island of freedom in a Communist sea. It is even more than a link with the Free World, a beacon of hope behind the Iron Curtain, an escape hatch for refugees.

West Berlin is all of that. But above all it has now become—as never before—the great testing place where our solemn commitments stretching back over the years since 1945, and Soviet ambitions now meet in basic confrontation.

It would be a mistake for others to look upon Berlin, because of its location, as a tempting target. The United States is there; the United Kingdom and France are there; the pledge of NATO is there—and the people of Berlin are there. It is as secure, in that sense, as the rest of us—for we cannot separate its safety from our own....

We do not want to fight—but we have fought before....

So long as the Communists insist that they are preparing to end by themselves **unilaterally** our rights in West Berlin and our commitments to its people, we must be prepared to defend those rights and those commitments....

The new preparations that we shall make to defend the peace are part of the long-term build-up in our strength which has been underway since January....

We have another sober responsibility. To recognize the possibilities of nuclear war in the missile age, without our citizens knowing what they should do and where they should go if bombs begin to fall, would be a failure of responsibility. In May, I pledged a new start on Civil Defense. Last week, I assigned, on the recommendation of the Civil Defense Director [Frank Ellis], basic responsibility for this program to the Secretary of Defense [Robert S. McNamara], to make certain it is administered and coordinated ... at the highest civilian level. Tomorrow, I am requesting of the Congress new funds for the following immediate objectives: to identify and mark space in existing structures—public and private—that could be used for

Shield: Military protection.

Unilaterally: Acting on their own.

fall-out shelters in case of attack; to stock those shelters with food, water, first-aid kits and other minimum essentials for survival; to increase their capacity; to improve our air-raid warning and fall-out detection systems, including a new household warning system which is now under development; and to take other measures that will be effective at an early date to save millions of lives if needed.

In the event of an attack, the lives of those families which are not hit in a nuclear blast and fire can still be saved—if they can be warned to take shelter and if that shelter is available. We owe that kind of insurance to our families—and to our country. In contrast to our friends in Europe, the need for this kind of protection is new to our shores. But the time to start is now. In the coming months, I hope to let every citizen know what steps he can take without delay to protect his family in case of attack....

We recognize the Soviet Union's historical concern about their security in Central and Eastern Europe, after a series of ravaging invasions, and we believe arrangements can be worked out which will help to meet those concerns, and make it possible for both security and freedom to exist in this troubled area....

The world is not deceived by the Communist attempt to label Berlin as a hot-bed of war. There is peace in Berlin today. The source of world trouble and tension is Moscow, not Berlin. And if war begins, it will have begun in Moscow and not Berlin....

And the challenge is not to us alone. It is a challenge to every nation which asserts its **sovereignty** under a system of liberty. It is a challenge to all those who want a world of free choice. It is a special challenge to the **Atlantic Community**—the heartland of human freedom....

The solemn voice each of us gave to West Berlin in time of peace will not be broken in time of danger. If we do not meet our commitments to Berlin, where will we later stand? If we are not true to our word there, all that we have achieved in collective security, which relies on these words, will mean nothing. And if there is one path above all others to war, it is the path of weakness and disunity.

Today, the endangered frontier of freedom runs through divided Berlin. We want it to remain a frontier of peace. This is the hope of every citizen of the Atlantic Community; every citizen of Eastern Europe; and, I am confident, every citizen of the Soviet Union. For I cannot believe that the Russian people—who bravely suffered enormous losses in the Second World War—would now wish to see the

Sovereignty: The independence of a political state.

Atlantic Community: A reference to NATO member nations.

peace upset once more in Germany. The Soviet government alone can convert Berlin's frontier of peace into a pretext for war....

I would like to close with a personal word....

Now, in the thermonuclear age, any mis-judgment on either side about the intentions of the other could rain more devastation in several hours than has been wrought in all the wars of human history....

I know that sometimes we get impatient, we wish for some immediate action that would end our perils. But I must tell you that there is no quick and easy solution. The Communists control over a billion people, and they recognize that if we should falter, their success would be imminent.

Thank you and good night.

We must look to long days ahead, which if we are courageous and persevering can bring us what we all desire.

What happened next ...

Khrushchev, who was vacationing at a Black Sea resort called Pitsunda, was outraged at Kennedy's speech. He called Kennedy's disarmament advisor, John Jay McCloy (1895–1989), who was in Moscow for talks, to come immediately to Pitsunda. Khrushchev growled that Kennedy's speech was practically a declaration of war. He threateningly added that if war was what Kennedy wanted, it is what he would get, even though it would most likely be a nuclear war. On August 4, 1961, Khrushchev met with communist leaders and expressed his opinions on Kennedy's words (see next excerpt).

Did you know ...

- By the mid- to late 1950s, Khrushchev had decided the Soviet Union could not keep pace with the U.S. military buildup. Instead, he focused on key military areas for strengthening. He then used an approach called "bluster and intimidation" to frighten the United States into thinking the Soviets were militarily much more powerful than they were. This approach explained much of his behavior during his meeting with the young American president. The U.S. officials did not know this was a calculated approach. Instead, they thought he was merely showing his determination and assertive personality to meet the United States head on in war.

- Khrushchev had no intention of starting a war over Berlin. In fact, Ulbricht made him very nervous with his aggressive suggestions.

- Soon after Kennedy's speech, which emphasized civil defense, yellow and black nuclear shelter signs appeared in cities throughout the United States. Individual U.S. citizens with the desire and monetary means built bomb shelters in their backyards in preparation for nuclear war.

- The stream of refugees from East Germany to the West continued until construction of the Berlin Wall began on August 13, 1961.

Consider the following ...

- What did President Kennedy say West Berlin was a symbol of? Why did he say this?

- Since West Berlin geographically seemed to be easy prey for a communist takeover, why do you think this did not happen?

- At your local public library, check your town's old newspapers for July 26 through August 1961 for local reaction to Kennedy's speech and civil defense plans.

For More Information

Books

Gelb, Norman. *The Berlin Wall: Kennedy, Khrushchev and a Showdown in the Heart of Europe.* New York: Times Books, 1986.

Grant, R. G. *The Berlin Wall.* Austin, TX: Raintree Steck-Vaughn, 1999.

Parrish, Thomas. *Berlin in the Balance, 1945–1949: The Blockade, the Airlift, the First Major Battle of the Cold War.* Reading, MA: Perseus Publishing, 1998.

Paterson, Thomas G., ed. *Kennedy's Quest For Victory: American Foreign Policy, 1961–1963*. New York: Random House, 1995.

Public Papers of the Presidents of the United States: John F. Kennedy, 1961. Washington, DC: U.S. Government Printing Office, 1961.

Web Site

John Fitzgerald Kennedy Library. http://www.cs.umb.edu/jfklibrary (accessed on September 17, 2003).

Nikita Khrushchev

*Excerpt from "Khrushchev's Secret Speech
on the Berlin Crisis, August 1961"*

Excerpted from *Cold War International
History Project Virtual Archive* **(Web site)**

> "If [Kennedy] starts a war
> then he would probably
> become the last
> president of the United
> States of America."

In this excerpt from "Khrushchev's Secret Speech on the Berlin Crisis, August 1961," Soviet premier Nikita Khrushchev (1894–1971) spoke to his Communist Party leaders. These leaders included Soviet foreign minister Andrei Gromyko (1909–1989); the leaders of Bulgaria, Hungary, Poland, Czechoslovakia, and Rumania; and most importantly, Walter Ulbricht (1893–1973) of East Germany. He was responding to the radio and television address of U.S. president John F. Kennedy (1917–1963; served 1961–63) on July 25, 1961. Kennedy was speaking to American citizens about Berlin and Khrushchev. Much of Khrushchev's speech revolved around his conversation with U.S. envoy John J. McCloy (1895–1989), a disarmament expert who happened to be in Moscow at the time of Kennedy's speech. First, Khrushchev stressed that the Soviets must continue to push for a German peace treaty that would permanently separate East and West Germany, giving independent country status to both. (The United States would agree only to a reunited Germany.)

The excerpt begins with Khrushchev considering whether or not the United States will go to war over German

Soviet leader Nikita Khrushchev pounds his fist on the podium while giving a speech. *Reproduced by permission of AP/Wide World Photos.*

reunification and over West Berlin, where the Western powers maintained a military presence. Khrushchev spoke of the possibility of nuclear war and his belief that pursuing a German peace treaty was worth the risk of war. He also gave his impression of the young president. He described Kennedy as a "rather unknown quantity ... a light-weight," hardly capable of influencing the U.S. government.

Khrushchev vowed to meet the Western powers on a strong and equal basis if war came. He also defended Soviet involvement in East Germany as a vital buffer between the Soviet Union and the West.

Things to remember while reading the excerpt from "Khrushchev's Secret Speech on the Berlin Crisis, August 1961":

- It was imperative that Khrushchev maintain a very hard line in front of his fellow communist leaders.

- Khrushchev believed the young Kennedy did not measure up to past U.S. statesmen and was confident that he could frighten and overwhelm the new president.

- The original translated version of Khrushchev's speech that follows includes text in brackets generally meant to clarify certain passages; in some instances, the original Russian word or phrase is included as well.

Excerpt from "Khrushchev's Secret Speech on the Berlin Crisis, August 1961"

*[There was always an understanding ... that the West] would **intimidate** us, call out all spirits against us to test our courage, our **acumen** and our will.... As for me and my colleagues in the state and party leadership, we think that the **adversary** [the United States] proved to be less staunch [zhestokii] than we had estimated.... We expected there would be more blustering and ... so far the worst spurt of intimidation was in the Kennedy speech [on 25 July 1961].... Kennedy spoke [to frighten us] and then got scared himself [referring to Kennedy strengthening U.S. civil defense]....*

Immediately after Kennedy delivered his speech I spoke with [U.S. envoy John J. McCloy]. We had a long conversation, talking about disarmament instead of talking, as we needed to, about Germany and conclusion of a peace treaty on West Berlin. So I suggested: come to my place [Black Sea resort in Pitsunda] tomorrow and we will continue our conversation....

*I said [to McCloy]: "I don't understand what sort of disarmament we can talk about, when Kennedy in his speech declared war on us and set down his conditions. What can I say? Please tell your president that we accept his ultimatum and his terms and will respond **in kind**...."*

He then said ... [that] Kennedy did not mean it, he meant to negotiate. I responded: "Mr. McCloy, but you said you did not read Kennedy's speech?" He faltered [zamialsia], for clearly he knew about the content of the speech....

"You want to frighten us," I went on [to McCloy]. "You convinced yourself, that Khrushchev will never go to war ... so you

Intimidate: Frighten.

Acumen: Keen insight.

Adversary: Opponent.

In kind: In the same way.

scare us [expecting] us to retreat. True, we will not declare war, but we will not withdraw either, if you push it on us. We will respond to your war in kind...."

I told him to let Kennedy know ... that if he starts a war then he would probably become the last president of the United States of America....

[Khrushchev said he had met Italian Prime Minister Amintore Fanfani, who came to Moscow **ostensibly** at his own initiative, but in fact at Kennedy's prodding.]

[Khrushchev reports that he told Fanfani:] We have means [to retaliate]. Kennedy himself acknowledged, that there is equality of forces, i.e. the Soviet Union has as many hydrogen and atomic weapons as they have. I agree with that, [although] we did not crunch numbers. [But, if you recognize that] let us speak about equal opportunities. Instead they [Western leaders] behave as if they were a father dealing with a toddler: if it doesn't come their way [the Soviets do not agree on a peace treaty with a united Germany], they threaten to pull our ears.... We already passed that age, we wear long trousers, not short ones....

I told Fanfani yesterday: "I don't believe, though, there will be war. What am I counting on? I believe in your [Western leaders'] common sense. Do you know who will argue most against war? [West German chancellor Konrad] Adenauer. [Because, if the war starts] there will not be a single stone left in place in Germany...."

[British Prime Minister Harold Macmillan visited Moscow in 1959 and told Khrushchev that war was impossible. Khrushchev presumes that Western leaders continue to act on that conviction.] Macmillan could not have lost his mind since then. He considered war impossible then and, suddenly, now he changes his mind? No, no. The outcome of modern war will be decided by atomic weapons....

Can we clash? Possibly.... I told Fanfani, that [the American state] is a barely governed state.... Kennedy himself hardly influences the direction and development of policies [politiki] in the American state.... The American Senate and other [state] organizations are very similar to our **Veche of Novgorod**.... One party there defeated the other when it tore off half of the beards of another party.... They shouted, yelled, pulled each other's beards, and in such a way resolved the question who was right....

Hence anything is possible in the United States. War is also possible. They can unleash it. There are more stable situations in Eng-

Ostensibly: Appearing to be.

Veche of Novgorod: A ruling assembly of citizens of the Russian city of Novgorod from the late ninth century through the late fifteenth century.

land, France, Italy, Germany. I would even say that, when our "friend" [U.S. secretary of state John Foster] Dulles was alive, they had more stability [in the United States]. I told McCloy about it....

I told McCloy, that if they deploy one division in Germany, we will respond with two divisions, if they declare mobilization, we will do the same. If they mobilize such and such numbers, we will put out 150–200 divisions, as many as necessary. We are considering now ... to deploy tanks defensively along the entire border [between the GDR (German Democratic Republic, East Germany) and the FRG (Federal Republic of Germany, West Germany)]. In short, we have to seal every weak spot they might look for....

[Khrushchev admitted the GDR cost the Soviets much more than they needed for their own defense.] Each division there costs us many times more, than if it had been located [on the Soviet territory]. Some might say, why do we need the GDR, we are strong, we have **armaments** and all, and we will stand on our borders. This would have really been a narrow nationalist vision [a point of view considering only the Soviet Union]....

Summing up, our Central Committee and government believe, that now preparations are proceeding better, but there will be a thaw, and, more importantly, a cooling down.... We have to work out our tactics now and perhaps it is already the right time.

What happened next ...

After Kennedy's speech and Khrushchev's reply, thousands and thousands of East Germans crossed into West Berlin. They sensed something was about to happen. Then, in the early morning hours of August 13, 1961, Khrushchev made his move on Berlin. It was not with tanks, guns, or missiles but jackhammers and rolls of barbed wire. He ordered the construction of the Berlin Wall.

Did you know ...

- In part of Khrushchev's talk not excerpted here, he sounded as if the Soviets also used domino theory thinking. He

Armaments: Weapons.

YOU ARE LEAVING
THE AMERICAN SECTOR

ВЫ ВЫЕЗЖАЕТЕ ИЗ
АМЕРИКАНСКОГО СЕКТОРА

VOUS SORTEZ
DU SECTEUR AMERICAIN

SIE VERLASSEN DEN AMERIKANISCHEN SEKTOR

West Berliners watch concrete plates being unloaded, to reinforce the Berlin Wall and help prevent escapes. *Reproduced by permission of AP/Wide World Photos.*

stated that if Germany were united, East Germany would disappear and be absorbed under the Western powers. Then Poland, Czechoslovakia, and the Soviet Union would be next to fall, like dominos, to the Western powers. Dean G. Acheson (1893–1971), secretary of state under President Harry S. Truman (1884–1972; served 1945–53), had earlier expressed the same domino concern in connection with the likelihood of countries in Western Europe, the Middle East, or Africa falling to communism.

- Even though East Germany had the highest standard of living of Eastern European countries, East Germans continued to vote with their feet—and headed west through Berlin.

Consider the following ...

- Look back to the introduction to this entire chapter and the introduction to the first excerpt. Find the overriding reason that the Soviets wanted a German peace treaty recognizing both separate countries of East and West Germany.

- For all his blustering, Khrushchev says he does not really believe there will be a war. Why?

- What impression of President Kennedy did Khrushchev have during his talk?

For More Information

Books

Frankland, Mark. *Khrushchev.* New York: Stein and Day, 1979.

Khrushchev, Nikita S. *Khrushchev Remembers.* Boston: Little, Brown, 1970.

Khrushchev, Nikita S. *Khrushchev Remembers: The Last Testament.* Boston: Little, Brown, 1974.

Khrushchev, Sergei. *Nikita Khrushchev: Creation of a Superpower.* University Park: Pennsylvania State University Press, 2000.

Web Site

Woodrow Wilson International Center for Scholars. "Khrushchev's Secret Speech on the Berlin Crisis, August 1961." *Cold War International History Project Virtual Archive.* http://wwics.si.edu/index.cfm?fuseaction=library.document&topic_id=1409&id=680 (accessed on September 17, 2003).

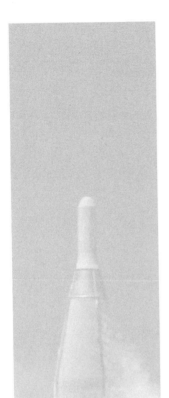

John F. Kennedy

Excerpt from "Remarks in the Rudolph Wild Platz, Berlin, June 26, 1963"

Originally published in *Public Papers of the Presidents of the United States: John F. Kennedy, 1963*

"All free men, wherever they may live, are citizens of Berlin, and, therefore, as a free man, I take pride in the words, 'Ich bin ein Berliner [I am a Berliner].'"

On August 12, 1961, twenty-five hundred East Germans crossed over into West Berlin to work and live under freedom and democracy. Although through the 1950s approximately three million East Germans had crossed into West Berlin with most proceeding to West Germany, that number for one day was unusually high. After U.S. president John F. Kennedy (1917–1963; served 1961–63) gave a speech regarding Berlin on July 25 and Soviet premier Nikita Khrushchev (1894–1971) responded on August 4 (see first and second excerpts in this chapter), it was clear to many East Germans that the days of relatively unrestricted crossover through Berlin might well be coming to an end.

With German peace treaty negotiations stalemated, Walter Ulbricht (1893–1973), leader of East Germany, was screaming for Khrushchev to stop the exodus. Ulbricht's answer to the heavy crossover was a Soviet military action to take over West Berlin and declare it part of East Germany. Khrushchev, despite his own boisterous talk, knew Ulbricht's solution was too aggressive and was likely to risk war—nuclear war—with the West. Khrushchev decided to put in place an old plan—one developed years earlier. He would construct a wall running along the sector lines of the Soviet-occupied East Berlin and the West Berlin sectors occupied by the United States, Britain, and France. He would seal off the Western sectors from East Berlin, thereby halting the crossing of refugees from East Berlin into West Berlin.

As noted on the *History Today* Web site, Daniel Schorr, former Eastern European bureau correspondent for CBS news, recalled, "I had gone to Berlin [in the summer of 1961] because it was clear something was happening there. On August 12, 2,500 people crossed over [from East to West]. The East Germans couldn't let this [stream of refugees] go on. At 2:30 in the morning, I got a call from my camera-man. He said something very strange was going on at the sector border and that I should come down, so—grum-

Journalist Daniel Schorr, who covered for CBS the events surrounding the construction of the Berlin Wall. *Reproduced by permission of AP/Wide World Photos.*

bling—I got out of bed and went. Under floodlights and guarded by soldiers, engineering crews were using jackham-mers to sink posts in the ground. Between these posts they were unrolling sheets of barbed wire. By 7 A.M., West Berliners were there, hooting and jeering."

By morning, the border between East and West was closed. Berliners with family members living in various sec-tors of the city, who until this moment had enjoyed free movement through all sectors, found themselves split apart. Commuter trains carrying East Berliners to their jobs in the West were halted at the crossing and could not proceed.

Meanwhile that same morning across the Atlantic Ocean, President Kennedy was setting out from Hyannis Port, Massachusetts, with his family for a day of sailing on their yacht, the *Marlin*. According to *Time* magazine reporter Hugh Sidey in the November 20, 1989, issue, an army major on duty at the Kennedy compound ran into the surf in his full uniform to give the Berlin bulletin to Brigadier General

U.S. president John F. Kennedy (standing, far left, in car) looks at the cheering crowd during a ticker tape parade upon his arrival in Berlin, West Germany, on June 26, 1963. *Reproduced by permission of AP/Wide World Photos.*

Chester Clifton (1913–1991), who was swimming offshore. Clifton was the president's military aide. Clifton signaled the *Marlin* to shore and informed Kennedy of what had transpired in Berlin the previous night. Kennedy was astounded. Out of at least forty contingency plans, building a wall through Berlin had never been discussed. Sidey further reported that Kennedy, back in the Oval Office, told Clifton that the Wall would stay until the Soviets tired of it. Kennedy said, "We could have sent tanks over and knocked the Wall down. What then? They build another one back a hundred yards? We knock that down, then we go to war." Kennedy knew a "wall" was better than a "war." As long as the Soviets and East Germans left West Berlin alone, Kennedy would not act militarily.

Khrushchev's risky guess had paid off. There would be no war as long as West Berlin was not threatened. Khrushchev had successfully stopped the flow of refugees out of East Berlin, as Ulbricht demanded. Many historians believe

Khrushchev had a second reason for the wall—to seal Ulbricht in so that he would not take matters into his own hands and start a war.

Very limited access was granted to West Berliners to occasionally go into East Berlin at only a few specific crossing points. Other Westerners, including U.S. citizens, could only cross into East Berlin at the Friedrichstrasse Crossing, commonly called Checkpoint Charlie. Many thought of Checkpoint Charlie as where the communist East came face to face with the democratic West.

It was to Checkpoint Charlie that President Kennedy came on June 26, 1963, when he visited West Berlin. Asking aides to remain back, Kennedy alone climbed up a viewing stand and peered into the gray of East Berlin. Shortly thereafter, he delivered one of the most memorable speeches of his presidency, a presidency filled with rousing, eloquent speeches. Having set aside the original speech, he spoke from the heart to the 250,000 gathered West Berliners. If anyone did not understand the differences between a free world and a communist world, Kennedy called out repeatedly, "Let them come to Berlin." He ended dramatically with "Ich bin ein Berliner (I am a Berliner)."

Things to remember while reading the excerpt from "Remarks in the Rudolph Wild Platz, Berlin, June 26, 1963":

- By the time Kennedy visited Berlin, the wall had been in place one year and ten months. Many East Germans had lost their lives trying to escape over, under, and through the wall.

- The wall was an ugly testament to the divisions brought about during the Cold War. Because the wall showed that the only way to keep people under a communist system was to force them to stay, the wall was a propaganda symbol for the West.

- By June 1963, Kennedy had shown his strength as a leader and was already loved by Europeans despite his relative youth.

Excerpt from "Remarks in the Rudolph Wild Platz, Berlin, June 26, 1963"

There are many people in the world who really don't understand, or say they don't, what is the great issue between the free world and the Communist world. Let them come to Berlin. There are some who say that communism is the wave of the future. Let them come to Berlin. And there are some who say in Europe and elsewhere we can work with the Communists. Let them come to Berlin. And there are even a few who say that it is true that communism is an evil system, but it permits us to make economic progress. Lass' sie nach Berlin kommen. *Let them come to Berlin.*

Freedom has many difficulties and democracy is not perfect, but we have never had to put a wall up to keep our people in, to prevent them from leaving us. I want to say, on behalf of my countrymen, who live many miles away on the other side of the Atlantic, who are far distant from you, that they take the greatest pride that they have been able to share with you, even from a distance, the story of the last 18 years. I know of no town, no city, that has been besieged for 18 years that still lives with the vitality and the force, and the hope and the determination of the city of West Berlin. While the wall is the most obvious and vivid demonstration of the failures of the Communist system, for all the world to see, we take no satisfaction in it, for it is, as your Mayor has said, an offense not only against history but an offense against humanity, separating families, dividing husbands and wives and brothers and sisters, and dividing a people who wish to be joined together.

What is true of this city is true of Germany—real, lasting peace in Europe can never be assured as long as one German out of four is denied the elementary right of free men, and that is to make a free choice. In 18 years of peace and good faith, this generation of Germans has earned the right to be free, including the right to unite their families and their nation in lasting peace, with good will to all people. You live in a defended island of freedom, but your life is part of the main. So let me ask you, as I close, to lift your eyes beyond the dangers of today, to the hopes of tomorrow, beyond the freedom merely of this city of Berlin, or your country of Germany, to the advance of freedom everywhere, beyond the wall to the day of peace with justice, beyond yourselves and ourselves to all mankind.

*Freedom is **indivisible**, and when one man is enslaved, all are not free. When all are free, then we can look forward to that day when this city will be joined as one and this country and this great Continent of Europe in a peaceful and hopeful globe. When that day finally comes, as it will, the people of West Berlin can take sober satisfaction in the fact that they were in the front lines for almost two decades.*

All free men, wherever they may live, are citizens of Berlin, and, therefore, as a free man, I take pride in the words, "Ich bin ein Berliner [I am a Berliner]."

U.S. president John F. Kennedy (fourth from right on podium) looks over at the Brandenburg Gate of the Berlin Wall on June 26, 1963. Red flags drape the gate so that Kennedy cannot see behind it.
Reproduced by permission of AP/Wide World Photos.

What happened next ...

The wall remained for twenty-eight years. West Berlin's economy prospered while East Berlin's languished.

Indivisible: Not separated into parts.

A copy of a note card used by U.S. president John F. Kennedy during his Berlin speech in June 1963. The first line shows Kennedy's phonetic version of his famous line "Ich bin ein Berliner." *Reproduced by permission of the Corbis Corporation.*

On October 7, 1989, Soviet leader Mikhail Gorbachev (1931–) visited East Germany to promote reform in East Germany. Two days later, amid fireworks and celebration, the gates opened and the wall began coming down.

Did you know ...

- The fence sealing off West Berlin's perimeter was 103 miles (166 kilometers) long. The wall that ran through the city was 28.5 miles (46 kilometers) long. The barbed wire fence in the city portion was replaced by a concrete wall topped by a round concrete pipe that was impossible to grasp by someone trying to climb over the wall.

- Around the wall was a no-man's land of guard towers, land mines, a guard patrol track, structures to destroy tires, and plenty of coiled barbed wire.

- On October 27, 1961, a few months after the wall went up, a dispute over passport procedures at Checkpoint Charlie escalated way beyond its importance. Soviet tanks moved up and directly faced U.S. tanks. Diplomatic efforts prevented shots from being fired. Some historians believe this confrontation at Checkpoint Charlie came as close as any during the Cold War to igniting a hot war.

Consider the following …

- Explain what the wall, called the "Wall of Shame" in West Berlin, came to symbolize.

- Why did Kennedy not use military force to immediately bring the wall down?

- Imagine and tell what it must have been like to be a member of a family split apart by the wall. Remember the wall remained in place for twenty-eight years and there was no Internet.

For More Information

Books

Dallek, Robert. *An Unfinished Life: John F. Kennedy, 1917–1963.* Boston: Little, Brown and Company, 2003.

Public Papers of the Presidents of the United States: John F. Kennedy, 1963. Washington, DC: U.S. Government Printing Office, 1964.

Tusa, Ann. *The Last Division: A History of Berlin, 1945–1989.* Reading, MA: Addison-Wesley, 1997.

Wyden, Peter. *Wall: The Inside Story of Divided Berlin.* New York: Simon and Schuster, 1989.

Web Site

Rempel, Gerhard. "The Berlin Wall." *History Today.* http://mars.acnet.wnec.edu/~grempel/courses/germany/lectures/39wall.html (accessed on September 17, 2003).

Sidey, Hugh. "President Kennedy at the Construction." *Time.com: The Berlin Wall: Ten Years After.* http://www.time.com/time/daily/special/berlin/sidey.html (accessed on September 17, 2003).

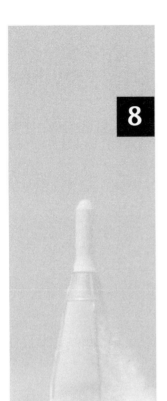

8 Cuban Missile Crisis

On January 1, 1959, revolutionary Fidel Castro (1926–) established himself as leader of the small island of Cuba, 90 miles (145 kilometers) off the coast of Florida. At the time, Soviet leader Nikita Khrushchev (1894–1971) and other Soviet leaders took no notice. Considered unimportant to Soviet interests, the Cuban Soviet embassy had shut its doors in 1952. There were no Soviet representatives in Cuba in 1959.

The American media at first offered positive reports about Castro. They labeled him a daring, educated soldier interested in improving the lives of Cubans. On the other hand, Soviet intelligence reported to Moscow that Castro was the usual Central American dictator who was most likely closely affiliated with the U.S. government. Castro, however, was determined to choose his own independent path. He angered many wealthy and middle-class Cubans, many of whom had fled to the United States, by breaking up their large properties and giving parcels to common citizens to work. His intention to end America's domination of much of Cuba's economy, such as the sugar industry and oil refineries, was soon apparent. Also, Castro refused to hold free elections as he had promised.

Castro was quickly becoming troublesome in the eyes of U.S. leaders, including President Dwight D. Eisenhower (1890–1969; served 1953–61). Among Soviets, it was Khrushchev who first took notice. The Soviets set up economic ties with Cuba as the U.S.-Cuban relationship worsened. As early as the mid-1960s, intelligence coming in from the National Security Agency (NSA) indicated that the Soviets were sending arms and advisors to Cuba. The NSA's Signal Intelligence (SIGINT) was America's prime intelligence organization for listening in on and analyzing foreign communications.

Cuban leader Fidel Castro.
Reproduced by permission of AP/Wide World Photos.

In September 1960, Khrushchev and Castro met and warmly greeted each other at the United Nations in New York City. Soon, Castro publicly aligned Cuba with the Soviet Union. On January 3, 1961, Cuba and the United States severed all diplomatic ties. Khrushchev privately delighted in the realization that communism had gained a foothold in the Americas. (The Americas include North America, Central America, and South America, which together make up the Western Hemisphere.) President Eisenhower was privately dismayed that Cuba had gone communist. He authorized funds to train Cuban exiles to invade Cuba and take back the island. This invasion, known as the Bay of Pigs, took place on April 17, 1961, under the new U.S. president, John F. Kennedy (1917–1963; served 1961–63). Castro learned of the invasion ahead of time, and his Soviet-made tanks defeated the exiles quickly. The Bay of Pigs invasion failed miserably.

By May 1961, SIGINT reported radio chatter from Cuba about antiaircraft radar systems. Over the next twelve months, Soviet arms and advisors continued to arrive in Cuba. For the U.S. military and government officials aware of the situation, Cuba was quietly becoming a nightmare. Nevertheless, they took some reassurance that Moscow, through diplomatic channels, insisted that all Soviet military buildup in Cuba was only defensive for Cuba's protection should the United States or others try again to invade and topple Castro. For Moscow and Khrushchev, Cuba was a strategic military dream: it was only 90 miles (145 kilometers) from the United States.

By the spring of 1962, Khrushchev had decided on a plan of action in keeping with his "bluster and intimidation" plan. Its main tool being Khrushchev's exaggerated talk, "bluster and intimidation" was a calculated approach to make the United States believe the Soviets and the United States had approximately the same nuclear-weapon capabilities. In actuality the U.S. capabilities, at least in number of weapons, far surpassed those of the Soviets.

Khrushchev for some years had been furious over U.S. placement of missiles with nuclear warheads aimed at the Soviet Union in Turkey, Italy, and Great Britain. Khrushchev decided to secretly install in Cuba forty missile launchers, each armed with two missiles topped with nuclear warheads. By July 1962, Soviet ships carrying missile equipment were on their way to Cuba. As the cargo arrived, missile launch sites were prepared.

In August and September 1962, the intercepted intelligence chatter turned alarming. SIGINT reported that apparently Soviet surface-to-air missiles (SAMs) had been shipped to Cuba. SAMs could shoot down high-flying U.S. Air Force reconnaissance (spy-photography) aircraft such as the U-2. The U.S. military reasoned correctly that if the Soviets were sending missiles as sophisticated as SAMs, then they must have secret operations on Cuba that needed protection.

The first excerpt that follows comes from the book *Thirteen Days: A Memoir of the Cuban Missile Crisis*, by U.S. attorney general Robert Kennedy (1925–1968). In the excerpt, Kennedy, also the president's brother, describes the meetings of the Executive Committee (Ex-Comm) of the National Security Council. Ex-Comm was quickly assembled by President Kennedy to analyze and make suggestions as to what to do about the Soviet missile placement. Once a response was decided upon, President Kennedy informed the American people of the crisis.

The second excerpt comes from President Kennedy's "Radio and Television Report to the American People on the

Soviet Arms Buildup in Cuba, October 22, 1962." Over the six days that followed the speech, the United States and Soviet Union went to the brink of nuclear war. The third excerpt is from Khrushchev's communiqué, or message, to President Kennedy on October 28, 1962, accepting an end to the crisis. The communiqué is reprinted in *The Cuban Missile Crisis, 1962: National Security Archive Documents Reader.*

Robert F. Kennedy

Excerpt from Thirteen Days: A Memoir of the Cuban Missile Crisis
Originally published in 1969

"The strain and the hours without sleep were beginning to take their toll. However, ... those human weaknesses—impatience, fits of anger—are understandable. Each one of us was being asked to make a recommendation which would affect the future of all mankind, a recommendation which, if wrong and if accepted, could mean the destruction of the human race."

Throughout July, August, and September of 1962, Soviet ships arrived in Cuban ports. Their secret cargo, missile-site equipment, was unloaded and taken to missile launch construction sites around the island. On Sunday, October 14, 1962, a high-flying U.S. U-2 reconnaissance plane took photographs over Cuba. The photos were developed and analyzed on October 15. The chilling evidence that medium-range Soviet missiles were at a construction site known as San Cristobal was in the hands of U.S. officials.

On Tuesday, October 16, at 9:00 A.M., Kennedy's national security advisor, McGeorge Bundy (1919–1996), presented and explained the photographs to the president. Kennedy, immediately realizing the gravity of the situation, gathered a small group of trusted and brilliant senior officials from his presidential cabinet, the National Security Council (NSC), and the military. The group became known as Ex-Comm, abbreviated from Executive Committee of the NSC. The NSC was part of the executive branch of government and advised the president on America's security issues. Ex-Comm's discussions on October 16 and 17 explored a whole

range of proposals, from doing nothing immediately to a full invasion of Cuba involving both ground and air attacks. All members agreed on one goal from the start—the missiles must leave Cuba one way or another.

On Thursday, October 18, intelligence reports given to Ex-Comm indicated medium-range missiles could be ready for launch within twenty-four hours. The excerpt from *Thirteen Days: A Memoir of the Cuban Missile Crisis* begins with Ex-Comm's activities the night of October 18. The excerpt takes readers to Saturday afternoon, October 20, when President Kennedy decided to impose a naval blockade around Cuba. All ships approaching Cuba would be stopped, searched, and could only proceed if no military equipment was onboard.

U.S. president John F. Kennedy (left, near second window) meets with his Cabinet to discuss the Cuban Missile Crisis in October 1962. *Reproduced by permission of the Corbis Corporation.*

Things to remember while reading the excerpt from *Thirteen Days: A Memoir of the Cuban Missile Crisis*:

- Of the forty missile launchers planned to be installed in Cuba, twenty-four were medium-range launchers. Each

launcher was armed with two missiles topped with nuclear warheads. The medium-range missiles could travel 1,100 miles (1,770 kilometers). All the southeastern United States, from Dallas, Texas, to Washington, D.C., was in range. The sixteen long-range missile launchers were not yet in place. Once they were readied, the only major U.S. city they could not reach was Seattle, Washington.

- Ex-Comm members at first had no definitive plan to make the Soviets remove the missiles. Instead, they brainstormed back and forth, with most members changing their minds several times.

- During the entire crisis period, a slight move or misstep or single voiced command on either side could have unleashed a nuclear holocaust.

Robert F. Kennedy. *Courtesy of the National Archives and Records Administration.*

Blockade: A build-up of naval ships around an area; during the Cuban Missile Crisis, the United States installed a blockade around Cuba, to prevent more Soviet ships from reaching Cuba.

Committee: The Executive Committee of the National Security Council, to discuss the Cuban Missile Crisis.

Ensued: Followed.

Excerpt from Thirteen Days: A Memoir of the Cuban Missile Crisis

By Thursday night [October 18], *there was a majority opinion in our group for a **blockade**. Our **committee** went from the State Department to the White House around 9:15 that night. In order to avoid the suspicion that would have **ensued** from the presence of a long line of limousines, we all went in my car—*[CIA director] *John McCone,* [chairman of the Joint Chiefs of Staff] *Maxwell Taylor, the driver, and myself all crowded together in the front seat, and six others sitting in back.*

We explained our recommendations to the President. At the beginning, the meeting seemed to proceed in an orderly and satisfactory way. However, as people talked, as the President raised probing questions, minds and opinions began to change again, and not

only on small points. For some, it was from one extreme to another—supporting an air attack at the beginning of the meeting and, by the time we left the White House, supporting no action at all.

*The President, not at all satisfied, sent us back to our **deliberations**. Because any other site would arouse suspicion, he returned to his regular schedule and his campaign speaking engagements.*

The next morning [Friday, October 19], at our meeting at the State Department, there were sharp disagreements again. The strain and the hours without sleep were beginning to take their toll. However, even many years later, those human weaknesses—impatience, fits of anger—are understandable. Each one of us was being asked to make a recommendation which would affect the future of all mankind, a recommendation which, if wrong and if accepted, could mean the destruction of the human race. That kind of pressure does strange things to a human being, even to brilliant, self-confident, mature, experienced men. For some it brings out charac-

U.S. president John F. Kennedy (right) meets with Soviet foreign minister Andrey Gromyko shortly before the Cuban Missile Crisis began in October 1962. *Reproduced by permission of AP/Wide World Photos.*

Deliberations: Discussions considering all sides of an issue.

Cuban Missile Crisis: Robert F. Kennedy

U.S. attorney general
Robert Kennedy (left)
consults with his brother,
President John F. Kennedy.
*Reproduced by permission of
AP/Wide World Photos.*

*teristics and strengths that perhaps even they never knew they had,
and for others the pressure is too overwhelming.*

*Our situation was made more difficult by the fact that there
was no obvious or simple solution. A dogmatism, a certainty of
viewpoint, was simply not possible. For every position there were **inherent** weaknesses; and those opposed would point them out, often
with devastating effects.*

*Finally, we agreed on a procedure by which we felt we could
give some intelligent recommendations to the President. We knew
that time was running out and that delay was not possible. We split
into groups to write up our respective recommendations, beginning
with an outline of the president's speech to the nation and the
whole course of action thereafter, trying to anticipate all possible
contingencies and setting forth recommendations as to how to
react to them.*

Inherent: Natural.

Contingencies: Outcomes.

Dissected: Analyzed.

*In the early afternoon [still Friday], we exchanged papers, each
group **dissected** and criticized the other, and then the papers were*

returned to the original group to develop further answers. *Gradually from all this came the outline of **definitive** plans. For the group that advocated the blockade, it was an outline of the legal basis for our action, an agenda for a meeting of the **Organization of American States**, recommendations for the role of the United Nations, the military procedures for stopping ships, and, finally, the circumstances under which military force might be used. For the group that advocated immediate military action, it was an outline of the areas to be attacked, a defense of our position in the United Nations, suggestions as to how to obtain support from Latin American countries, and a proposed communication to Khrushchev to convince him of the inadvisability of moving militarily against us in the Caribbean, Berlin [former capital of Germany], or elsewhere in the world.*

During all these deliberations, we all spoke as equals. There was no rank, and, in fact, we did not even have a chairman.... The conversations were completely uninhibited and unrestricted. Everyone had an equal opportunity to express himself and to be heard directly. It was a tremendously advantageous procedure that does not frequently occur within the executive branch of the government, where rank is often so important.

We met all day Friday and Friday night. Then again early Saturday [October 20] morning we were back at the State Department. I talked to the President several times on Friday. He was hoping to be able to meet with us early enough to decide on a course of action and then broadcast it to the nation Sunday night [October 21]. Saturday morning at 10:00 o'clock I called the President at the Blackstone Hotel in Chicago and told him we were ready to meet with him. It was now up to one single man. No committee was going to make this decision. He canceled his trip and returned to Washington.

*As he was returning to Washington, our armed forces across the world were put on alert. Telephoning from our meeting in the State Department, Secretary [of Defense Robert S.] McNamara ordered four **tactical air squadrons** placed at readiness for an air strike, in case the President decided to accept that recommendation.*

The President arrived back at the White House at 1:40 p.m. [Saturday, October 20] and went for a swim. I sat on the side of the pool, and we talked. At 2:30 we walked up to the Oval Room.

The meeting went on until ten minutes after five. Convened as a formal meeting of the National Security Council, it was a larger group of people who met, some of whom had not participated in

Definitive: Definite.

Organization of American States: An alliance of nations from North and Latin America that sought to maintain political stability in the region for protection and cooperation.

Tactical air squadrons: Short-range bombers for flexible use.

the deliberations up to that time. Bob McNamara presented the arguments for the blockade; others presented the arguments for the military attack....

The President made his decision that afternoon in favor of the blockade.

What happened next ...

With plans for the blockade firm, on Sunday, October 21, President Kennedy canceled the remainder of his scheduled campaign appearances over the next few weeks. Kennedy requested the television networks clear their scheduled programs on Monday evening, October 22, for an urgent broadcast to the nation. In prime time at 7:00 P.M. Eastern time President Kennedy addressed the nation.

Did you know ...

- Ex-Comm met almost around the clock. The meetings were free-wheeling brainstorming sessions at which everyone could speak.

- With an eye to history, President Kennedy had all of the meetings tape recorded. The participants were unaware of this so spoke freely. In the 1990s, with the Cold War ended, the tapes were released for study.

- The term "quarantine" was chosen to be used instead of "blockade," since blockades were illegal under international law and considered acts of war.

- Not wanting to let on anything was wrong until a plan of action was decided on, President Kennedy had continued his planned schedule of campaign appearances supporting various Democratic candidates for the 1962 November mid-term elections through Saturday morning of October 20.

- Each Soviet nuclear warhead in Cuba carried an explosive power equal to 1 million tons (900,000 metric tons) of TNT. At the end of World War II (1939–45), the bomb that destroyed Hiroshima, Japan, had the explosive power of only 13,000 tons (11,800 metric tons) of TNT.

Consider the following ...

- Ex-Comm eventually divided into two groups: those who wanted a full military invasion of Cuba and those who favored the blockade. Pick a side, explain your choice, and predict the consequences.

- At your local library, locate the book *The Kennedy Tapes: Inside the White House During the Cuban Missile Crisis.* Follow the reasoning over a period of days of one individual, for instance General Maxwell Taylor (1901–1987) or Secretary of Defense Robert McNamara (1916–).

- Describe the range of emotions no doubt encountered at the meeting on October 16 between national security advisor McGeorge Bundy and President Kennedy.

For More Information

Books

Allison, Graham T., and Philip Zelikow. *Essence of Decision: Explaining the Cuban Missile Crisis.* 2nd ed. New York: Longman, 1999.

Kennedy, Robert F. *Thirteen Days: A Memoir of the Cuban Missile Crisis.* New York: W. W. Norton, 1969.

May, Ernest R., and Philip D. Zelikow, eds. *The Kennedy Tapes: Inside the White House During the Cuban Missile Crisis.* New York: W. W. Norton, 2002.

Thompson, Robert S. *The Missiles of October: The Declassified Story of John F. Kennedy and the Cuban Missile Crisis.* New York: Simon & Schuster, 1992.

John F. Kennedy

Excerpt from "Radio and Television Report to the American People on the Soviet Arms Buildup in Cuba, October 22, 1962"

Originally published in *Public Papers of the Presidents of the United States: John F. Kennedy, 1962*, published in 1963

"It shall be the policy of this Nation to regard any nuclear missile launched from Cuba against any nation in the Western Hemisphere as an attack by the Soviet Union on the United States, requiring a full retaliatory response upon the Soviet Union."

President John F. Kennedy (1917–1963; served 1961–63) addressed the American people on the evening of Monday, October 22, 1962, to inform them about the crisis in Cuba. He explained the United States had undeniable evidence that Soviet missiles were in place in Cuba to provide "nuclear strike capability against the Western Hemisphere," consisting of North, Central, and South America. Kennedy announced that a naval "quarantine" of Cuba would begin on Wednesday morning, October 24. That meant that all ships approaching Cuba would be stopped, searched, and could only proceed if no military equipment was onboard. This was essentially the same thing as a blockade, but because blockades were illegal under international law and considered an act of war, the term "quarantine" was used instead.

Kennedy also announced that the U.S. military was on full-alert status; that any nuclear missile launched by the Soviets would be met with a "full retaliatory response" aimed at the Soviet Union; called for an immediate meeting of international peacekeeping organizations; and called on Soviet premier Nikita Khrushchev (1894–1971) "to halt and elimi-

nate this clandestine [secret], reckless, and provocative [challenging] threat to world peace."

A Cuban refugee in Miami, Florida, watches U.S. president John F. Kennedy address the nation on TV. *Reproduced by permission of the Corbis Corporation.*

Things to remember while reading the excerpt from "Radio and Television Report to the American People on the Soviet Arms Buildup in Cuba, October 22, 1962":

- President Kennedy believed the blockade most likely would not trigger an immediate nuclear war. It gave Khrushchev time and a way to withdraw from the situation.

- Grim-faced leaders in Moscow gathered to await Kennedy's words, not knowing what his plan of action would be.

- U.S. leaders had decided they would never back down from their demand that the missiles be removed.

Excerpt from "Radio and Television Report to the American People on the Soviet Arms Buildup in Cuba, October 22, 1962"

Good evening, my fellow citizens:

*This Government, as promised, has maintained the closest **surveillance** of the Soviet military buildup on the island of Cuba. Within the past week, unmistakable evidence has established the fact that a series of offensive missile sites is now in preparation on that imprisoned island. The purpose of these bases can be none other than to provide a nuclear strike capability against the Western Hemisphere.*

*Upon receiving the first preliminary hard information of this nature last Tuesday morning at 9 A.M., I directed that our surveillance be **stepped up.** And having now confirmed and completed our evaluation of the evidence and our decision on a course of action, this Government feels **obliged** to report this new crisis to you in fullest detail.*

*The characteristics of these new missile sites indicate two distinct types of installations. Several of them include medium-range **ballistic missiles,** capable of carrying a nuclear warhead for a distance of more than 1,000 nautical miles. Each of these missiles, in short, is capable of striking Washington, D.C., the Panama Canal, **Cape Canaveral,** Mexico City, or any other city in the southeastern part of the United States, in Central America, or in the Caribbean area.*

Additional sites not yet completed appear to be designed for intermediate range ballistic missiles—capable of traveling more than twice as far—and thus capable of striking most of the major cities in the Western Hemisphere, ranging as far north as Hudson Bay, Canada, and as far south as Lima, Peru. In addition, jet bombers, capable of carrying nuclear weapons, are now being uncrated and assembled in Cuba, while the necessary air bases are being prepared.

*This urgent transformation of Cuba into an important strategic base—by the presence of these large, long-range, and clearly offensive weapons of sudden mass destruction—constitutes an **explicit** threat to the peace and security of all the Americas....*

This action also contradicts the repeated assurances of Soviet spokesmen, both publicly and privately delivered, that the arms

Surveillance: Watchfulness.

Stepped up: Intensified.

Obliged: That it is necessary.

Ballistic missiles: Projectiles with maximum flight performance and the ability to hit specific targets.

Cape Canaveral: The site in Florida from which the National Aeronautics and Space Administration (NASA), the U.S. space agency, launches its rockets.

Explicit: Clear.

buildup in Cuba would **retain its original defensive character**, and that the Soviet Union had no need or desire to station **strategic missiles** on the territory of any other nation....

Nuclear weapons are so destructive and ballistic missiles are so swift, that any substantially increased possibility of their use or any sudden change in their **deployment** may well be regarded as a definite threat to peace.

For many years, both the Soviet Union and the United States, recognizing this fact, have deployed strategic nuclear weapons with great care, never upsetting the **precarious status quo** which insured that these weapons would not be used in the absence of some vital challenge. Our own strategic missiles have never been transferred to the territory of any other nation under a **cloak** of secrecy and deception; and our history—unlike that of the Soviets since the end of World War II—demonstrates that we have no desire to dominate or conquer any other nation or impose our system upon its people. Nevertheless, American citizens have become adjusted to living daily on the bull's-eye of Soviet missiles located inside the U.S.S.R. or in submarines.

In that sense, missiles in Cuba add to an already clear and present danger—although it should be noted the nations of Latin America have never previously been subjected to a potential nuclear threat....

We will not prematurely or unnecessarily risk the costs of worldwide nuclear war in which **even the fruits of victory would be ashes in our mouth**—but neither will we shrink from that risk at any time it must be faced.

Acting, therefore, in the defense of our own security and of the entire Western Hemisphere, and under the authority entrusted to me by the Constitution as endorsed by the resolution of the Congress, I have directed that the following initial steps be taken immediately:

First: To halt this offensive buildup, a strict **quarantine** on all offensive military equipment under shipment to Cuba is being initiated. All ships of any kind bound for Cuba from whatever nation or port will, if found to contain cargoes of offensive weapons, be turned back. This quarantine will be extended, if needed, to other types of cargo and carriers. We are not at this time, however, denying the necessities of life as the Soviets attempted to do in their Berlin blockade of 1948.

Second: I have directed the continued and increased close surveillance of Cuba and its military buildup.... Should these offensive

Retain its original defensive character: Exist to defend Cuba only.

Strategic missiles: Long-range missiles designed to offensively attack and destroy an enemy's capability to wage war.

Deployment: Strategic placement.

Precarious status quo: Uncertain existing condition.

Cloak: Disguise.

Even the fruits of victory would be ashes in our mouth: Even in victory, the United States would suffer great devastation.

Quarantine: Blockade; this term was chosen because international law prohibited blockades.

*military preparations continue, thus increasing the threat to the hemisphere, further action will be justified. I have directed the Armed Forces to prepare for any **eventualities**....*

*Third: It shall be the policy of this Nation to regard any nuclear missile launched from Cuba against any nation in the Western Hemisphere as an attack by the Soviet Union on the United States, requiring a full **retaliatory** response upon the Soviet Union.*

*Fourth: As a necessary military precaution, I have reinforced our base at **Guantanamo**, evacuated today the **dependents** of our personnel there, and ordered additional military units to be on a stand-by alert basis.*

*Fifth: We are calling tonight for an immediate meeting of the Organ of Consultation under the **Organization of American States**, to consider this threat to hemispheric security....*

*Sixth: Under the Charter of the United Nations, we are asking tonight that an emergency meeting of the Security Council be **convoked** without delay to take action against this latest Soviet threat to world peace. Our resolution will call for the prompt dismantling and withdrawal of all offensive weapons in Cuba, under the supervision of U.N. observers, before the quarantine can be lifted.*

*Seventh and finally: I call upon Chairman Khrushchev to halt and eliminate this **clandestine**, reckless, and **provocative** threat to world peace and to stable relations between our two nations. I call upon him further to abandon this course of world domination, and to join in an historic effort to end the perilous arms race and to transform the history of man. He has an opportunity now to move the world back from the **abyss** of destruction—by returning to his government's own words that it had no need to station missiles outside its own territory, and withdrawing these weapons from Cuba—by **refraining from** any action which will widen or deepen the present crisis—and then by participating in a search for peaceful and permanent solutions....*

We have no wish to war with the Soviet Union—for we are a peaceful people who desire to live in peace with all other peoples.

*But it is difficult to settle or even discuss these problems in an atmosphere of **intimidation**. That is why this latest Soviet threat—or any other threat which is made either independently or in response to our actions this week—must and will be met with determination. Any hostile move anywhere in the world against the*

Eventualities: Possible outcomes.

Retaliatory: Strike back in return.

Guantanamo: A U.S. military base on the east end of Cuba.

Dependents: Families.

Organization of American States: An alliance of nations from North and Latin America that sought to maintain political stability in the region for protection and cooperation.

Convoked: Called together.

Clandestine: Secret.

Provocative: Challenging.

Abyss: Edge.

Refraining from: Halting.

Intimidation: Threatening behavior.

*safety and freedom of peoples to whom we are committed—includ-
ing in particular the brave people of West Berlin—will be met by
whatever action is needed....*

*My fellow citizens: let no one doubt that this is a difficult and
dangerous effort on which we have set out. No one can foresee precisely what course it will take or what costs or **casualties** will be in-
curred....*

*The path we have chosen for the present is full of hazards, as
all paths are—but it is the one most consistent with our character
and courage as a nation and our commitments around the world.
The cost of freedom is always high—but Americans have always
paid it. And one path we shall never choose, and that is the path of
surrender or **submission.***

*Our goal is not the victory of might, but the **vindication** of
right—not peace at the expense of freedom, but both peace and
freedom, here in this hemisphere, and, we hope, around the world.
God willing, that goal will be achieved.*

Thank you and good night.

What happened next ...

On Tuesday, October 23, Khrushchev vowed Soviet
vessels would continue on course to Cuba. If stopped by
American naval ships, Soviet submarines, stationed around
Cuba and armed with nuclear warheads, would fire. It was
apparent to all sides that the world was at the brink of nuclear war. U Thant (1909–1974), the secretary general of the
United Nations, pleaded with the superpowers to refrain
from plunging the world into a nuclear holocaust.

Twenty-four hours later, on Wednesday morning, October 24, the United States began the quarantine as
Kennedy's speech had promised. The world held its collective
breath. Many historians believe that morning provided the
Cold War's most intense and terrifying moments.
Khrushchev sent a message to Kennedy calling the quarantine "an act of aggression."

Casualties: Losses.

Submission: Giving in.

Vindication: Upholding.

Russian men read coverage of the Cuban Missile Crisis in the Russian newspaper *Pravda*. *Reproduced by permission of the Corbis Corporation.*

Given Khrushchev's statement to Kennedy, the next events seemed almost miraculous. The U.S. communications intelligence service (SIGINT) reported to President Kennedy that interception of radio messages from Soviet vessels approaching Cuba indicated the Soviets were stopping short of the quarantine circle. In fact, when SIGINT plotted the location of the Soviet vessels they were stopped dead in the water outside the ring of U.S. ships. They were avoiding confrontation. As noted in Dino A. Brugioni's *Eyeball to Eyeball: The Inside Story of the Cuban Missile Crisis,* U.S. secretary of state Dean Rusk (1909–1994) commented, "We're eyeball to eyeball and I think the other fellow just blinked." Sergei Khrushchev (1935–), son of Nikita Khrushchev, reported in his 2000 book *Nikita Khrushchev: and the Creation of a Superpower* that his father believed, "the one who decides to blink first doesn't have weaker nerves but possesses greater wisdom."

Did you know ...

- Anatoly Dobrynin (1919–), the Soviet ambassador to the United States, had no knowledge of the Soviet missiles in

Cuba. A text of Kennedy's speech was given to him before Kennedy went on television. Dobrynin was dumbfounded and had to gather himself together before he could relay the speech to Moscow.

- Although the United States had been targeted for some time by nuclear missiles located in the Soviet Union, Central and South America had never before been within reach of nuclear weapons.

- The missiles in Cuba were the first Soviet missiles located outside the Soviet Union. The United States had missiles with nuclear warheads placed in Turkey, Italy, and Great Britain, all within easy range of the Soviet Union.

Consider the following ...

- Stand in the shoes of President Kennedy or Soviet Premier Khrushchev. What would you have done the morning of October 24? Remember you carry the responsibility of the world's safety on your shoulders.

- Kennedy suggested it was impossible to discuss peace between the superpowers when the Soviets intimidated the United States with the Cuban missiles. What do you think the Soviets thought about having U.S. missiles relatively close in Turkey, Italy, and Great Britain and pointed at their country?

- Explain Kennedy's statement that even victory would be "ashes in our mouth."

For More Information

Books

Brubaker, Paul E. *The Cuban Missile Crisis in American History.* Berkeley Heights, NJ: Enslow, 2001.

Brugioni, Dino A. *Eyeball to Eyeball: The Inside Story of the Cuban Missile Crisis.* New York: Random House, 1991.

Dallek, Robert. *An Unfinished Life: John F. Kennedy, 1917–1963.* Boston: Little, Brown, 2003.

Fursenko, Aleksandr, and Timothy Naftali. *"One Hell of a Gamble": Khrushchev, Castro & Kennedy, 1958–1964.* New York: W. W. Norton, 2000.

Khrushchev, Sergei. *Nikita Khrushchev: Creation of a Superpower.* University Park: Pennsylvania State University Press, 2000.

Paterson, Thomas G., ed. *Kennedy's Quest for Victory: American Foreign Policy, 1961–1963.* New York: Random House, 1995.

Web Site

"The World on the Brink: John F. Kennedy and the Cuban Missile Crisis." *John Fitzgerald Kennedy Library.* http://www.jfklibrary.org/cmc_exhibit_2002.html (accessed on September 20, 2003).

Nikita Khrushchev

Excerpt from "Communiqué to President Kennedy Accepting an End to the Missile Crisis, October 28, 1962"

Originally published in *The Cuban Missile Crisis, 1962: National Security Archive Documents Reader*, 1992

On Wednesday, October 24, 1962, the first day of the U.S. naval quarantine, or blockade, designed to prevent Soviet ships carrying military equipment from reaching the island of Cuba, the U.S. military was at alert level DEFCON 2 (DEFense CONdition 2). DEFCON 2 is the last level before DEFCON 1, which means a nuclear war is imminent or has begun. At no other time in U.S. history had the level been at DEFCON 2. Then by midday, the Soviet ships apparently had stopped in the water and not challenged the U.S. ships forming the quarantine ring. On Thursday, October 25, the Soviet vessels carrying military equipment indeed turned around and headed back to the Soviet Union. However, this did not end the crisis. It was only a momentary breather because missiles with nuclear warheads already on site on the island remained.

By Friday, October 26, Attorney General Robert Kennedy (1925–1968), at the request of his brother, President John F. Kennedy (1917–1963; served 1961–63), was having "backdoor" meetings with the Soviet ambassador to the United States, Anatoly Dobrynin (1919–). That evening, Soviet leader Nikita Khrushchev (1894–1971) sent President Kennedy a letter

"I very well understand your anxiety and the anxiety of the United States people in connection with the fact that the weapons which you describe as "offensive" are, in fact, grim weapons. Both you and I understand what kind of weapon they are."

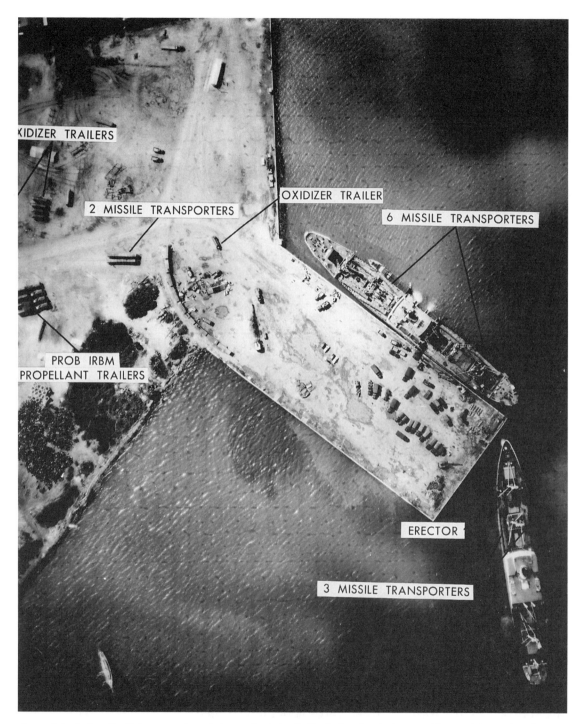

An aerial photo of a Cuban naval port shows Soviet missiles being loaded onto ships on November 5, 1962. *Reproduced by permission of AP/Wide World Photos.*

offering to remove the missiles already located on the island if President Kennedy would assure him that the United States would not invade Cuba. That same evening, Dobrynin and Attorney General Kennedy met, and Dobrynin hinted that the United States should remove the U.S. missiles located in Turkey. On Saturday morning, Khrushchev sent President Kennedy yet another letter demanding those missiles in Turkey be removed if the Soviets agreed to remove the missiles in Cuba.

Before President Kennedy could reply to either of Khrushchev's letters, more rapid-fire events turned Saturday, October 27, into "Black Saturday." It was so named because many thought it was the day the world came closest to annihilation. Two incidents occurred involving U.S. U-2 reconnaissance (spy-photography) aircraft. In the first instance, a U-2 flying over Alaska drifted into Soviet airspace. The Soviets took the incident as a test of their defense system. The second incident occurred over Cuba, where a U-2 was shot down and the pilot killed. By the afternoon, the U.S. military and various members of Congress were pressing President Kennedy hard for an immediate invasion of Cuba.

Ignoring much of the uproar and staying intensely focused, Attorney General Kennedy came up with a simple compromise. He told the president to ignore the second letter from Khrushchev and accept the terms of the first—promising Khrushchev the United States would not invade Cuba and would halt the quarantine if he removed the missiles. This was the public part of the agreement. Then, privately, Dobrynin got his assurance that the missiles in Turkey would be removed. The next morning, Sunday, October 28, Khrushchev sent a message to President Kennedy agreeing to remove the missiles from Cuba. The following is an excerpt from Khrushchev's October 28 message.

Things to remember while reading the excerpt from "Communiqué to President Kennedy Accepting an End to the Missile Crisis, October 28, 1962":

- President Kennedy was under intense U.S. military and congressional pressure to invade Cuba.

- Sergei Khrushchev (1935–), son of Nikita Khrushchev, writes in his book *Nikita Khrushchev: Creation of a Superpower,* "When Father argued at a meeting of the Soviet leadership in favor of withdrawing the missiles, he made this unprecedented statement: 'We have to help Kennedy withstand pressure from the hawks [supporters of war]. They are demanding an immediate military invasion.'" Khrushchev knew an invasion would lead to nuclear war.

- Nikita Khrushchev agreed to a U.S. president's "promise" not to invade Cuba again. According to Sergei Khrushchev, this would have been "inconceivable" only a few years earlier.

Excerpt from "Communiqué to President Kennedy Accepting an End to the Missile Crisis, October 28, 1962"

*Esteemed Mr. President: I have received your message of October 27, 1962. I express my satisfaction and gratitude for the **sense of proportion** and understanding of the responsibility **borne** by you at present for the preservation of peace throughout the world which you have shown. I very well understand your anxiety and the anxiety of the United States people in connection with the fact that the weapons which you describe as "offensive" are, in fact, grim weapons. Both you and I understand what kind of weapon they are.*

*In order to complete with greater speed the **liquidation** of the conflict dangerous to the cause of peace, to give confidence to all people longing for peace, and to calm the American people, who, I am certain, want peace as much as the people of the Soviet Union, the Soviet Government, in addition to previously issued instructions on the **cessation** of further work at building sites for the weapons, has issued a new order on the dismantling of the weapons which you describe as "offensive," and their crating and return to the Soviet Union.*

Mr. President, I would like to repeat once more what I had already written to you in my preceding letters—that the Soviet Government has placed at the disposal of the Cuban Government economic aid, as well as arms, inasmuch as Cuba and the Cuban

Esteemed: Respected.

Sense of proportion: Appreciation of the seriousness.

Borne: Carried.

Liquidation: End.

Cessation: Halting.

people have constantly been under the continuous danger of an invasion [from the United States]....

We stationed them there in order that no attack should be made against Cuba and that no rash action should be permitted to take place.

I regard with respect and trust your statement in your message of October 27, 1962, that no attack will be made on Cuba—that no invasion will take place—not only by the United States, but also by other countries of the Western Hemisphere, as your message pointed out. Then the motives which promoted us to give aid of this nature to Cuba cease. They are no longer **applicable**, hence we have instructed our officers—and these means, as I have already stated, are in the hands of Soviet officers—to take necessary measures for stopping the building of the **said projects** and their dismantling and return to the Soviet Union....

I note with satisfaction that you have responded to my wish that the said dangerous situation should be liquidated and also that conditions should be created for a more thoughtful appraisal of the

A U.S. destroyer sails near a Russian freighter in preparation for an inspection of a presumed cargo of missiles being withdrawn from Cuba in November 1962. An American patrol plane flies overhead. *Reproduced by permission of AP/Wide World Photos.*

Applicable: Relevant.

Said projects: Missile sites.

Fortieth Anniversary Meeting of Cuban Missile Crisis Participants

In mid-October 2002, forty years after the Cuban Missile Crisis, an anniversary reunion of many of those involved in the crisis convened in Havana, Cuba. Kevin Sullivan of the Washington Post Foreign Service reported on the gathering, which included the highest-level government officials and crewmen manning the ships. Sullivan wrote that President Fidel Castro (1926–) of Cuba, "his famous black beard gone thunderstorm grey ... still spoke in rambling circles ... still a master entertainer, funny and excitable." Graying Russian generals were also present and Sullivan explained, "They had not lost the Soviet gift for cement-thick oratory [speech], giving long speeches about throw-weights and tonnages," as if everyone understood such terms. Across the conference table sat the Americans, Sullivan noted: "Surviving members of President John F. Kennedy's administration were lined up like a living page from a history book." Kennedy's secretary of defense Robert S. McNamara (1916–); historian Arthur M. Schlesinger Jr. (1917–); Kennedy's speech writer Theodore C. Sorensen (1928–); Ethel Kennedy (1928–), widow of President Kennedy's brother and attorney general Robert Kennedy (1925–1968); and Kennedy's aide Richard Goodwin (1931–).

Thomas S. Blanton (1955–), director of a research group called the National Security Archive, located at George Washington University in Washington, D.C., had organized the meeting in cooperation with the Cuban government. Blanton provided the participants newly declassified documents for their review. Fascinating accounts and remembrances were shared by retired U.S. Navy captain William Ecker, seventy-eight years of age, who had piloted a low-flying F-8 fighter jet that photographed Soviet missile

*international situation which is **fraught** with great dangers in our age of thermonuclear weapons, rocket technology ... global rockets, and other lethal weapons. All people are interested in insuring peace. Therefore, we who are **invested** with trust and great responsibility must not permit an **exacerbation** of the situation and must liquidate the breeding grounds where a dangerous situation has been created fraught with serious consequences for the cause of peace. If we succeed along with you and with the aid of other people of good will in liquidating this tense situation, we must also concern ourselves to see that other dangerous conflicts do not arise which might lead to a world thermonuclear catastrophe....*

Mr. President, I trust your statement. However, on the other hand, there are responsible people who would like to carry out an in-

Fraught: Filled.

Invested: Given authority or power.

Exacerbation: Increased severity.

sites in Cuba. Likewise, former Central Intelligence Agency (CIA) analyst Dino Brugioni, eighty years of age, spoke of interpreting the first photographs from a U-2 spy plane that clearly showed Soviet missiles in Cuba. Russian attendees spoke up and said they "never intended to fire the nuclear missiles." But Brugioni bantered back that his photographs showed the warheads on trucks parked right by the missiles. The most spellbinding reminiscence Sullivan recounted came from Vadim Orlov, a crewman on a Soviet submarine in the waters around Cuba, and J. W. Peterson, a crewman on a U.S. destroyer above Orlov's submarine. Sullivan reports:

> There was pandemonium on the Soviet B-59 submarine. A U.S. destroyer was lobbing depth charges into the water as a warning: Surface or you will be attacked. The explosions pounded the sub's hull like blasts from a sledgehammer. Oxygen was running out. Crewmen were fainting.

> Tensions were extreme: It was Oct. 27, 1962, the height of the Cuban missile crisis.

> Officers on the Soviet [sub] were screaming for the captain to sink the U.S. ship. What the Americans did not know nearly blew up the world: The Soviet sub, and three others in the waters off Cuba, each carried one torpedo tipped with a nuclear warhead....

> Former defense secretary Robert S. McNamara said that a nuclear attack on a U.S. ship could easily have escalated into a full-scale nuclear exchange between the United States and the Soviet Union.

> Orlov ... said that came within one word of happening: The sub was authorized to fire its nuclear torpedo with the approval of three officers aboard; two wanted to shoot, the third said no.

> "A guy named Arkhipov saved the world," said Thomas S. Blanton."

(From "Forty Years After Missile Crisis: Players Swap Stories in Cuba," by Kevin Sullivan. Washington Post, October 13, 2002, page A28.)

---

*vasion of Cuba at this time, and in such a way to spark off a war. If we take practical steps and announce the dismantling and evacuation of the appropriate means from Cuba, then, doing that, we wish to establish at the same time the confidence of the Cuban people that we are with them and are not **divesting** ourselves of the responsibility of granting help to them.*

*We are convinced that the people of all countries, like yourself, Mr. President, will understand me correctly. We do not issue threats. We desire only peace. Our country is now on the **upsurge**. Our people are enjoying the fruits of their peaceful labor....*

*We value peace, perhaps even more than other people, because we experienced the **terrible war against Hitler**. However, our peo-*

Divesting: Freeing.

Upsurge: Rise.

Terrible war against Hitler: A reference to the invasion of the Soviet Union by Germany and its Nazi leader Adolf Hitler, during World War II.

U.S. president John F. Kennedy tells the nation that the Cuban Missile Crisis is over. *Reproduced by permission of AP/Wide World Photos.*

ple will not **flinch in the face of** any ordeal. Our people trust their government, and we assure our people and the world public that the Soviet government will not allow itself to be provoked.

Should the **provocateurs** unleash a war, they would not escape the grave consequences of such a war. However, we are confident that reason will triumph. War will not be unleashed and the peace and security of people will be insured....

With respect for you, Khrushchev. October 28, 1962.

Flinch in the face of: Shy away from.

Provocateurs: Instigators; those who stir up action.

What happened next ...

With the agreement, both sides immediately breathed easier. The U.S. military alert level went to DEFCON

5, the lowest level of military concern. Khrushchev proceeded to bring the missiles back to the Soviet Union. Both sides claimed victory. President Kennedy had achieved the goal of moving the missiles out of Cuba. Khrushchev had gotten a promise of protection for communist Cuba. As of 2003, the United States had never invaded Cuba. Both Khrushchev and Kennedy claimed victory that a nuclear war was avoided.

The primary consequence of the Cuban Missile Crisis was that the American public now believed that the Soviet Union's nuclear capabilities equalled those of the United States. Citizens would not listen to numbers that showed the United States with far more missiles. As far as Americans were concerned, each country could totally annihilate the other—or, for that matter, all life on earth. It was the last of the Cold War "missile bluff" diplomacies.

Both sides had so frightened the other during the Cuban Missile Crisis that the first serious negotiations in controlling nuclear weaponry began in August 1963. The United States, the Soviet Union, and Great Britain—which also had nuclear capabilities—signed the Limited Test-Ban Treaty to ban nuclear testing underwater, in the atmosphere, and in outer space.

Did you know ...

- For the first time in Cold War history, the two superpower leaders negotiated not with mutual public threats and propaganda but in reasoned secret personal correspondence.

- Knowing mutual dialogue and a new trust had averted a disaster for the world, President Kennedy asked the news media to tone down their shouts of victory as Khrushchev withdrew the missiles from Cuba.

- In June 1963, a direct hot line was set up between the Kremlin (Soviet government headquarters) in Moscow and the White House in Washington, D.C., to reduce the chance of nuclear war through miscalculation or misunderstanding.

Consider the following ...

- The Cuban Missile Crisis is rarely thought of in terms of positive outcomes. Find and list at least five good results or consequences (for either the Americans or the Soviets or both) stemming from the Cuban Missile Crisis.

- One of the reasons Khrushchev brought Soviet missiles to Cuba was to protect Cuba from invasion. Could this have been accomplished with less drastic tactics? What might be another underlying reason Khrushchev wanted missiles in Cuba?

- Do you think the Soviets really intended to fire the missiles at the United States? Why or why not?

For More Information

Books

Chrisp, Peter. *Cuban Missile Crisis.* Milwaukee, WI: World Almanac Library, 2002.

Finkelstein, Norman H. *Thirteen Days/Ninety Miles: The Cuban Missile Crisis.* New York: J. Messner, 1994.

Frankland, Mark. *Khrushchev.* New York: Stein and Day, 1979.

Huchthausen, Peter A., and Alexander Hoyt. *October Fury.* Hoboken, NJ: Wiley & Sons, 2002.

Khrushchev, Nikita S. Edited by Strobe Talbott. *Khrushchev Remembers.* Boston: Little, Brown, 1970.

Khrushchev, Sergei. *Nikita Khrushchev: Creation of a Superpower.* University Park: Pennsylvania State University Press, 2000.

Changing Superpower Relations in the 1970s and 1980s

9

Cold War rivalry in the 1960s was marked by dramatic tense events and often bloody hot spots. The Cold War was a prolonged conflict for world dominance from 1945 to 1991 between the two superpowers, the democratic, capitalist United States and the communist Soviet Union. The weapons of conflict were commonly words of propaganda and threats. During the John F. Kennedy (1917–1963; served 1961–63) and Lyndon B. Johnson (1908–1973; served 1963–69) presidential years from 1961 to 1969, the U.S. foreign policy of containment, to contain communism from spreading around the globe, suffered two major setbacks.

First, Soviet relations with Cuba cemented and firmly set the island nation as a communist stronghold 90 miles (145 kilometers) from the Florida coast. Second, by 1969, the Vietnam War (1954–75), a major hot spot of the Cold War, had proved unwinnable for the United States. The U.S. government consistently underestimated communist North Vietnam's will to continue fighting and overestimated the U.S. citizens' support of the war. The seemingly endless war led to President Johnson's decision not to run for reelection in

1968. Republican candidate and former vice president Richard M. Nixon (1913–1994; served 1969–74) won the November 1968 presidential election. Nixon pledged during the campaign to end U.S. involvement in Vietnam.

Although the end of the Vietnam War would not come for several years, by beginning the withdrawal process, Nixon recognized America had limits to its power to contain every occasional communist rebel group threatening to gain power in a country. In the first excerpt in this chapter, "Informal Remarks in Guam with Newsmen (Nixon Doctrine), July 25, 1969," President Nixon stressed that the United States must always be interested and involved in the Asian nations but not necessarily impose its form of government there.

By 1969, a considerable rift between the two largest communist nations, the Soviet Union and the People's Republic of China (PRC), had developed. President Nixon and national security advisor Henry Kissinger (1923–) skillfully exploited this rift, to the advantage of the United States. The Soviet Union dreaded the idea that the United States might become friendly with the PRC. That is exactly what Nixon and Kissinger set out to do. First Kissinger quietly became the first U.S. government representative to visit China since the communist takeover in 1949. Kissinger's visit paved the way for a very public visit by the president and the first lady, Pat Nixon (1912–1993) in February 1972. In the second excerpt, "Remarks at Andrews Air Force Base on Returning from the People's Republic of China, February 28, 1972," Nixon reports on his amazing visit to China.

The Soviet Union, threatened by the improved U.S.-PRC relations, decided they too must improve relations with the United States. This was the precise response Nixon and Kissinger had hoped for. Over the next few years, not only did diplomatic communications open up between the United States and China, but Nixon and Soviet premier Leonid Brezhnev (1906–1982) began a new era in U.S.-Soviet relations known as détente, or an easing of international tensions.

Détente depended on the personalities of Nixon, Kissinger, and Brezhnev. Unfortunately, détente became entangled in a web of U.S. domestic politics. In August 1974, Nixon became the first president in U.S. history to resign, after a domestic political scandal known as Watergate. The scandal stemmed from the June 1972 burglarizing of the offices of the Democratic National Committee (located in the Watergate building in Washington, D.C.) and the cover-up that followed. With the departure of Nixon, a departure that seemed totally unnecessary to the Soviets, détente began to flounder.

Vice President Gerald R. Ford (1913–; served 1974–77) replaced Nixon and maintained the policies of détente, but the Soviets were skeptical if détente would continue. Nevertheless, on August 1, 1975, President Ford, Soviet premier Brezhnev, and leaders from numerous other countries gathered in Finland to sign the Helsinki Accords. The Accords addressed geographic issues in Europe; promised cooperation in trade, cultural exchanges, and scientific areas; and dealt with humanitarian issues. Ford and Brezhnev overcame critics in their respective countries to sign the Accords. The signing was the high point of détente.

As the 1976 presidential campaign got into full swing, two key candidates, U.S. senator Henry Jackson (1912–1983) of Washington state (a Democrat) and former California governor Ronald Reagan (1911–) (a Republican) forcefully opposed détente. They convinced many Americans that détente played up Soviet strengths and U.S. weaknesses. The ultimate victor in the race was Democratic candidate Jimmy Carter (1924–; served 1977–81), former governor of Georgia. Carter had almost no foreign affairs experience and changed his approach toward the Soviets several times in his one term in office. As a result, tensions steadily heated up.

In 1980, Carter lost his reelection bid to Reagan. When Reagan took office in 1981, the superpower rivalry escalated. Reagan's campaign was full of strong anticommunist rhetoric. Historians refer to the Carter and early Reagan presidential years as the "freeze" in superpower relations. In the early 1980s, the military budgets of both the United States and the Soviet Union rose dramatically, affecting the economies of both nations.

Reagan was reelected in November 1984. Within only a few months, in March 1985, Mikhail Gorbachev (1931–) assumed leadership of the Soviet Union. Gorbachev, outgoing, intelligent, and articulate, was determined to take his country down a different path. Reagan began to listen to Gorbachev's offers of arms reduction and opening of trade relations. The two met four times between 1985 and 1988 to work out differences between the Soviet Union and the United States. Their second meeting in October 1986 in Reykjavik, Iceland, brought a common understanding toward the goal of actual reductions in nuclear weapons. In the third excerpt, "Address to the Nation on the Meetings with Soviet General Secretary Gorbachev in Iceland, October 13, 1986," Reagan reported to Americans on his meeting in Iceland with Gorbachev.

Richard M. Nixon

Excerpt from "Informal Remarks in Guam with Newsmen (Nixon Doctrine), July 25, 1969"

Originally published in *Public Papers of the Presidents of the United States: Richard M. Nixon, 1969,* **published in 1971**

Despite conflicts in Europe, particularly in Berlin, Germany, Indochina proved to be the region that consumed America's energies, finances, and resources during the mid- and late 1960s. Indochina is a region of Southeast Asia extending south from the southern border of the People's Republic of China (PRC), commonly referred to as China, along the eastern portion of a large peninsula extending into the South China Sea. Indochina comprises three countries—Vietnam, Cambodia, and Laos.

In 1954, Vietnam was divided into the communist North Vietnam and the democratic, U.S.-influenced South Vietnam. However, there was no peace in Vietnam. Immediately, communist forces began waging guerrilla warfare in the South, and the United States, by lending assistance to the South, became increasingly involved in the conflict. Between 1965 and 1968, North Vietnam received at least $2 billion in military aid and economic assistance from the Soviets and the Chinese. By 1968, over five hundred thousand U.S. troops were in Vietnam trying to keep South Vietnam from falling to the communists. Approximately fifty thousand U.S. soldiers

"As far as our role is concerned, we must avoid that kind of policy that will make countries in Asia so dependent upon us that we are dragged into conflicts such as the one that we have in Vietnam. This is going to be a difficult line to follow. It is one, however, that I think, with proper planning, we can develop."

U.S. president Richard Nixon calls on a reporter at a press conference in 1969.
Reproduced by permission of the Corbis Corporation.

lost their lives there. When Richard M. Nixon (1913–1994; served 1969–74) assumed the U.S. presidency in January 1969, he pledged to the American people, very weary of the Vietnam War (1954–75), to end U.S. involvement.

In mid-1969, Nixon nudged Americans and American foreign policy toward a new way of thinking about all of the Pacific Rim, including Asia and Indochina. By withdrawing from Vietnam, Nixon recognized that America had limits to its power. He also called to the attention of communist-fearing Americans that the communist world outside the Soviet Union was not poised to consume the United States. Instead, the communist world had many centers that sporadically rose and fell in power and were almost never joined to one another. Because Nixon understood this, the Nixon Doctrine became defined as a shift in American foreign commitments—away from immediately sending American troops to wherever a communist rebel group threatened to gain control in a country. In this excerpt from "Informal Remarks in Guam with Newsmen (Nixon Doctrine), July 25, 1969," Nixon stressed that the United States must be highly involved in the Pacific Rim and develop a "long-range view" there. (Guam is a territory of the United States located in the Mariana Islands of the southwest Pacific region.) At the same time, the United States would no longer be the world's policeman and hoped to never again be involved in a Vietnamlike entanglement.

Things to remember while reading the excerpt from "Informal Remarks in Guam with Newsmen (Nixon Doctrine), July 25, 1969":

- Major U.S. conflicts generally radiated from the Pacific Rim area—an attack on Pearl Harbor, Hawaii, by Japan threw the United States into World War II (1939–45). The Korean War (1950–53) and Vietnam War both occurred in Asia.

- Thinking along more peaceful lines, much of the Pacific Rim was experiencing dramatic economic growth that could present the U.S. economy with great trade potential.

Excerpt from "Informal Remarks in Guam with Newsmen (Nixon Doctrine), July 25, 1969"

UNITED STATES ROLE IN ASIA

Now, insofar as this phase of the trip is concerned, and I will speak first to the Asian phase … I think what would be of greatest interest to you before we go to your questions is to give you the perspective that I have with regard to Asia and America's role in Asia.

As you know, my background here goes back a few years. It was in 1953 that I first visited this area. That trip was very extensive.… It provided an opportunity to meet the leaders, but more than that to know the countries in a very effective way.…

Now, a word about what is a very consuming interest in Asia. A consuming interest, I say, because it is one that I have had for a number of years, and one that now, as I look at the perspective of history, becomes even more imperative.

The United States is going to be facing, we hope before too long—no one can say how long, but before too long—a major decision: What will be its role in Asia and in the Pacific after the end of the war in Vietnam? We will be facing that decision, but also the Asian nations will be wondering about what that decision is.

When I talked to Prime Minister [John Grey] Gorton [of Australia], for example, he indicated, in the conversations he had had with a number of Asian leaders, they all wondered whether the United States, because of its frustration over the war in Vietnam, because of its earlier frustration over the war in Korea—whether the United States would continue to play a significant role in Asia, … whether we would withdraw from the Pacific and play a minor role.

This is a decision that will have to be made, of course, as the war comes to an end. But the time to develop the thinking which will *go into that decision is now. I think that one of the weaknesses in American foreign policy is that too often we react rather **precipitately** to events as they occur. We fail to have the perspective and the long-range view which is essential for a policy that will be **viable**....*

I am convinced that the way to avoid becoming involved in another war in Asia is for the United States to continue to play a significant role.... Whether we like it or not, geography makes us a Pacific power.

Also, as we look over the historical perspective, while World War II began in Europe, for the United States it began in the Pacific. It came from Asia. The Korean war came from Asia. The Vietnamese war came from Asia.

So, as we consider our past history, the United States involvement in war so often has been tied to our Pacific policy, or our lack of a Pacific policy, as the case might be.

*As we look at Asia today, we see that the major world power which adopts a very aggressive attitude and a **belligerent** attitude in its foreign policy, Communist China, of course, is in Asia, and we find that the two minor world powers—minor, although they do have significant strength as we have learned—that most greatly threaten the peace of the world, that adapt the most belligerent foreign policy, are in Asia, North Korea and, of course, North Vietnam.*

When we consider those factors we, I think, realize that if we are thinking down the road, down the long road—not just 4 years, 5 years, but 10, 15, or 20—that if we are going to have peace in the world, that potentially the greatest threat to that peace will be in the Pacific.

I do not mean to suggest that the Mideast is not a potential threat to the peace of the world and that there are not problems in Latin America that concern us, or in Africa and, of course, over it all, we see the great potential conflict between the United States and the Soviet Union, the East-West conflict between the two super powers.

But as far as those other areas are concerned, the possibility of finding some kind of solution, I think is potentially greater than it is in the Asian area.

*Pursuing that line of reasoning a bit further then, I would like to put it in a more positive sense: When we look at the problems in Asia, the threat to peace that is presented by the growing power of Communist China, the belligerence of North Korea and North Vietnam, we should not let that **obscure** the great promise that is here.*

Precipitately: Quickly and thoughtlessly.

Viable: Workable for the long term.

Belligerent: Warlike.

Obscure: Hide.

*As I have often said, the fastest rate of growth in the world is occurring in non-Communist Asia. Japan, in the last 10 years, has tripled its **GNP**; South Korea has doubled its GNP; Taiwan has doubled its GNP; Thailand has doubled its GNP. The same is true of Singapore and of Malaysia....*

So, what I am trying to suggest is this: As we look at Asia, it poses, in my view, over the long haul, looking down to the end of the century, the greatest threat to the peace of the world, and, for that reason the United States should continue to play a significant role. It also poses, it seems to me, the greatest hope for progress in the world....

We must recognize that there are two great, new factors which you will see, a very great growth of nationalism ... national pride is becoming a major factor, regional pride is becoming a major factor.

The second factor is one that is going to, I believe, have a major impact on the future of Asia, and it is something that we must take into account. Asians will say in every country that we visit that they do not want to be dictated to from the outside, Asia for the Asians. And that is what we want, and that is the role we should play. We should assist, but we should not dictate.

At this time, the political and economic plans that they are gradually developing are very hopeful. We will give assistance to those plans. We, of course, will keep the treaty commitments that we have.

But as far as our role is concerned, we must avoid that kind of policy that will make countries in Asia so dependent upon us that we are dragged into conflicts such as the one that we have in Vietnam.

This is going to be a difficult line to follow. It is one, however, that I think, with proper planning, we can develop.

What happened next ...

Holding his promise to end U.S. involvement in Vietnam, Nixon had dispatched national security advisor Henry Kissinger (1923–) for secret negotiations with the communist North Vietnamese to end the war. The talks were not produc-

GNP: Gross national product, the value of goods and services produced by a nation during a given period of time.

tive, so Nixon and Kissinger looked to the Soviet Union and China to help in bringing an end to the war. In reality, in spite of their military aid to the North, neither had much influence over the North Vietnamese. U.S. military leaders became convinced the only way to end the conflict was to destroy the North supply lines originating in the neighboring countries of Cambodia and Laos. Secret bombing commenced but did not remain secret for long. Shocked and outraged, many Americans viewed this action as an escalation of the war rather than as a beginning to an end. Nevertheless, by October 1972, secret peace talks became more productive. On January 27, 1973, a cease-fire went into effect. The last U.S. soldiers left Vietnam on March 29. The relentless North Vietnamese, however, took to the offensive again and gained control of the South by early 1975. The war then ended as the communists gained control of all of Vietnam.

Did you know ...

- The bombing in Cambodia and Laos led to violent outbursts on America's college campuses. Four students were killed at Kent State University in Kent, Ohio, in May 1970 when national guardsmen opened fire on antiwar protesters.

- Laos and Cambodia also fell to the communists, but the communist spread then halted as it came up against more prosperous countries such as Thailand. The Nixon Doctrine appeared vindicated. Communism would not devour all of Asia.

- The United States became a major player in the booming Asian economies, as President Nixon had hoped.

Consider the following ...

- Consider the involvement of the U.S. economy with Asia at the beginning of the twenty-first century. Explain how the Nixon Doctrine, despite its critics in the United States, appears to have been very farsighted.

- The United States did not become involved in another major military conflict using air and ground troops until the Persian Gulf War of 1991. Think of the Korean War, the Vietnam War, and the Nixon Doctrine to offer some reasons why.

For More Information

Books

Ambrose, Stephen E. *Nixon.* 3 vols. New York: Simon & Schuster, 1987–1991.

Anderson, David L. *The Columbia Guide to the Vietnam War.* New York: Columbia University Press, 2002.

Berman, Larry. *No Peace, No Honor: Nixon, Kissinger, and Betrayal in Vietnam.* New York: Free Press, 2001.

Herring, George C. *America's Longest War: The United States and Vietnam, 1950–1975.* 2nd ed. New York: Knopf, 1988.

Isaacson, Walter. *Kissinger: A Biography.* New York: Simon & Schuster, 1992.

Kissinger, Henry. *Diplomacy.* New York: Simon & Schuster, 1996.

Public Papers of the Presidents of the United States: Richard M. Nixon, 1969. Washington, DC: U.S. Government Printing Office, 1971.

Web Site

The Richard Nixon Library and Birthplace. http://www.nixonfoundation. org (accessed on September 20, 2003).

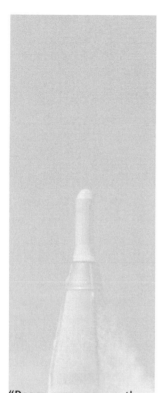

Richard M. Nixon

Excerpt from "Remarks at Andrews Air Force Base on Returning from the People's Republic of China, February 28, 1972"

Originally published in *Public Papers of the Presidents of the United States: Richard M. Nixon, 1972*, published in 1974

"Peace means more than the mere absence of war. In a technical sense, we were at peace with the People's Republic of China before this trip, but a gulf of almost 12,000 miles and 22 years of noncommunication and hostility separated [us].... We have started the long process of building a bridge across that gulf...."

While U.S. president Richard M. Nixon (1913–1994; served 1969–74) in 1969 and 1970 was trying to remove the United States from the Vietnam War (1954–75), tensions between the People's Republic of China (PRC), or simply China, and the Soviet Union were at an all-time high. Along their 3,000-mile (4,828-kilometer) common border, sporadic fighting broke out between Soviet and Chinese troops. Soviet leader Leonid Brezhnev (1906–1982) had introduced the Brezhnev Doctrine, which proclaimed the right of the Soviet Union to intervene in the internal affairs of any other communist country. The Chinese angrily assumed the Soviets included them under this doctrine. China was also displeased that the Soviets had not shared in any meaningful way industrial and military technology.

To take advantage of the rocky relationship between the world's two largest communist countries, President Nixon secretly sent his national security advisor, Henry Kissinger (1923–), to Warsaw, Poland, in 1970 to meet with Chinese officials. Fearful of Soviet aggression, China was eager to improve relations with the powerful United States. Believing China was

supplying the communist North Vietnamese with weapons, President Nixon hoped China could be persuaded to halt the supplies so that he could pull out U.S. troops faster. Both Nixon and Kissinger believed that if the Soviets thought the United States and China were becoming allies, then the Soviets would also push for better relations with the United States.

Kissinger's secret talks led the way for a visit to China by the president and the first lady, Pat Nixon (1912–1993) in February 1972. Portions of the visit were televised back to the United States. In this excerpt, Nixon had just returned to Washington, D.C., aboard *Air Force One*. Nixon describes agreements between the United States and China announced in a joint communiqué, or statement. The joint statement was released to the Chinese in Shanghai, China, and to Americans by the White House.

Nixon's only disappointment with the meeting was that the Chinese did not agree to halt support for the North

Vietnamese. As a result of the open communications, however, tensions over the Vietnam War as well as over the Nationalist Chinese government located in Taiwan since 1949 were greatly lessened.

Things to remember while reading the excerpt from "Remarks at Andrews Air Force Base on Returning from the People's Republic of China, February 28, 1972":

- There had been no communication between the People's Republic of China and the United States in twenty-two years, since the communist takeover in 1949.

- It was obvious Nixon had applied his Nixon Doctrine (see earlier excerpt in this chapter) when he stated that the United States was opposed to "domination of the Pacific area by any one power" and that the United States would broaden cultural exchanges, trade, and further communications with China. Nixon had stressed that the United States must be highly involved in the Pacific area nations, but should no longer be the world's policeman.

- Nixon and Chinese leader Mao Zedong (1893–1976) communicated despite vastly different fundamental philosophies of how people should be allowed to live.

Excerpt from "Remarks at Andrews Air Force Base on Returning from the People's Republic of China, February 28, 1972"

Mr. Vice President, members of the Congress, members of the Cabinet, members of the diplomatic corps, and ladies and gentlemen:

Because of the superb efforts of the hardworking members of the press who accompanied us—they got even less sleep than I did—millions of Americans in this past week have seen more of China than I did. Consequently, tonight I would like to talk to you

not about what we saw but about what we did, to sum up the results of the trip and to put it in perspective.

When I announced this trip last July, I described it as a journey for peace. In the last 30 years, Americans have in three different wars gone off by the hundreds of thousands to fight, and some to die, in Asia and in the Pacific. One of the central motives behind my journey to China was to prevent that from happening a fourth time to another generation of Americans.

As I have often said, peace means more than the mere absence of war. In a technical sense, we were at peace with the People's Republic of China before this trip, but a gulf of almost 12,000 miles and 22 years of noncommunication and hostility separated the United States of America from the 750 million people who live in the People's Republic of China, and that is one-fourth of all the people in the world.

As a result of this trip, we have started the long process of building a bridge across that gulf, and even now we have something bet-

U.S. secretary of state William Rogers (left) sits next to President Richard Nixon and Chinese leader Zhou Enlai at a meeting in Peking, China, in February 1972. *Reproduced by permission of AP/Wide World Photos.*

ter than the mere absence of war. Not only have we completed a week of intensive talks at the highest levels, we have set up a procedure whereby we can continue to have discussions in the future. We have demonstrated that nations with very deep and fundamental differences can learn to discuss those differences calmly, rationally, and frankly, without compromising their principles. This is the basis of a structure for peace, where we can talk about differences rather than fight about them.

The primary goal of this trip was to reestablish communication with the People's Republic of China after a generation of hostility. We achieved that goal.

Let me turn now to our joint communiqué.

We did not bring back any written or unwritten agreements that will guarantee peace in our time. We did not bring home any magic formula which will make unnecessary the efforts of the American people to continue to maintain the strength so that we can continue to be free.

We made some necessary and important beginnings, however, in several areas. We entered into agreements to expand cultural, educational, and journalistic contacts between the Chinese and the American people. We agreed to work to begin and broaden trade between our two countries. We have agreed that the communications that have now been established between our governments will be strengthened and expanded.

Most important, we have agreed on some rules of international conduct which will reduce the risk of confrontation and war in Asia and in the Pacific.

We agreed that we are opposed to domination of the Pacific area by any one power. We agreed that international disputes should be settled without the use of the threat of force and we agreed that we are prepared to apply this principle to our mutual relations.

With respect to Taiwan [the noncommunist Republic of China located on the island of Taiwan], *we stated our established policy that our forces overseas will be reduced gradually as tensions ease, and that our ultimate objective is to withdraw our forces as a peaceful settlement is achieved.*

We have agreed that we will not negotiate the fate of other nations behind their backs, and we did not do so at Peking. There were no secret deals of any kind. We have done all this without giving up any United States commitment to any other country.

In our talks, the talks that I had with the leaders of the People's Republic and that the Secretary of State had with the office of the Government of the People's Republic in the foreign affairs area, we both realized that a bridge of understanding that spans almost 12,000 miles and 22 years of hostility can't be built in one week of discussions. But we have agreed to begin to build that bridge, recognizing that our work will require years of patient effort. We made no attempt to pretend that major differences did not exist between our two governments, because they do exist.

*This communique was unique in honestly setting forth differences rather than trying to cover them up with diplomatic **doubletalk**....*

We hope ... this journey for peace will grow and prosper into a more enduring structure for peace and security in the Western Pacific.

But peace is too urgent to wait for centuries. We must seize the moment to move toward that goal now, and this is what we have done on this journey.

As I am sure you realize, it was a great experience for us to see the timeless wonders of ancient China, the changes that are being made in modern China. And one fact stands out, among many others, from my talks with the Chinese leaders: It is their total belief, their total dedication, to their system of government. That is their right, just as it is the right of any country to choose the kind of government it wants.

But as I return from this trip, just as has been the case on my return from other trips abroad which have taken me to over 80 countries, I come back to America with an even stronger faith in our system of government.

As I flew across America today, all the way from Alaska, over the Rockies, the Plains, and then on to Washington, I thought of the greatness of our country and, most of all, I thought of the freedom, the opportunity, the progress that 200 million Americans are privileged to enjoy. I realized again this is a beautiful country. And tonight my prayer and my hope is that as a result of this trip, our children will have a better chance to grow up in a peaceful world.

Thank you.

Doubletalk: Deliberate use of unclear or evasive language.

What happened next ...

Nixon's historic China trip was a turning point in the Cold War. The Cold War was a prolonged conflict for world dominance from 1945 to 1991 between the two superpowers, the democratic, capitalist United States and the communist Soviet Union. The weapons of conflict were commonly words of propaganda and threats. Nixon's trip paved the way for full diplomatic relations with China seven years later in 1979. Cultural exchanges of educators and planning of tourist travel began. The most important immediate effect was that the Soviet Union felt a great deal of pressure with a U.S.-China alignment.

Kissinger continued his secret, so-called "back door" trips. This time, he went to Moscow both to speak of peace talks on Vietnam and to discuss points of U.S.-Soviet disagreement in the Strategic Arms Limitation Talks (SALT I). Just as he had in China, Kissinger paved the way for President Nixon to visit Moscow in what would be another historic meeting. Nixon went to Moscow even though he knew the Soviets were arming the North Vietnamese and although he had just ordered another heavy bombing campaign against Hanoi, the capital of North Vietnam. Nixon and Brezhnev met in Moscow on May 22, 1972. They signed the SALT I treaty for the first time, scaling back the arms race by setting limits on the numbers of certain weapons. The costs of the arms race were fast becoming overwhelming for both countries. They significantly reduced the chance of nuclear war by establishing a working relationship between the United States and the Soviet Union.

Did you know ...

- Almost one-fourth of the population of the world lived in China at the time.

- Nixon, as a young congressman in the late 1940s and 1950s, had staked his early reputation on fierce anticommunism. In 1972, he toasted leaders of the two largest communist nations. Political times change and Nixon adapted.

- The most famous scene brought to Americans of the China trip was President and Mrs. Nixon walking along the Great Wall of China with other Chinese and U.S. government officials.

Consider the following ...

- Find in the excerpt and then list all areas where the United States and China made communicative progress at the February meeting.

- What did Nixon stress as his number one reason for traveling to China?

- Research the life of Henry Kissinger and his role in diplomacy during the Cold War.

For More Information

Books

Aitken, Jonathan. *Nixon: A Life*. London: Weidenfeld and Nicolson, 1993.

Jian, Chen. *Mao's China and the Cold War*. Chapel Hill: University of North Carolina Press, 2001.

Keith, Ronald C. *The Diplomacy of Zhou Enlai*. New York: Macmillan, 1989.

Kissinger, Henry. *The White House Years*. Boston: Little, Brown, 1979.

Nixon, Richard M. *The Memoirs of Richard Nixon*. New York: Grosset and Dunlap, 1978.

Public Papers of the Presidents of the United States: Richard M. Nixon, 1972. Washington, DC: U.S. Government Printing Office, 1974.

Schaller, Michael. *The United States and China: Into the 21st Century*. 3rd ed. New York: Oxford University Press, 2002.

Spence, Jonathan D. *Mao Zedong*. New York: Viking, 1999.

Thornton, Richard C. *The Nixon-Kissinger Years: Reshaping America's Foreign Policy*. New York: Paragon House, 1989.

Ronald Reagan

Excerpt from "Address to the Nation on the Meetings with Soviet General Secretary Gorbachev in Iceland, October 13, 1986"

Originally published in *Public Papers of the Presidents of the United States: Ronald Reagan, 1986, Book 2*, published in 1989

"The implications of these talks are enormous.... We proposed the most sweeping ... arms control proposal in history. We offered the complete elimination of all ballistic missiles—Soviet and American—from the face of the Earth by 1996. While we parted company with this American offer still on the table, we are closer than ever before to agreements that could lead to a safer world without nuclear weapons."

With the Watergate scandal–driven resignation of U.S. president Richard M. Nixon (1913–1994; served 1969–74), the erratic foreign policies of President Jimmy Carter (1924–; served 1977–81), and the strong anticommunist stance of President Ronald Reagan (1911–; served 1981–89), U.S.-Soviet relations in the early 1980s were in a deep freeze. Détente, an easing of international tensions, had long stalled. Both the United States and the Soviet Union were spending vast sums on the military arms race.

U.S.-Soviet arms-reduction talks had stalled by the early 1980s. A key reason was a proposed new U.S. missile system called the Strategic Defense Initiative (SDI). The new missile system was announced by President Reagan in March 1983. It became commonly known as the "Star Wars" project, named after the popular science-fiction movie of the time, because SDI involved a protective shield of laser-armed satellites in space. Together the missile, rockets, and laser beams would search out and destroy enemy missiles fired toward U.S. targets. The project would require vast sums of money, would be highly complex, and quite possibly might not work. Reagan persisted with the Star Wars project, even though the Soviets would feel compelled to develop a similar system despite the severe strain that would put on their weak economy. Soviet premier Yuri Andropov (1914–1984) charged that Star Wars violated the Outer Space Treaty of 1967. Disgruntled, he proclaimed that the arms race now had no bounds. The year 1983 was one of great tension in the Cold War superpower rivalry.

The SDI program and other arms development programs gave President Reagan an increasing sense of U.S. nuclear superiority and a feeling of security. The overall result was that Reagan, negotiating from his position of strength, became a bit more accommodating toward the Soviets. Also, the November 1984 presidential election campaign was heating up. Under pressure from opposing Democratic candidates for president, Reagan realized he must soften his approach somewhat and commit to arms control talks if he had hopes of Congress funding his massive Star Wars program and hopes of reelection.

In February 1984, Andropov died and was replaced by another old-guard Soviet communist leader, Konstantin Chernenko (1911–1985). Chernenko was not eager to negotiate with Reagan. He wanted to see if Reagan was going to win reelection that fall. He did—by easily defeating former vice president Walter Mondale (1928–)—and he began his second term in January 1985. Not long afterwards, Chernenko died on March 10. The U.S.S.R.'s series of aging communist leaders, fiercely anti–United States, and unable to halt the economic state of stagnation in the Soviet Union, came to an end. By late evening on March 10, the Politburo, the key policy-making body of the Soviet Communist Party, elected fifty-four-year-old Mikhail Gorbachev (1931–) to lead the Soviet Union.

Vice President George Bush (1924–) and Secretary of State George Shultz (1920–) represented the United States at Chernenko's funeral. While in Moscow, they spoke with Gorbachev. Upon returning to the United States, Bush and Shultz informed Reagan that significant changes for the Soviet Union were on the horizon. They believed Gorbachev was a Soviet leader that they could possibly work with.

Gorbachev adopted a plan for Soviet economic recovery and opened up Soviet society to greater freedom of expression. To get his economic recovery program underway, he cut back economic aid to Third World nations, including

Reagan's Early Tough Talk About the Soviets

In January 1981, Republican Ronald Reagan was inaugurated as the fortieth president of the United States. Reagan had spoken in fiercely anticommunist rhetoric during his campaign. With no desire to bargain with the Soviets on arms control or anything else, he held a hard-line stance in the early years of his presidency. To illustrate this stance, he labeled the Soviet Union the "focus of evil in the modern world." His "focus of evil" speech was made to a national convention of ministers on March 8, 1983. The following is an excerpt containing his famous words:

Whatever sad episodes exist in our past, any objective observer must hold a positive view of American history, a history that has been the story of hopes fulfilled and dreams made into reality. Especially in this century, America has kept alight the torch of freedom, but not just for ourselves but for millions of others around the world.

And this brings me to my final point today. During my first press confer-ence as President, in answer to a direct question, I pointed out that, as good Marxist-Leninists, the Soviet leaders have openly and publicly declared that the only morality they recognize is that which will further their cause, which is world revolution. I think I should point out I was only quoting Lenin, their guiding spirit, who said in 1920 that they repudiate all morality that proceeds from supernatural ideas—that's their name for religion.

This doesn't mean we should isolate ourselves and refuse to seek an understanding with them. I intend to do everything I can to persuade them of our peaceful intent, to remind them that it was the West that refused to use its nuclear monopoly in the forties and fifties for territorial gain and which now proposes a 50 percent cut in strategic ballistic missiles and the elimination of an entire class of land-based, intermediate-range nuclear missiles.

At the same time, however, they must be made to understand we will never compromise our principles and standards. We will never give away our freedom. We will never abandon our belief in God. And

Nicaragua, Cambodia, Angola, and Ethiopia. (Third World countries are poor underdeveloped or economically developing nations in Africa, Asia, and Latin America.) Gorbachev began withdrawing Soviet troops from Afghanistan. The Soviets had tried to prop up a procommunist government in Afghanistan but had become entangled in an unsuccessful decade-long conflict that resembled the earlier U.S. involvement in Vietnam. Gorbachev then boldly proposed an end to the arms race and an end to the Cold War. He desired immediate talks with President Reagan. With most Soviets living in relative poverty, Gorbachev knew that the only way to begin significant social we will never stop searching for a genuine peace....

Yes, let us pray for the salvation of all of those who live in that totalitarian darkness [those who live under a government that does not allow differing opinions and exercises total control over all aspects of an individual's life]—pray they will discover the joy of knowing God. But until they do, let us be aware that while they preach the supremacy [highest authority] of the state, declare its omnipotence [all-powerful force or quality] over individual man, and predict its eventual domination of all peoples on the Earth, they are the focus of evil in the modern world.

While America's military strength is important, let me add here that I've always maintained that the struggle now going on for the world will never be decided by bombs or rockets, by armies or military might. The real crisis we face today is a spiritual one; at root, it is a test of moral will and faith.

I believe we shall rise to the challenge. I believe that communism is another sad, bizarre chapter in human history whose last pages even now are being written. I believe this because the source of our strength in the quest for human freedom is not material, but spiritual. And because it knows no limitation, it must terrify and ultimately triumph over those who would enslave their fellow man.

God bless you, and thank you very much.

Nineteen years after Reagan's remarks, U.S. president George W. Bush (1946–; served 2001–) made similar remarks in front of the U.S. Congress concerning what he called the "axis of evil" in 2002—Iraq, Iran, and North Korea. Bush had harkened back to wording used during World War II (1939–45)—the Axis powers referring to U.S. enemies Germany, Italy, and Japan—and to Reagan's Cold War words.

(Excerpt from "Remarks at the Annual Convention of the National Association of Evangelicals, in Orlando, Florida, March 8, 1983." Published in *Public Papers of the Presidents of the United States: Ronald Reagan, 1983, Book 1, January 1 to July 1, 1983*. Washington, DC: U.S. Government Printing Office.)

changes was to end the arms race with the United States that drained much of the Soviets' economic resources.

Reagan, still suspicious of Soviet intentions, met first with Gorbachev in Geneva, Switzerland, in November 1985. The meeting was designed primarily to build confidence and a personal relationship between the leaders. One year later, the two met again, in October 1986, in Reykjavik, Iceland. To the Americans' surprise, Gorbachev proposed a broad detailed plan to reduce arms. A major obstacle, however, continued to be Reagan's Star Wars program. Despite this obstacle, some as-

U.S. president Ronald
Reagan (left) grimly walks
alongside Soviet leader
Mikhail Gorbachev
following a disappointing
close to their October 1986
summit in Reykjavik,
Iceland. Gorbachev
continued to insist that
Reagan and the Americans
do away with their Star
Wars missile program, to
which Reagan would not
agree. *Reproduced by
permission of the Corbis
Corporation.*

tounding common understandings were personally reached between Reagan and Gorbachev at Reykjavik. These included a
desire to eliminate all intermediate-range missiles located in
Europe, to eliminate all ballistic missiles over a ten-year period,
and to make other major reductions involving bombers and
tactical (short-range) weapons. The two leaders left Iceland dis-
appointed that they did not accomplish more, but they looked
forward to figuring out how to accomplish these goals. The following excerpt is from a televised address by Reagan to the
American people reporting on the progress made at Reykjavik.

Things to remember while reading the excerpt from "Address to the Nation on the Meetings with Soviet General Secretary Gorbachev in Iceland, October 13, 1986":

- Only three years earlier, the arms race had appeared to
  have no limits.

- For the first time, the two superpower leaders talked of actually eliminating entire classes of nuclear weapons.

- If the United States actually developed a working Star Wars defense shield, then it could attack the Soviet Union with no fear of Soviet retaliation. Economically, the Soviets had no hope of developing such a program on their own, so they had to continue serious negotiations with the United States.

Excerpt from "Address to the Nation on the Meetings with Soviet General Secretary Gorbachev in Iceland, October 13, 1986"

Good evening. As most of you know, I've just returned from meetings in Iceland with the leader of the Soviet Union, General Secretary Gorbachev. As I did last year when I returned from the summit conference in Geneva [the first summit meeting between Reagan and Gorbachev in 1985], *I want to take a few moments tonight to share with you what took place in these discussions. The implications of these talks are enormous and only just beginning to be understood. We proposed the most sweeping and generous arms control proposal in history. We offered the complete elimination of all **ballistic missiles**—Soviet and American—from the face of the Earth by 1996. While we parted company with this American offer still on the table, we are closer than ever before to agreements that could lead to a safer world without nuclear weapons....*

Before I report on our talks, though, allow me to set the stage by explaining two things that were very much a part of our talks: one a treaty and the other a defense against nuclear missiles, which we're trying to develop. Now, you've heard their titles a thousand times—the ABM treaty [signed in 1972 with both sides agreeing to limit the number of antiballistic missiles—defensive missiles to shoot down incoming offensive missiles] *and SDI. Well, those letters stand for ABM, antiballistic missile; SDI, Strategic Defense Initiative* ["Star Wars" program]....

So, here we are at Iceland for our second such meeting. In the first, and in the months in between, we have discussed ways to reduce and in fact eliminate nuclear weapons entirely....

Ballistic missiles: Nuclear-tipped missiles capable of being programmed to hit specific targets by taking an arcing path.

*But by their choice, the main subject was arms control. We discussed the **emplacement** of intermediate-range missiles in Europe and Asia and seemed to be in agreement they could be drastically reduced. Both sides seemed willing to find a way to reduce, even to zero, the strategic ballistic missiles we have aimed at each other. This then brought up the subject of SDI.*

*I offered a proposal that we continue our present research. And if and when we reached the stage of testing, we would sign, now, a treaty that would permit Soviet observation of such tests. And if the program was practical, we would both eliminate our **offensive missiles**, and then we would share the **benefits** of advanced defenses. I explained that even though we would have done away with our offensive ballistic missiles, having the defense would protect against cheating or the possibility of a madman, sometime, deciding to create nuclear missiles. After all, the world now knows how to make them. I likened it to our keeping our gas masks, even though the nations of the world had outlawed poison gas after World War I. We seemed to be making progress on reducing weaponry, although the General Secretary was registering opposition to SDI and proposing a pledge to observe ABM for a number of years as the day was ending....*

*The Soviets had asked for a 10-year delay in the **deployment** of SDI programs. In an effort to see how we could satisfy their concerns— while protecting our principles and security—we proposed a 10-year period in which we began with the reduction of all strategic nuclear arms, bombers, air-launched **cruise missiles**, intercontinental ballistic missiles, submarine-launched ballistic missiles and the weapons they carry. They would be reduced 50 percent in the first 5 years. During the next 5 years, we would continue by eliminating all remaining offensive ballistic missiles, of all ranges. And during that time, we would proceed with research, development, and testing of SDI—all done in conformity with ABM provisions. At the 10-year point, with all ballistic missiles eliminated, we could proceed to deploy advanced defenses, at the same time permitting the Soviets to do likewise.*

And here the debate began. The General Secretary wanted wording that, in effect, would have kept us from developing the SDI for the entire 10 years. In effect, he was killing SDI. And unless I agreed, all that work toward eliminating nuclear weapons would go down the drain—canceled. I told him I had pledged to the American people that I would not trade away SDI, there was no way I could tell our people their government would not protect them against nuclear destruction. I went to Reykjavik determined that everything was

Emplacement: Placement.

Offensive missiles: Missiles primarily intended to destroy each other.

Benefits: Technological knowledge.

Deployment: Strategic placement.

Cruise missiles: Long-range, jet-propelled missiles guided by remote control.

negotiable except two things: our freedom and our future. I'm still optimistic that a way will be found. The door is open, and the opportunity to begin eliminating the nuclear threat is within reach.

So you can see, we made progress in Iceland. And we will continue to make progress if we pursue a **prudent**, deliberate, and above all, realistic approach with the Soviets. From the earliest days of our administration this has been our policy. We made it clear we had no illusions about the Soviets or their ultimate intentions. We were publicly **candid** about the critical, moral distinctions between **totalitarianism** and democracy. We declared the principal objective of American foreign policy to be not just the prevention of war, but the extension of freedom. And we stressed our commitment to the growth of democratic government and democratic institutions around the world. And that's why we assisted freedom fighters who are resisting the **imposition** of totalitarian rule in Afghanistan, Nicaragua, Angola, Cambodia, and elsewhere. And finally, we began work on what I believe most spurred the Soviets to negotiate seriously: rebuilding our military strength, reconstructing our strategic deterrence, and above all, beginning work on the Strategic Defense Initiative....

I realize some Americans may be asking tonight: Why not accept Mr. Gorbachev's demand? Why not give up SDI for this agreement? Well, the answer, my friends, is simple. SDI is America's insurance policy that the Soviet Union would keep the commitments made at Reykjavik. SDI is America's security guarantee if the Soviets should—as they have done too often in the past—fail to comply with their solemn commitments. SDI is what brought the Soviets back to arms control talks at Geneva and Iceland. SDI is the key to a world without nuclear weapons. The Soviets understand this. They have devoted far more resources, for a lot longer time than we, to their own SDI. The world's only operational missile defense today surrounds Moscow, the capital of the Soviet Union.

What Mr. Gorbachev was demanding at Reykjavik was that the United States agree to a new version of a 14-year-old ABM treaty that the Soviet Union has already violated. I told him we don't make those kinds of deals in the United States. And the American people should reflect on these critical questions: How does a defense of the United States threaten the Soviet Union or anyone else? Why are the Soviets so **adamant** that America remain forever vulnerable to Soviet rocket attack? As of today, all free nations are utterly defenseless against Soviet missiles—fired either by accident or design. Why does the Soviet Union insist that we remain so—forever?

Prudent: Wise.

Candid: Honest.

Totalitarianism: A highly centralized form of government that has total control over the population.

Imposition: Forced burden.

Adamant: Determined.

So, my fellow Americans, I cannot promise, nor can any President promise, that the talks in Iceland or any future discussion with Mr. Gorbachev will lead inevitably to great breakthroughs or momentous treaty signing....

So, if there's one impression I carry away with me from these October talks, it is that, unlike the past, we're dealing now from a position of strength. And for that reason, we have it within our grasp to move speedily with the Soviets toward even more breakthroughs.... So, there's reason, good reason for hope. I saw evidence of this in the progress we made in the talks with Mr. Gorbachev.

What happened next ...

In February 1987, Gorbachev dropped all his demands that Reagan abandon Star Wars. That cleared the way for removing all intermediate-range nuclear force (INF) missiles in Europe, both U.S. missiles aimed at the Soviets and Soviet missiles in Eastern Europe aimed at the United States. Reagan and Gorbachev signed the historic INF Treaty on December 8, 1987, in Washington, D.C., at their third meeting.

For their fourth meeting, Reagan went to Moscow in June 1988 to show support for Gorbachev's domestic reform in the Soviet Union. It was the first visit of a U.S. president to Moscow in fourteen years, since Richard Nixon visited in 1974. In December 1988, Gorbachev traveled to New York City to speak before the United Nations' General Assembly. There, he gave a dramatic speech promoting democracy and individual liberty (see next chapter). The Cold War was indeed winding down.

Did you know ...

• Under the INF treaty, the United States would destroy 850 missiles and dismantle approximately 1,000 nuclear warheads. The Soviet Union would destroy 1,800 missiles and 3,000 nuclear warheads.

- On July 25, 1988, Soviet foreign minister Eduard Shevardnadze (1928–) made the startling and sweeping statement that the entire decades-old arms race with the United States was a massively mistaken policy.

- Ultimately, Congress refused to adequately fund Star Wars and it died with the Cold War.

Once foes, Soviet leader Mikhail Gorbachev (left) and U.S. president Ronald Reagan developed a close relationship. *Photograph by Bill FitzPatrick. Reproduced by permission of Getty Images.*

Consider the following ...

- Although under criticism from many in the United States, Reagan insisted on his Star Wars program. List the various reasons he may have had for this determination. Also list reasons why many opposed it.

- What are the major reasons Gorbachev chose to pursue serious arms elimination talks?

- Consider and write down your reflections on what emotions must have been involved as Reagan and Gorbachev, leaders of nations that had been bitter enemies for forty years, sat down for talks.

For More Information

Books

Fischer, Beth A. *The Reagan Reversal: Foreign Policy and the End of the Cold War.* Columbia: University of Missouri Press, 1997.

FitzGerald, Frances. *Way Out There in the Blue: Reagan, Stars Wars, and the End of the Cold War.* New York: Simon and Schuster, 2000.

Gorbachev, Mikhail. *Memoirs.* New York: Doubleday, 1995.

Gorbachev, Mikhail. *Perestroika: New Thinking for Our Country and the World.* New York: Harper & Row, 1987.

Mandelbaum, Michael, and Strobe Talbott. *Reagan and Gorbachev.* New York: Vintage Books, 1987.

McCauley, Martin. *Gorbachev.* New York: Longman, 1998.

Public Papers of the Presidents of the United States: Ronald Reagan, 1986, Book 2. Washington, DC: U.S. Government Printing Office, 1989.

Winik, Jay. *On the Brink: The Dramatic, Behind-the-Scenes Saga of the Reagan Era and the Men and Women Who Won the Cold War.* New York: Simon and Schuster, 1996.

Web Site

Reagan Library and Museum. http://www.reagan.utexas.edu (accessed on September 21, 2003).

End of the Cold War   10

Between 1985 and 1988, U.S. president Ronald Reagan (1911–; served 1981–89) and Soviet leader Mikhail Gorbachev (1931–) brought major changes to relations between the two Cold War rivals. At a second summit meeting between the two leaders held in Reykjavik, Iceland, in October 1986, Gorbachev surprised Reagan and the U.S. delegation with detailed proposals for major reductions in nuclear arms. It was becoming much clearer to the Americans that Gorbachev was indeed pressing for major changes both within the Soviet Union and in its international relations. Although no formal agreements were reached at Reykjavik, the two leaders agreed in principle to pursue certain major goals in arms reduction.

Negotiations through the following year led to the intermediate-range nuclear force treaty (INF) signed by Reagan and Gorbachev on December 8, 1987. It was a historic moment. Not only were the number of some types of nuclear weapons to be reduced, but other types were eliminated altogether.

With their working relationship continuing to grow, in June 1988, Reagan journeyed to Moscow for a fourth meeting with Gorbachev to express support for the Soviet re-

Soviet leader Mikhail Gorbachev addresses his Russian comrades in Moscow on November 2, 1987. *Photograph by Peter Turnley. Reproduced by permission of the Corbis Corporation.*

forms Gorbachev was pressing in the Soviet communist system. Gorbachev also continued to make changes in foreign policy by withdrawing Soviet troops from Afghanistan after a decade of bloody warfare during which the Soviets tried to prop up an unpopular pro-Soviet government.

To gain greater acceptance of the Soviet Union in the world community of nations, Gorbachev journeyed to New York City in December 1988 to speak before the United Nations (UN) General Assembly. In the first excerpt from Gorbachev's "Address to the 43rd United Nations General Assembly Session, December 7, 1988," the Soviet leader stressed the depth of change coming to his nation and the desire for more peaceful international relations. To provide continued proof of his intentions, Gorbachev traveled to the People's Republic of China in May 1989 to end years of hostile relations between the two communist giants.

Although U.S.-Soviet relations had warmed considerably through 1988, the new U.S. president George Bush

(1924–; served 1989–93), inaugurated in January 1989, had run a strong anticommunist presidential campaign. His campaign was typical of many other campaigns during the previous four decades. Even though he was Reagan's vice president through all eight years of Reagan's administration, he was critical of what he considered Reagan's rush to work with Gorbachev. He and his advisors worried that Gorbachev's reforms would quickly lose favor in the Soviet Union and that hard-line communists would regain control. Bush was fearful of reducing nuclear arms too quickly. However, Reagan and other world leaders urged Bush to continue U.S. support for Gorbachev. Gorbachev even continued reducing Soviet nuclear arms without getting Bush's agreement to do likewise.

By early 1989, change was coming faster than anyone, including Gorbachev, had anticipated. Bush and others worried about political stability and chaos in Eastern Europe. First Poland, followed by Hungary, East Germany, Czecho-

As communist governments fell, so did the symbols of past regimes, In Bucharest, Hungary, toppled statues of Romanian leader Petru Groza (left) and Soviet leader Vladimir I. Lenin lie on the ground. *Photograph by Barry Lewis. Reproduced by permission of the Corbis Corporation.*

slovakia, and Romania threw out their communist governments. The most dramatic moment was the dismantling of the Berlin Wall in November 1989. The wall had divided communist East Berlin from the democratic West Berlin since 1961. Unrest was similarly growing with the Soviet Union's fifteen republics. Bush became increasingly worried that the Soviet nuclear arsenal could fall into the hands of terrorists or remaining groups of hard-line communists. By May 1989, Bush had begun responding cautiously with further reductions in conventional forces in Europe. Then he agreed to personally meet with Gorbachev in December 1989 on a ship in a harbor in Malta in the eastern Mediterranean Sea. The second excerpt, from "At Historic Crossroads: Documents on the December 1989 Malta Summit," relays the public comments of both Bush and Gorbachev at the conclusion of their session.

Events within the Soviet Union unfolded at an ever quicker pace through 1990 and 1991. The Soviet economy continued to deteriorate, and Gorbachev was losing favor with both the communist hard-liners on one side, who thought his reforms went too far, and the Soviet public, who wanted greater freedoms and economic relief. By August 1991, the final downfall of Gorbachev and the Soviet Union had come. Following a brief failed coup by communist hard-liners to topple Gorbachev and reverse his reforms, the Communist Party was banned in various Soviet republics. The seat of power shifted from Gorbachev, president of the Soviet Union, to Boris Yeltsin (1931–), president of the Russian republic and a promoter of much more dramatic democratic and economic reform. The Soviet republics began achieving independence from Soviet rule on August 24, with the three Baltic States of Estonia, Latvia, and Lithuania leading the way.

By December 25, 1991, Gorbachev stepped down as president, and the Soviet Union ceased to exist a few days later. The Baltic States and the twelve remaining Soviet republics formed a new type of alliance as independent nations. Shortly after the fall of the Soviet Union, President George Bush chose the annual State of the Union address to Congress and the American people to officially proclaim victory for the United States in the Cold War. The third excerpt is from "End of Cold War: Address Before a Joint Session of

the Congress on the State of the Union, January 28, 1992."
The address provides Bush's proclamation and a first look at
new directions in a new post–Cold War era.

Mikhail Gorbachev

Excerpt from "Address to the 43rd United Nations General Assembly Session, December 7, 1988"

Found in *United Nations General Assembly, Provisional Verbatim Record of the Seventy-Second Meeting*

"We are witnessing the emergence of a new, historic reality: a turning away from the principle of super-armament to the principle of reasonable defense sufficiency."

On December 7, 1988, Soviet leader Mikhail Gorbachev (1931–) spoke to the General Assembly of the United Nations (UN) at the UN headquarters in New York City. Gorbachev was general secretary of the Central Committee of the Communist Party of the Soviet Union and president of the Presidium of the Supreme Soviet of the Union of Soviet Socialist Republics (U.S.S.R.). In other words, he was head of both the Soviet Communist Party and the government of the Soviet Union. The speech would mark another major step toward ending the Cold War, a prolonged conflict for world dominance from 1945 to 1991 between the two superpowers, the democratic, capitalist United States and the communist Soviet Union. The occasion of the speech also came several weeks before U.S. president Ronald Reagan (1911–; served 1981–89) ended his term of office and George Bush (1924–; served 1989–93) began his.

Before the entire world, Gorbachev plainly announced the Soviet reforms that he had begun over the previous three years. Describing his reforms as containing "a tremendous potential for peace and international co-opera-

tion," Gorbachev charted a course never heard expressed by a Soviet leader before. He spoke of "profound social change" and "new nations and States." People, he claimed, were "longing for independence, democracy and social justice." He declared this was in large part due to the growing mass media that brought a greater exchange of ideas around the world. Keeping societies closed to the outside world, such as the Soviet society since the 1920s, was no longer practical.

Related to this change was a globalization of trade. No country could economically develop and thrive without taking part in the newly developing worldwide economic system. At this time, Gorbachev still held fast to maintaining communist rule, though with a reformed Communist Party allowing greater personal freedoms and public participation. He spoke of respecting differing viewpoints and tolerance among the nations, of living "side by side with others, while remaining different." Gorbachev stressed a key step toward greater world stability was disarmament, and he desired to

Soviet leader Mikhail Gorbachev addresses the United Nations in December 1988. He announced cuts in the Soviet military budget as well as a withdrawal of fifty thousand troops from Eastern Europe. *Photograph by Robert Maass. Reproduced by permission of the Corbis Corporation.*

build on the INF treaty signed the previous December. He called for "radical economic reform" by lessening government control of industry and business. Gorbachev thanked President Reagan and U.S. secretary of state George Shultz (1920–) for supporting his reforms. In conclusion, he expressed a desire to continue the growing relationship with the United States through newly elected president Bush.

Things to remember while reading "Address to the 43rd United Nations General Assembly Session, December 7, 1988":

- Mikhail Gorbachev came into the Soviet leadership position in 1985 when the economy was in disarray and the United States, under President Reagan, was pursuing another period of expensive rapid arms buildup. Soviet citizens had lost faith in the communist system and dramatic reform was desperately needed.

- Reagan and Shultz had overcome hard-line anticommunist opposition in the U.S. administration to negotiate arms control agreements and support Gorbachev's efforts at Soviet reform.

- Gorbachev differed from previous Soviet leaders by being from a later generation, being college-educated, and being quite socially outgoing in public.

Excerpt from "Address to the 43rd United Nations General Assembly Session, December 7, 1988"

*We have come here to show our respect for the United Nations, which increasingly has been **manifesting** its ability to act as a unique international center in the service of peace and security....*

*The role played by the Soviet Union in world affairs is well known, and in view of the revolutionary **perestroika** under way in our country, which contains a tremendous potential for peace and*

Manifesting: Demonstrating.

Perestroika: Mikhail Gorbachev's policy of economic and government reforms.

international co-operation, we are now particularly interested in being properly understood.

That is why we have come here to address this most authoritative world body and to share our thoughts with it. We want it to be the first to learn of our new, important decisions....

*We are witnessing the most profound social change. Whether in the East or the South, the West or the North, hundreds of millions of people, new nations and States, new public movements and **ideologies** have moved to the forefront of history. Broad-based and frequently turbulent popular movements have given expression ... to a longing for independence, democracy and social justice. The idea of **democratizing** the entire world order has become a powerful socio-political force....*

*Thanks to the advances in mass media and means of transportation the world seems to have become more visible and **tangible**. International communication has become easier than ever before. Today, the preservation of any kind of closed society is hardly possible. This calls for a radical review of approaches to the totality of the problems of international co-operation as a major element of universal security. The world economy is becoming a single organism, and no State, whatever its social system or economic status, can develop normally outside it....*

*However, concurrently with wars, **animosities** and divisions among peoples and countries, another trend, with equally objective causes, was gaining momentum: the process of the emergence of a mutually interrelated and integral world. Today, further world progress is possible only through a search for universal human consensus as we move forward to a new world order....*

The international community must learn how it can shape and guide developments in such a way as to preserve our civilization and to make it safe for all and more conducive to normal life....

In the past differences were often a factor causing mutual rejection. Now, they have a chance of becoming a factor for mutual enrichment and mutual attraction.

Behind differences in social systems, in ways of life and in preferences for certain values, stand different interests. There is no escaping that fact....

This objective fact calls for respect for the views and positions of others, tolerance, a willingness to perceive something different as

Ideologies: Body of beliefs.

Democratizing: Changing foreign governments into democracies, in which they have multiple political parties and free public elections.

Tangible: Real; valuable.

Animosities: Resentment toward each other, possibly leading to armed conflict.

not necessarily bad or hostile, and an ability to learn to live side by side with others, while remaining different and not always agreeing with each other....

These are our reflections on the patterns of world development on the threshold of the twenty-first century....

Forces have already emerged in the world that in one way or another stimulate the arrival of a period of peace....

*Those politicians whose activities used to be geared to the Cold War and sometimes linked with its most critical phases are now drawing appropriate conclusions. Of all people, they find it particularly hard to abandon old **stereotypes** and past practices, and, if even they are changing course, it is clear that, when new generations take over, opportunities will increase in number.*

In short, the understanding of the need for a period of peace is gaining ground and beginning to prevail. This has made it possible to take the first real steps towards creating a healthier international environment and towards disarmament....

The whole world welcomes the efforts of this Organization [United Nations]....

Under the sign of democratization, perestroika has now spread to politics, the economy, intellectual life and ideology.

We have initiated a radical economic reform. We have gained experience. At the start of next year, the entire national economy will be directed to new forms and methods of operation....

Let me now turn to the main issue without which none of the problems of the coming century can be solved: disarmament.

*International development and communications have been distorted by the arms race and the militarization of thinking. As the Assembly will know, on 15 January 1986 the Soviet Union put forward a programme for building a nuclear-weapon-free world. Translated into actual negotiating positions, it has already produced material results. Tomorrow marks the first anniversary of the signing of the Treaty between the United States of America and the Union of Soviet Socialist Republics on the elimination of their Intermediate-Range and Shorter-Range Missiles—the INF Treaty. I am therefore particularly pleased to note that the implementation of the Treaty—the elimination of missiles—is proceeding normally in an atmosphere of trust and businesslike work. **A large breach** has thus been made in a seemingly unbreakable wall of suspicion and animosity. We are*

Stereotypes: Common, oversimplified opinions of a group of people.

A large breach: Much progress.

witnessing the emergence of a new, historic reality: a turning away from the principle of super-armament to the principle of reasonable defense sufficiency....

Finally, since I am here on American soil, and also for other obvious reasons, I have to turn to the subject of our relations with this great country. I had a chance to appreciate the full measure of its hospitality during my memorable visit to Washington exactly a year ago. Relations between the Soviet Union and the United States of America have a history of five and a half decades. As the world has changed, so have the nature, role and place of those relations in world politics. For too long they developed along the lines of confrontation and sometimes animosity, either **overt** or **covert**. But in the last few years the entire world has been able to breathe a sigh of relief, thanks to the changes for the better in the substance and the atmosphere of the relationship between Moscow and Washington.

No one intends to underestimate the seriousness of our differences and the toughness of our outstanding problems. We have, however, already graduated from the primary school of learning to understand each other and seek solutions in both our own and the common interest.

The USSR and the United States have built the largest nuclear and missile **arsenals**; but it is those two countries that, having become specifically aware of their responsibility, have been the first to conclude a treaty on the reduction and physical elimination of a portion of their armaments which posed a threat to both of them and to all other countries. Both countries possess the greatest and most sophisticated military secrets; but it is those two countries that have laid a basis for and are further developing a system of mutual verification both of the elimination of armaments and of the reduction and prohibition of their production. It is those two countries that are accumulating experience for future **bilateral** and **multilateral** agreements.

We value this. We acknowledge and appreciate the contributions made by President Ronald Reagan and by the members of his Administration, particularly Mr. George Shultz.

All this is our joint investment in a venture of historic importance. We must not lose that investment, or leave it idle.

The next United States administration, headed by President-elect George Bush, will find in us a partner who is ready—without long pauses or backtracking—to continue the dialogue in a spirit of realism, openness and goodwill, with a willingness to achieve con-

Overt: Open.

Covert: Secret.

Arsenals: Collection of weapons.

Bilateral: Interaction between two countries.

Multilateral: Interaction between more than two countries.

crete results working on the agenda which covers the main issues of Soviet/United States relations and world politics....

We are not inclined to simplify the situation in the world.

Yes, the trend towards disarmament has been given a powerful impetus, and the process is gaining a momentum of its own. But it has not yet become irreversible.

Yes, the willingness to give up confrontation in favor of dialogue and co-operation is being felt strongly. But it is still far from becoming a permanent feature in the practice of international relations.

Yes, movement towards a nuclear-weapon-free and non-violent world is capable of radically transforming the political and intellectual identity of our planet. But only the first steps have been taken, and even they have been met with mistrust in certain influential quarters and face resistance.

*The legacy and the **inertia** of the past continue to be felt....*

We are meeting at the end of a year which has meant so much for the United Nations and on the eve of a year from which we all expect so much.

I should like to believe that our hopes will be matched by our joint efforts to put an end to an era of wars, confrontation and regional conflicts, to aggressions against nature, to the terror of hunger and poverty as well as to political terrorism.

That is our common goal and we can only reach it together....

What happened next ...

Not long after the UN speech, Gorbachev introduced major political reforms within the Soviet Union. A revised Soviet constitution created a new parliament known as the Congress of People's Deputies. To fill seats in the new parliament, elections were held in the various fifteen Soviet republics in March. Gorbachev was surprised how badly hard-line communist candidates had lost. One new reform-minded communist who won was Boris Yeltsin (1931–) in the highly important Moscow district of Russia. Gorbachev had not expected

Inertia: Something moving at its own pace until affected by something else.

such a shift in political power away from the Communist Party. On the international scene, President Bush's new secretary of state, James Baker (1930–), and Soviet foreign minister Eduard Shevardnadze (1928–) met several times through the early months of 1989, forming a close working relationship.

Did you know …

- During his visit to the UN headquarters in New York City, Gorbachev posed with President Ronald Reagan and President-elect George Bush in front of the Statue of Liberty. It later proved a powerful image representing the fall of communism and the end of the Cold War.

- President George Bush's secretary of defense Richard Cheney (1941–) warned Bush against aiding Gorbachev, predicting the reforms would fail and hard-line communists would regain control. Other advisors would warn that Gorbachev's reforms were a trick to weaken the United States by agreeing to disarmament measures. This was old-line, long-adhered-to U.S. philosophy concerning the Soviet Union. Letting go of this line of thinking was difficult for many old-line U.S. diplomats.

- A major feature of Gorbachev's UN speech was his renouncing longtime communist assumptions that conflict between capitalism and communism was inevitable.

- In the speech, Gorbachev shocked other nations by announcing a withdrawal of a half million Soviet troops

Soviet leader Mikhail Gorbachev (left), U.S. president Ronald Reagan, and Vice President George Bush look at the Statue of Liberty in December 1988. *Reproduced by permission of the Corbis Corporation.*

and thousands of heavy conventional weapons from Eastern Europe.

Consider the following ...

- Gorbachev claimed that mass media made it almost impossible for a government to maintain a strict control over a society closed to outside influences. What kinds of influences do you think young Soviets may have been exposed to in the 1970s and 1980s?

- Why do you suppose Gorbachev did not intend to end communism, but basically reform it?

- What did Gorbachev mean when he asserted that U.S.-Soviet relations through the Cold War were "distorted by the arms race and the militarization of thinking" and that "the first steps" of disarmament "have been met with mistrust in certain influential quarters"?

For More Information

Books

Gorbachev, Mikhail, and Zdenek Mlynar. *Conversations with Gorbachev.* New York: Columbia University Press, 2002.

Kelly, Nigel. *Fall of the Berlin Wall: The Cold War Ends.* Chicago: Heineman Library, 2001.

Mandelbaum, Michael. *The Ideas That Conquered the World: Peace, Democracy, and Free Markets in the Twenty-First Century.* New York: PublicAffairs, 2002.

McCauley, Martin. *Gorbachev.* New York: Longman, 1998.

Morrison, Donald, ed. *Mikhail S. Gorbachev: An Intimate Biography.* New York: Time Books, 1988.

Stokes, Gale. *The Walls Came Tumbling Down: The Collapse of Communism in Eastern Europe.* New York: Oxford University Press, 1993.

United Nations General Assembly, Provisional Verbatim Record of the Seventy-Second Meeting, A/43/PV.72, December 8, 1988. New York: United Nations, 1988.

Web Site

Mikhail Sergeyevich Gorbachev. http://www.mikhailgorbachev.org (accessed on September 22, 2003).

George Bush and Mikhail Gorbachev

Excerpt from "At Historic Crossroads: Documents on the December 1989 Malta Summit"

Published in *Cold War International History Project Bulletin*, Issue 12/13, Fall/Winter 2001

Following the fall of communism in Eastern Europe and increasing unrest within the Soviet Union, it was clearer to President George Bush (1924–; served 1989–93) and his secretary of state, James A. Baker (1930–), that change was real in the former Soviet empire and a prospect of substantial political instability loomed large. Bush had at first been cool to showing support for Gorbachev. He was coming to decide that it would be best for the United States if Gorbachev's reforms were successful and if some degree of social order was maintained without the hard-line communists taking control once again.

Immediately following the collapse of communism in Eastern Europe, Bush met with Gorbachev on a ship off the island nation of Malta in the Mediterranean Sea. The historic talks began as a major storm was raging, tossing the ship to and fro in the bay where it was anchored. In the Soviet Union, ethnic tensions were rising in some Soviet republics pressing for independence. Potential political chaos was looming. The two leaders ended their session by making a joint public statement.

> "We have managed to avoid a large-scale war for 45 years. This single fact alone says that not everything was so bad in the past. Nevertheless, one conclusion is obvious—reliance on force, on military superiority, and the associated arms race have not been justified. Our two countries obviously understand this better than others."
>
> —*Mikhail Gorbachev*

First, Bush spoke on his increased desire to see Soviet reforms succeed. Bush offered steps to provide improved trade and financial assistance, but he stressed that the United States was not offering aid to "save" the Soviet Union but rather a cooperative venture in helping the Soviets see their reforms through. This also included letting the Soviets become more participatory in world economic markets. Bush also addressed the reduction of chemical weapons, strategic nuclear weapons, and major reductions in conventional forces in Europe.

Gorbachev responded with great pleasure that Bush was willing to increase U.S. assistance to his reform efforts. He again denounced the Cold War's arms race and confrontations over differing philosophies. He warned that military leaders on both sides were locked into a Cold War mentality of military aggressiveness. Gorbachev spoke of "a united, integrated European economy" and greater involvement of China as well—"a regrouping of forces in the world."

A first step, according to Gorbachev, was a promise "that the Soviet Union will not start a war under any circumstances." He added that the Soviets no longer considered the United

U.S. president George Bush greets Soviet leader Mikhail Gorbachev at the December 1989 Malta Summit.
Photograph by Wally McNamee. Reproduced by permission of the Corbis Corporation.

States as an enemy. It was urgent to end the arms race and reduce weapons as soon as possible and become military cooperators rather than confronters. Turning to domestic issues, Gorbachev asserted that a "main principle" of the "new thinking is the right of each country to ... choose without outside interference ... a certain social and economic system." Unknown at this time was the fact that the Soviet Union would exist for only one more year.

Things to remember while reading the excerpt from "At Historic Crossroads: Documents on the December 1989 Malta Summit":

- President Bush was very hesitant to support Gorbachev's reforms. This excerpt clearly shows Gorbachev's expression of urgency and Bush's more reserved but growing support.

- Bush had previously held various government positions involved in Cold War politics, such as U.S. representative to the United Nations, director of the Central Intelligence Agency (CIA), and U.S. representative to communist China.

- Communist governments in Eastern Europe had just fallen during the past several months. The Soviet empire was dramatically shrinking to its own borders, with social unrest growing within.

Excerpt from "At Historic Crossroads: Documents on the December 1989 Malta Summit"

G. Bush: We have already had productive discussions. I would like for you to allow me to describe some ideas of the American side in summary form....

*About our attitude to **perestroika** ... that the world would be better off for* perestroika's *success....*

But you can be confident that you are dealing with a U.S. administration and also with a Congress that wants your reforms to be successful.

I would now like to describe a number of positive steps which, in our opinion, could define in general terms the direction of our joint work to prepare for an official summit meeting in the U.S.

Some comments about economic questions. I want to inform you that my administration intends to take steps directed at preventing the Jackson-Vanik amendment which prohibits granting the Soviet Union most-favored nation status, from going into force....

Perestroika: Mikhail Gorbachev's policy of economic and government reforms.

*I would also like to report that the administration has adopted
a policy of repealing the Stevenson and Byrd amendments which restrict the possibility of granting credits to the Soviet side.*

*These measures, which the administration is proposing right
now in the area of Soviet-American relations, are restrained ... in
the appropriate spirit: they are not at all directed at demonstrating
American superiority. And in this sense, as we understand it, they
correspond with your attitude. We in the U.S., of course, are deeply
confident of the advantages of our way of economic management.
But that is not the issue right now. We have been striving to draw
up our proposals so as not to create the impression that America "is
saving" the Soviet Union. We are not talking about an aid program,
but a cooperative program.*

*After the Jackson-Vanik amendment is repealed, favorable con-
ditions will arise to remove the restrictions on granting credits. The
American administration is not thinking about granting aid but
about creating conditions for the development of effective coopera-*

tion on economic issues. We have in mind sending the Soviet side our proposals on this matter in the form of a document. It concerns a number of serious projects in the areas of finance, statistics, market operations, etc....

I would like to say a few words to explain our position regarding the Soviet side's desire to gain observer status at **GATT** ... We are [now] in favor of the Soviet side being granted observer status at GATT. In doing so, we are proceeding from the belief that Soviet participation in GATT would help it familiarize itself with the conditions, the functioning, and the development of the world market....

You know that my administration is in favor of ridding mankind of chemical weapons....

On the practical level this means that even in the near future both sides could reach agreement about a considerable reduction of chemical weapon stockpiles, bringing this amount to 20% of the amount of CW [chemical warfare] agents the U.S. presently has in its arsenal....

About conventional weapons. Although serious efforts will be needed for this.... It appears in this regard that we could put forward such a goal: to orient ourselves toward signing agreements about radical reductions of conventional forces in Europe in 1990....

Concerning the issue of a future agreement about reducing strategic offensive weapons....

The resolution of the issue of preventing the **proliferation** of missiles and missile technology is gaining ever greater significance at the present time....

M. S. Gorbachev: Thank you for your interesting ideas. It's possible that this is the best evidence that the administration of President Bush has shaped its policy in the Soviet-American direction. I intend to touch on several specific issues later.

But right now I would like to make a number of comments of a philosophical nature. It seems to me that it is very important for us to talk with you about what conclusions can be drawn from past experience, from the Cold War. What has happened remains in history. Such, if you will, is the privilege of the historical process. However, to try to analyze the course of previous events—this is our direct responsibility. Why is this necessary? Certainly we can say that we have all ended up at historical crossroads. Completely new problems have arisen before humanity which people had not previously antic-

GATT: General Agreement on Tariffs and Trade; established in 1948 to promote world trade.

Proliferation: Increase in numbers.

ipated. And what about it—will we decide them using old approaches? Simply nothing would come out of this.

By no means should everything that has happened be considered in a negative light. We have managed to avoid a large-scale war for 45 years. This single fact alone says that not everything was so bad in the past. Nevertheless, one conclusion is obvious—reliance on force, on military superiority, and the associated arms race have not been justified. Our two countries obviously understand this better than others.

And confrontation arising from ideological convictions has not justified itself either; as a result of this we ended up swearing at one another. We reached a dangerous brink and it is good that we managed to stop. It is good that now mutual trust between our countries has emerged....

Cold War methods, methods of confrontation, have suffered defeat in strategic terms. We have recognized this. And ordinary people have possibly understood this even better. I do not want to preach here. People simply **meddle** in policymaking. Ecological problems, problems of preserving natural resources, and problems connected with the negative consequences of technological progress have arisen. All of this is completely understandable since we are essentially talking about the issue of survival. And this kind of public sentiment is strongly affecting us, the politicians.

Therefore we together—the U.S.S.R. and the U.S.—can do a lot at this stage to radically change our old approaches. We had felt this even in our contacts with the Reagan administration. And this process continues right now. Look how we have confided in one another.

We lag behind the mood of the people at the political level. And this is understandable since various forces influence leaders. It is good that [Chief of the General Staff] Marshall Akhromeyev and your [National Security] Adviser, [Brent] Scowcroft, understand the problems which arise in the military field. But there are people in both countries—and there are many of them—who simply scare us. Many people working in the defense sector are used to their profession and for whom it is not easy to change their way of thinking. And all the same, this process has begun.

Why have I begun with this? The thesis is consistently advanced in American political circles that the Soviet Union "has begun its perestroika and is changing policy under the influence of the Cold War policy." They say that everything is collapsing in Eastern Europe

Meddle: Interfere.

and [that] this also *"confirms the correctness of those who relied on Cold War methods."* And if this is so, then nothing needs to be changed in this policy. We need to increase strong arm pressure and prepare more baskets in order to catch more fruit. Mr. President, this is a dangerous delusion.

I have noticed that you see all this. I know that you have to listen to representatives of different circles. However, your public statements, as well as specific proposals directed at the development of cooperation between the U.S.S.R. and U.S. which you spoke of today, mean that President Bush has formed a certain idea about the world, and it corresponds to the challenges of the time....

*Initially, I was even thinking of expressing something of a **reproach**. To say that the President of the United States has not once expressed his support for perestroika, wished it success, and noted that the Soviet Union itself should deal with its own reforms. What we were expecting from the President of the United States was not only statements, but specific steps in accordance with these statements.*

Now there are both statements and these steps. I am drawing this conclusion having heard what you have just said. Despite the fact that these are only plans for steps. But this is very important.

*Second consideration. A great regrouping of forces is underway in the world. It is clear that we are going from a **bipolar** to a **multipolar** world. Whether we like it or not, we will have to deal with a united, integrated European economy. We could discuss the issue of Western Europe separately. Whether we want it or not, Japan is one more center of world politics. At one time you and I were talking about China. This is one more huge reality which neither we nor you should play against the other. And it is necessary to think about what to do, so that China does not feel excluded from all the processes which are taking place in the world....*

All these, I repeat, are huge events typical of a regrouping of forces in the world.

And what is waiting ahead for us with regard to the economy, the environment, and other problems? We need to think together about this, too.

We in the Soviet leadership have been reflecting about this for a long time and have come to the conclusion that the U.S. and U.S.S.R. are simply "doomed" to dialogue, coordination, and cooperation. There is no other choice.

Reproach: Disapproval.

Bipolar: Two equally opposed forces, such as the two superpowers.

Multipolar: More than two centers of power.

But to do this we need to get rid of the view of one another as enemies. Much of this stays in our brains. And we need to keep in mind that it is impossible to view our relations only at the military level.

*All this means that we are proposing a Soviet-American **condominium**.... We have only entered into the process of mutual understanding.*

Mr. President, yesterday I reacted very briefly to the ideas you expressed about military-political issues. Today it is our turn....

First of all, a new U.S. President should know that the Soviet Union will not start a war under any circumstances. This is so important that I would like to personally repeat this declaration to you. Moreover, the U.S.S.R. is prepared to no longer consider the U.S. as its enemy and openly say so. We are open to cooperation with America, including cooperation in the military sphere. That is the first thing.

Second point. We are in favor of ensuring mutual security through joint efforts. The Soviet leadership is devoted to a continuation of the process of disarmament in all directions. We consider it necessary and urgent to get past the arms race and prevent the creation of exotic new kinds of weapons....

The two of us have recognized that, as a result of the arms race, absolutely inconceivable military power was created on both sides. We have come to the common conclusion that such a situation was fraught with catastrophic [dangers]. We have started to act in the right direction and have displayed political will....

Summarizing what I have said, I would like to stress again with all my strength that we favor peaceful relations with the U.S. And proceeding from this very precondition we propose to transform the present military confrontation. This is the main thing....

It is necessary to proceed from an understanding of the enormous importance of the current changes. It is necessary to avoid possible mistakes and use the historic opportunities which are opening up to bring East and West together....

I stress that a special responsibility rests on the Soviet Union and the United States at this historic moment....

The main principle which we have adopted and which we follow in our new thinking is the right of each country to free choice, including the right to reexamine and change their original choice. This is very painful, but it is a fundamental right. The right to choose without

Condominium: Political sharing of power.

outside interference. The U.S. is devoted to a certain social and economic system which the American people have chosen. Let other people decide themselves, figuratively speaking, what God to pray to....

G. Bush: I understand you and agree.... We welcome the changes which are occurring with all our hearts.

M. S. Gorbachev: This is very important since, as I have said, the main thing is that the changes lead to greater openness in our relations with one another. We are beginning to be organically integrated and liberated from everything which divided us. What will this be called in the final account? I think—a new level of relations.

What happened next ...

By February 1990, public demonstrations were erupting against the Communist Party in various Soviet republics. In Moscow, hundreds of thousands of protesters turned out. To distance himself from the Communist Party after being its leader for five years, Gorbachev created a new governmental leadership position, the Soviet presidency. Gorbachev assumed the new position, for the first time separating Communist Party leadership from Soviet government leadership. In addition, other political parties besides the Communist Party were allowed for the first time since the communist takeover in 1917.

Through 1990, the Soviet economy continued its steep downward slide. Gorbachev's popularity on the home front was similarly declining. The Soviet Baltic States of Estonia, Latvia, and Lithuania were scrambling for independence from Soviet rule. During the previous year, Gorbachev stood by while communist rule ended in country after country in Eastern Europe. However, under pressure from party hard-liners, he responded with force when the Soviet republics tried to break away. When the Soviet republic of Lithuania attempted to gain independence, Gorbachev sent Soviet troops to the country and established an economic blockade. In reaction, Bush placed trade restrictions on the Soviets, causing Gorbachev to quickly back off.

A crowd watches as a crane lifts a large section out of the Berlin Wall. *Reproduced by permission of the Corbis Corporation.*

In May 1990, Gorbachev traveled to Washington, D.C., for another meeting with Bush to discuss the reunification of Germany. Since the fall of the Berlin Wall in November 1989, Gorbachev feared a new, strong, reunited Germany. He sought guarantees from Bush that Germany would not soon become a threat once again to Soviet security. Agreement was soon reached over a reunified Germany. East and West Germany merged on October 3, 1990. A new Europe was formed the next month as thirty-five nations signed the Charter of Paris. The charter declared support for democracy, human rights, social justice, and economic liberty. By February 1991, the Warsaw Pact, a military alliance of Eastern European countries formerly under Soviet control, disbanded. The Soviet Union itself would collapse over the next ten months. On December 25, 1991, Gorbachev announced his resignation as president of the Soviet Union, and the nation ceased to exist a few days later.

Did you know ...

- After the Malta summit, President Bush had a clearer understanding of Gorbachev's situation. If Gorbachev pressed reforms too hard, the hard-line communists would attack his policies. But if he did not press hard enough, the Soviet economic system would collapse.

- In 1990, Soviet president Gorbachev was awarded the Nobel Peace Prize for his Soviet reform efforts and named *Time* magazine's "Man of the Year."

- The first post–Cold War major conflict would be the Persian Gulf War (1990–91). In early 1991, President Bush led a broad coalition of nations under a UN resolution in liberating Kuwait from Iraqi invasion and occupation. Because of Soviet military and hard-line communist opposition to directly joining the coalition against Iraq, Gorbachev could only provide support through the UN.

- President Bush would travel to the Soviet republic of the Ukraine in August 1991 to publicly support Gorbachev's reforms. He warned Ukrainians against pushing for change too quickly and causing violent confrontations with the Soviets.

- The most important outcome of the Malta summit was a secret exchange of assurances. Gorbachev would avoid violence as much as possible as the Baltic States sought their independence, and Bush would not publicly criticize Gorbachev on this issue.

Consider the following ...

- Bush was concerned about moving too fast in agreements with Gorbachev, particularly on arms control. What were his concerns? What kinds of cooperation did Bush offer at Malta?

- Was Gorbachev able to achieve the reform goals he was seeking? If not, why?

- How would you react if you lived in a communist country that greatly controlled your everyday life, and neighboring communist countries were suddenly gaining considerably more freedoms?

For More Information

Books

Ash, Timothy G. *The Magic Lantern: The Revolution of '89 Witnessed in Warsaw, Budapest, Berlin, and Prague.* New York: Random House, 1990.

Ashlund, Anders. *Building Capitalism: The Transformation of the Former Soviet Bloc.* New York: Cambridge University Press, 2002.

Cold War International History Project Bulletin Issue 12/13 ("The End of the Cold War"), Fall/Winter 2001.

Greene, John R. *The Presidency of George Bush.* Lawrence: University Press of Kansas, 2000.

Hurst, Steven. *The Foreign Policy of the Bush Administration: In Search of a New World Order.* New York: Cassell, 1999.

Parmet, Herbert S. *George Bush: The Life of a Lone Star Yankee.* New York: Scribner, 1997.

Web Site

George Bush Presidential Library and Museum. http://bushlibrary.tamu.edu (accessed on September 22, 2003).

George Bush

Excerpt from "End of Cold War: Address Before a Joint Session of the Congress on the State of the Union, January 28, 1992"

Published in *Public Papers of the Presidents of the United States: George Bush, 1992–93, Book 1, January 1 to July 31, 1992,* published in 1993

By the fall of 1991, Soviet leader Mikhail Gorbachev (1931–) was finding that political changes in the Soviet Union's republics were increasingly out of his control. On December 31, 1991, the Soviet flag came down over the Kremlin in Moscow for the last time. Only days earlier, Gorbachev had resigned as president of the Soviet Union and turned over control of the Soviet nuclear arsenal to Boris Yeltsin (1931–), president of Russia. All the remaining republics declared independence and were soon admitted to the UN as new nations. Less than a month later, U.S. president George Bush (1924–; served 1989–93) was scheduled to give the annual State of the Union Address to a joint session of Congress and the world.

It was ideal timing for declaring the end of the Cold War (1945–91). Bush began by announcing, "I mean to speak tonight of big things, of big changes." In referring to the collapse of the Soviet Union over the past several months, Bush pronounced "communism died this year." Then in a bold statement, Bush proclaimed, "By the grace of God, America won the cold war." He then listed what changes this would

"Even as President, with the most fascinating possible vantage point, there were times when I was so busy managing progress and helping to lead change that I didn't always show the joy that was in my heart. But the biggest thing that has happened in the world in my life, in our lives, is this: By the grace of God, America won the cold war."

mean to the United States, such as decreased need for military readiness and greater attention to domestic issues. As he stated, the "world ... now recognizes one sole and prominent power, the United States of America." But that world trusts the United States "to do what's right."

Bush announced he was stopping B-2 bomber production and canceling a number of missile programs. Bush announced he would be meeting with Russian president Yeltsin to negotiate a new nuclear arms control treaty. He proclaimed the reductions would save some $50 billion over the next five years: "By 1997, we will have cut defenses by 30 percent." However, he did ask Congress for funding of a scaled-down Strategic Defense Initiative (SDI) to protect the United States from "limited nuclear attack ... because too many people in too many countries have access to nuclear arms."

Bush concluded by stating the new role of the United States in the post–Cold War era: "to lead in the support of freedom everywhere."

Things to remember while reading the excerpt from "End of Cold War":

- The beginning of the end of Gorbachev's role as Soviet leader came on August 19, 1991. On that day, Soviet Communist Party hard-liners opposing Gorbachev's reforms attempted a coup to overthrow the president. After only three days, the coup fell apart due to strong public opposition. Ironically, the ill-fated coup brought about the final demise of the Soviet Communist Party, the opposite result of what was intended. Although Gorbachev managed to regain his leadership position within days, his power and that of the Communist Party was lost. Boris Yeltsin, president of Russia, was the new holder of power. Soviet communism had essentially ended.

- The world had dramatically changed in an unbelievably short time—in just three years, from 1989 to 1991.

- The first Soviet republics to gain independence as separate nations were Estonia, Latvia, and Lithuania on August 24, 1991.

Excerpt from "End of Cold War"

Mr. Speaker and Mr. President, distinguished Members of Congress, honored guests, and fellow citizens:

I mean to speak tonight of big things, of big changes and the promises they hold, and of some big problems and how, together, we can solve them and move our country forward as the undisputed leader of the age.

We gather tonight at a dramatic and deeply promising time in our history and in the history of man on Earth. For in the past 12 months, the world has known changes of almost biblical proportions. And even now, months after the failed coup that doomed a failed system, I'm not sure we've absorbed the full impact, the full import of what happened. But communism died this year.

Even as President, with the most fascinating possible vantage point, there were times when I was so busy managing progress and helping to lead change that I didn't always show the joy that was in my heart. But the biggest thing that has happened in the world in my life, in our lives, is this: By the grace of God, America won the cold war.

I mean to speak this evening of the changes that can take place in our country, now that we can stop making the sacrifices we had to make when we had an avowed enemy that was a superpower. Now we can look homeward even more and move to set right what needs to be set right....

So now, for the first time in 35 years, our strategic bombers stand down. No longer are they on 'round-the-clock alert. Tomorrow our children will go to school and study history and how plants grow. And they won't have, as my children did, air raid drills in which they crawl under their desks and cover their heads in case of nuclear war. My grandchildren don't have to do that and won't have the bad dreams children had once, in decades past. There are still threats. But the long, drawn-out dread is over....

Much good can come from the prudent use of power. And much good can come of this: A world once divided into two armed camps now recognizes one sole and prominent power, the United States of America. And they regard this with no dread. For the world trusts us with power, and the world is right. They trust us to be fair and re-

strained. They trust us to be on the side of decency. They trust us to do what's right....

Two years ago, I began planning cuts in military spending that reflected the changes of the new era. But now, this year, with imperial communism gone, that process can be accelerated. Tonight I can tell you of dramatic changes in our strategic nuclear force. These are actions we are taking on our own because they are the right thing to do. After completing 20 planes for which we have begun procurement, we will shut down further production of the B-2 bombers. We will cancel the small ICBM program. We will cease production of new warheads for our sea-based ballistic missiles. We will stop all new production of the peacekeeper missile. And we will not purchase any more advanced cruise missiles.

This weekend I will meet at Camp David with Boris Yeltsin of the Russian Federation. I've informed president Yeltsin that if the Commonwealth, the former Soviet Union, will eliminate all land-based multiple-warhead ballistic missiles, I will do the following: We will eliminate all Peacekeeper missiles. We will reduce the number of warheads on Minuteman missiles to one and reduce the number of warheads on our sea-based missiles by about one-third. And we will convert a substantial portion of our strategic bombers to primarily con-

U.S. president George Bush delivers his State of the Union Address in January 1992. Vice President Dan Quayle is behind him.
Photograph by Martin Jeong. Reproduced by permission of the Corbis Corporation.

ventional use. President Yeltsin's early response has been very positive, and I expect our talks at Camp David to be fruitful.

I want you to know that for half a century American Presidents have longed to make such decisions and say such words. But even in the midst of celebration, we must keep caution as a friend. For the world is still a dangerous place. Only the dead have seen the end of conflict. And though yesterday's challenges are behind us, tomorrow's are being born....

*But do not misunderstand me. The reductions I have approved will save us an additional $50 billion over the next 5 years. By 1997, we will have cut defense by 30 percent since I took office. These cuts are deep, and you must know my resolve: This deep, and no deeper. To do less would be insensible to progress, but to do more would be ignorant of history. We must not go back to the days of "the hollow army." We cannot repeat the mistakes made twice in this century when **armistice** was followed by recklessness and defense was purged as if the world were permanently safe.*

I remind you this evening that I have asked for your support in funding a program to protect our country from limited nuclear missile attack. We must have this protection because too many people in too many countries have access to nuclear arms. And I urge you again to pass the Strategic Defense Initiative, SDI.

*There are those who say that now we can turn away from the world, that we have no special role, no special place. But we are the United States of America, the leader of the West that has become the leader of the world. And as long as I am President, I will continue to lead in support of freedom everywhere, not out of arrogance, not out of **altruism**, but for the safety and security of our children. This is a fact: Strength in the pursuit of peace is no vice; **isolationism** in the pursuit of security is no virtue.*

What happened next ...

Bush and Yeltsin negotiated new arms-reduction deals agreeing to eliminate all missiles that carried multiple warheads (MIRVs) and reducing the numbers of strategic nuclear warheads by several thousand. Bush would continue to deny significant economic aid to Yeltsin as he had with Gorbachev earlier.

Ironically, the change from the Cold War stalemate between two superpowers to that of one superpower led to greater instability in the world. With the end of communist domination over the diverse ethnic populations in its republics, bloody conflicts erupted. For example, war broke out between ethnic groups in the former Yugoslavia through the 1990s. Chechnya

Armistice: Military truce.

Altruism: An unselfish concern for the welfare of others.

Isolationism: A policy of avoiding official agreements with other nations in order to remain neutral.

Broken statues of such former Soviet leaders as Joseph Stalin (shown here) were common following the breakup of the Soviet Union. *Photograph by Chris Lisle. Reproduced by permission of the Corbis Corporation.*

attempted to establish independence from the Russian Federation, leading to Russian troops being dispatched in 1994. Fighting continued there into the twenty-first century. International terrorism also became a key concern, fueled by the September 11, 2001, attacks by Muslim extremists against the World Trade Center in New York City and the Pentagon in Virginia.

While Americans enjoyed unprecedented economic prosperity through the 1990s under the administration of President Bill Clinton (1946–; served 1993–2001), widespread economic hardships persisted in Russia and other former Soviet republics. Russian businesses were too inefficient to compete effectively on the open world market. Despite these severe problems, Boris Yeltsin managed to maintain leadership, even creating a new Russian constitution giving himself greater power. Finally, on December 31, 1999, he resigned under pressure owing to declining popularity.

Did you know ...

- The costs of the forty-five-year-old Cold War were steep for the United States. Tens of thousands of American troops were killed, primarily in the Korean War (1950–53) and Vietnam War (1954–75). A national debt of almost $4 trillion grew from the arms race and providing aid to friendly nations.

- President George Bush rode an incredibly high approval rating following defeat of Iraq in the Persian Gulf War and his proclamation of U.S. victory in the Cold War. Domestic economic problems, however, led to a nosedive in his ratings and eventual defeat to his Democratic opponent, Arkansas governor Bill Clinton, in the 1992 presidential election.

- President Bill Clinton inherited far different international problems than his numerous predecessors. The collapse of Soviet communist control led to many bloody ethnic confrontations, including those in Yugoslavia between Serbia, Slovenia, Croatia, Bosnia and Herzegovina, and Macedonia.

- Following his resignation as president of the Soviet Union, Gorbachev retired to a villa in Finland in addition to his main Moscow residence. Into the twenty-first century, he continued to lecture extensively abroad.

- With the United States the lone superpower in the world, focus would shift to a war on international terrorism, especially following the events of September 11, 2001.

Consider the following …

- Would the downfall of one of the world's two superpowers lead to a period of peace and prosperity?

- Some, like Bush, claimed the United States defeated the Soviet Union in the Cold War. Others asserted that the Soviet Union simply collapsed from its own economic and social limitations in a changing world, a path of self-destruction. Which do you think happened and why?

- The Soviet Union was replaced with a new federation of republics. What was it and how did it differ from the previous organization?

For More Information

Books

Beschloss, Michael R., and Strobe Talbott. *At the Highest Levels: The Inside Story of the End of the Cold War.* Boston: Little, Brown, 1994.

Bush, George, and Brent Scowcroft. *A World Transformed.* New York: Knopf, 1998.

Ciment, James. *The Young People's History of the United States.* New York: Barnes and Noble Books, 1998.

Kaplan, Robert D. *The Coming Anarchy: Shattering the Dreams of the Post Cold War.* New York: Random House, 2000.

Matlock, Jack F., Jr. *Autopsy of an Empire: The American Ambassador's Account of the Collapse of the Soviet Union.* New York: Random House, 1995.

Public Papers of the Presidents of the United States: George Bush, 1992–93, Book 1, January 1 to July 31, 1992. Washington, DC: U.S. Government Printing Office, 1993.

Text Permissions

Following is a list of the copyright holders who have granted us permission to reproduce excerpts from primary source documents in *Cold War: Primary Sources*. Every effort has been made to trace copyright; if omissions have been made, please contact us.

Copyrighted excerpts reproduced from the following periodicals:

Khrushchev, Sergei. "The Looking Glass." *American Heritage* (October 1999): pp. 36–38, 40, 42–46, 49–50. Copyright © 1999 *American Heritage*, A Division of Forbes, Inc. Reproduced by permission.

"The Reds Have a Standard Plan for Taking over a New Country." *Life Magazine* (June 7, 1948): pp. 36–37. Copyright © 1948, renewed 1976. Reproduced by permission.

Sullivan, Kevin. "Forty Years after the Missile Crisis: Players Swap Stories in Cuba." *Washington Post* (October 13, 2002): p. A28. Copyright © 2002, Washington Post Book

Copyrighted excerpts reproduced from the following book:

Where to Learn More

Books

Barson, Michael, and Steven Heller. *Red Scared! The Commie Menace in Propaganda and Popular Culture.* San Francisco: Chronicle Books, 2001.

Brubaker, Paul E. *The Cuban Missile Crisis in American History.* Berkeley Heights, NJ: Enslow, 2001.

Ciment, James. *The Young People's History of the United States.* New York: Barnes and Noble Books, 1998.

Collier, Christopher. *The United States in the Cold War.* New York: Benchmark Books/Marshall Cavendish, 2002.

FitzGerald, Frances. *Way Out There in the Blue: Reagan, Star Wars, and the End of the Cold War.* New York: Simon & Schuster, 2000.

Gaddis, John L. *We Now Know: Rethinking Cold War History.* New York: Oxford University Press, 1997.

Gates, Robert M. *From the Shadows: The Ultimate Insider's Story of Five Presidents and How They Won the Cold War.* New York: Simon & Schuster Trade Paperback, 1997.

Glynn, Patrick. *Closing Pandora's Box: Arms Races, Arms Control, and the History of the Cold War.* New York: Basic Books, 1992.

Grant, R. G. *The Berlin Wall.* Austin, TX: Raintree Steck-Vaughn, 1999.

Herring, George C. *America's Longest War: The United States and Vietnam, 1950–1975.* 2nd ed. New York: Knopf, 1988.

Huchthausen, Peter A., and Alexander Hoyt. *October Fury.* Hoboken, NJ: Wiley, 2002.

Isaacs, Jeremy, and Taylor Downing. *Cold War: An Illustrated History, 1945–1991.* Boston: Little, Brown, 1998.

Jacobs, William Jay. *Search for Peace: The Story of the United Nations.* New York: Atheneum, 1996.

Keep, John L. H. *A History of the Soviet Union, 1945–1991: Last of the Empires.* New York: Oxford University Press, 1995.

Kelly, Nigel. *Fall of the Berlin Wall: The Cold War Ends.* Chicago: Heineman Library, 2001.

Kort, Michael G. *The Cold War.* Brookfield, CT: Millbrook Press, 1994.

LaFeber, Walter. *America, Russia, and the Cold War, 1945–1996.* 8th ed. New York: McGraw-Hill, 1997.

Parrish, Thomas. *Berlin in the Balance, 1945–1949: The Blockade, the Airlift, the First Major Battle of the Cold War.* Reading, MA: Addison-Wesley, 1998.

Parrish, Thomas. *The Cold War Encyclopedia.* New York: Henry Holt, 1996.

Pietrusza, David. *The End of the Cold War.* San Diego, CA: Lucent, 1995.

Sherrow, Victoria. *Joseph McCarthy and the Cold War.* Woodbridge, CT: Blackbirch Press, 1999.

Sibley, Katherine A. S. *The Cold War.* Westport, CT: Greenwood Press, 1998.

Smith, Joseph. *The Cold War, 1945–1991.* 2nd ed. Malden, MA: Blackwell, 1998.

Stein, Conrad. *The Korean War: "The Forgotten War."* Springfield, NJ: Enslow, 1994.

Walker, Martin. *The Cold War: A History (Owl Book).* New York: Henry Holt, 1995.

Magazines

Hoover, J. Edgar. "How to Fight Communism." *Newsweek,* June 9, 1947.

Levine, Isaac Don. "Our First Line of Defense." *Plain Talk,* September 1949.

"X" (George F. Kennan). "The Sources of Soviet Conduct." *Foreign Affairs,* July 1947.

Novels

Brunner, Edward. *Cold War Poetry.* Urbana: University of Illinois Press, 2000.

Clancy, Tom. *The Hunt for Red October.* New York: Berkley Publishing Group, 1985.

Clancy, Tom. *Red Storm Rising*. New York: Berkley Publishing Group, 1987.

Clancy, Tom, and Martin Greenberg. *Tom Clancy's Power Plays: Cold War.* New York: Berkley Publishing Group, 2001.

George, Peter. *Dr. Strangelove, or How I Learned to Stop Worrying and Love the Bomb*. New York: Bantam Books, 1964.

Le Carre, John. *Spy Who Came in from the Cold*. New York: Coward, McCann & Geoghegan, 1978.

Littell, Robert. *The Company: A Novel of the CIA*. New York: Overlook Press, 2002.

Web Sites

The Atomic Archive. http://www.atomicarchive.com (accessed on September 26, 2003).

CNN Interactive: The Cold War Experience. http://www.CNN.com/SPECIALS/cold.war (accessed on September 26, 2003).

"Cold War History: 1949–1989." *U.S. Air Force Museum*. http://www.wpafb.af.mil/museum/history/coldwar/cw.htm (accessed on September 26, 2003)

The Dwight D. Eisenhower Library and Museum. http://www.eisenhower.utexas.edu (accessed on September 26, 2003).

George Bush Presidential Library and Museum. http://bushlibrary.tamu.edu (accessed on September 26, 2003).

Gerald R. Ford Library and Museum. http://www.ford.utexas.edu (accessed on September 26, 2003).

International Spy Museum. http://spymuseum.org (accessed on September 26, 2003).

John F. Kennedy Library and Museum. http://www.cs.umb.edu/jfklibrary/index.htm (accessed on September 26, 2003).

Lyndon B. Johnson Library and Museum. http://www.lbjlib.utexas.edu (accessed on September 26, 2003).

The Manhattan Project Heritage Preservation Association, Inc. http://www.childrenofthemanhattanproject.org (accessed on September 26, 2003).

National Atomic Museum. http://www.atomicmuseum.com (accessed on September 26, 2003).

National Security Agency. http://www.nsa.gov (accessed on September 26, 2003).

President Mikhail Sergeyevich Gorbachev. http://www.mikhailgorbachev.org (accessed on September 26, 2003).

The Richard Nixon Library and Birthplace. http://www.nixonfoundation.org (accessed on September 26, 2003).

Ronald Reagan Presidential Library. http://www.reagan.utexas.edu (accessed on September 26, 2003).

"Secrets, Lies, and Atomic Spies." *Nova Online.* http://www.pbs.org/wgbh/nova/venona (accessed on September 26, 2003).

Truman Presidential Museum & Library. http://www.trumanlibrary.org (accessed on September 26, 2003).

U.S. Central Intelligence Agency (CIA). http://www.cia.gov (accessed on September 26, 2003).

Woodrow Wilson International Center for Scholars. *The Cold War International History Project.* http://wwics.si.edu/index.cfm?fuseaction=topics.home&topic_id=1409 (accessed on September 26, 2003).

Index

Boldface indicates main entries and their page numbers; illustrations are marked by (ill.).

nationalism in, 271

Nixon Doctrine and, 264, 268–73, 276

Nixon, Richard M., and, 264, 267–73, 276

peace and, 107, 270–71, 277

Soviet Union and, 68

war and, 270, 277

"At Historic Crossroads: Documents on the December 1989 Malta Summit," 307–18

Atomic bombs, 69, 115, 116. *See also* Nuclear weapons

"Atoms for Peace." *See* "Peaceful Uses of Atomic Energy" speech

Attlee, Clement R., 16

B

Baker, James A., 305, 307

Ballistic missiles, 287–88, 302–3

Baltic States, 317–18, 320

Bay of Pigs, 233

Bentley, Elizabeth, 147–48

Beria, Lavrenty, 180

Berlin, 206 (ill.). *See also* Berlin Wall; East Berlin; West Berlin

airlift in, 205, 206 (ill.), 210

blockade in, 205

division of, 205

Eisenhower, Dwight D., and, 209

Kennedy, John F., and, 207, 208–15, 224–31

Khrushchev, Nikita, and, 207, 208–10, 217–23, 224–25

nuclear war and, 209, 210

peace and, 213–14

reunification of, 228–29

Berlin Wall, 222 (ill.), 229 (ill.), 316 (ill.)

Checkpoint Charlie, 227, 231

construction of, 207, 215, 221, 224–27, 230

crossing, 227, 231

fall of, 230, 296, 317

Kennedy, John F., and, 207, 224–31

Khrushchev, Nikita, and, 221, 224–25, 226–27

life of, 229

Ulbricht, Walter, and, 226–27

Big Three, 28

Black Saturday, 255

Blacklists, 142

Blanton, Thomas S., 258

Blockades

in Berlin, 205

Cuban Missile Crisis and, 237, 238, 241, 244, 247, 249–50, 253

Blunt, Anthony F., 50

Bogart, Humphrey, 143 (ill.)

Bolshevik Revolution, 2

Bradley, Omar, 86

Brezhnev Doctrine, 274

Brezhnev, Leonid, 264–65, 274, 280

Brinkmanship, 119–20, 190–91

Browder, Earl, 160

Brugioni, Dino A., 250, 259

Budget, 102, 119–20, 324

Bundy, McGeorge, 236

Burgess, Guy, 50

Bush, George, 305 (ill.), 308 (ill.), 310 (ill.), 322 (ill.)

"At Historic Crossroads: Documents on the December 1989 Malta Summit," 307–18

Baker, James A., and, 307

chemical weapons and, 311

Cheney, Richard, and, 305

Cold War's end and, 296–97, 319–25

disarmament and, 303–4, 305, 308, 311, 322, 323

economy and, 308, 309–11, 323, 324–25

election of, 294–95, 324–25

"End of Cold War: Address Before a Joint Session of the Congress on the State of the Union, January 28, 1992," 319–26

freedom and, 315, 320, 323

Germany and, 317

Gorbachev, Mikhail, and, 283, 294–97, 300, 303–4, 305, 307–18

isolationism and, 323

military and, 320, 322–23

nuclear weapons and, 295,
296, 303–4, 311, 320, 322–23
perestroika and, 309
Persian Gulf War and, 317, 324
power and, 320, 321–22
Reagan, Ronald, and, 283,
294–95
Soviet Union and, 294–97,
303–4, 305, 307–18
Strategic Defense Initiative
and, 320, 323
vice presidency of, 283, 295
Yeltsin, Boris, and, 322, 323
Bush, George W., 285
Byrnes, James F., 12, 13, 28, 29

C

Cambridge Spies, 50
Capitalism
Cominform and, 45
communism and, 5, 11, 48, 99,
128, 148, 149, 301–2, 305
economy and, 1
Europe and, 2–3
imperialism and, 27, 74
Khrushchev, Nikita, and, 196
property and, 1
Carter, Jimmy, 265, 282
Castro, Fidel, 232, 233 (ill.),
233–34, 258
Casualties. *See* Death
Central Intelligence Agency
(CIA), 49, 182
Chambers, Whittaker, 148
"The Chance for Peace," 89,
99–111, 188
Charter of Paris, 317
Chechnya, 323–24
Checkpoint Charlie, 227, 231
Chemical warfare, 311
Cheney, Richard, 305
Chernenko, Konstantin, 283
Chiang Kai-shek, 61–62, 64, 66
Children, 206 (ill.)
China. *See also* People's Republic
of China (PRC); Republic of
China (ROC); Taiwan
Acheson, Dean G., and, 65,
67–68
Brezhnev Doctrine and, 274
Brezhnev, Leonid, and, 274

communism in, 62, 64–70
containment and, 65–66,
67–68, 81
"Crimes of Stalin" speech and,
182
culture and, 278, 280
domino theory and, 70
Gorbachev, Mikhail, and, 294,
313
Japan and, 61, 64
Kissinger, Henry, and, 264,
274–75
Korean War and, 63, 80–81, 84,
86
MacArthur, Douglas, and, 63,
80–81, 84, 86
Marshall, George C., and, 65
Marshall Plan and, 65–66
Nationalists in, 61–62, 64–66
Nixon, Richard M., and, 69,
264, 270, 274–81
peace and, 277–78, 279
press and, 276
revolution in, 61–62, 64–70
Sino-Soviet Treaty and, 69
Soviet Union and, 65, 68, 69,
70, 264, 274, 294
Stalin, Joseph, and, 65, 70
Truman, Harry S., and, 62, 65,
67–68, 101
U.S. State Department and, 65,
67–68
Vietnam War and, 267, 272,
274–76
China Lobby, 62, 65
Churchill, Winston, 17 (ill.), 19
(ill.), 22 (ill.)
election of 1945 and, 16
"Iron Curtain speech" and, 4,
12–13, **16–24**, 25, 26, 28–29
peace and, 110
Stalin, Joseph, and, 19, 23
Truman, Harry S., and, 12, 16
World War I and, 20
World War II and, 16–17, 21
Yalta Conference and, 18
CIA. *See* Central Intelligence
Agency (CIA)
CIS. *See* Commonwealth of Inde-
pendent States (CIS)
Civil Defense, 212–13, 215
Civil rights, 127, 133, 142. *See
also* Freedom

Clausewitz, Karl von, 192
Clayton, Will, 43
Clifton, Chester, 226
Clinton, Bill, 324, 325
Closed societies, 4
Cohn, Roy, 167 (ill.)
Cold War
  beginning of, 1–4
  costs of, 324
  end of, 293–97, 319–25
  fear and, 185, 186, 198
  Khrushchev, Sergei, on,
    185–86, 192–93
  nuclear weapons and, 192–93
Comecon. *See* Council of Mutual
  Economic Assistance (Come-
  con)
Cominform. *See* Communist In-
  formation Bureau (Comin-
  form)
Comintern, 19
Commonwealth of Independent
  States (CIS), 296. *See also*
  Russia; Soviet Union
**"Communiqué to President
  Kennedy Accepting an End
  to the Missile Crisis, October 28, 1962," 253–62**
Communism. *See also* Communist Party
  Acheson, Dean G., and, 35–36
  Asia and, 211
  Bolshevik Revolution and, 2
  capitalism and, 5, 11, 48, 99,
    128, 148, 149, 301–2, 305
  in China, 62, 64–70
  closed societies and, 4
  collapse of, 295–97, 307, 309,
    315
  Comintern and, 19
  Communist Party and, 1, 150
  in Czechoslovakia, 50, 53, 54,
    56, 67
  democracy and, 26, 36, 123,
    124, 127, 128, 141, 142, 166,
    170, 204, 289
  domino theory and, 35–36, 40
  Dulles, John Foster, and, 110
  in Eastern Bloc, 16–24, 295–96,
    307, 309, 315
  economy and, 1–2, 4, 204
  education and, 127–32,
    141–42, 146, 148–65, 174

elections and, 1, 149, 151, 156,
  160, 204
espionage and, 170
Europe and, 56
fascism and, 158
Federal Bureau of Investigation
  and, 125–32, 161
in France, 43, 49
freedom and, 36, 38–40, 72,
  74, 151–52
fronts for, 157–58
in Greece, 32–33, 34–41
growth of, 152–53, 168–70
Hoover, J. Edgar, and, 123–24,
  125–33, 147, 153
in Italy, 43, 49
labor and, 128–29, 131, 132,
  149, 158
Lenin, Vladimir I., and, 64,
  127–28, 128–29
Marx, Karl, and, 2, 6, 64
Marxism and, 2, 6
National Education Association
  and, 163
Nixon, Richard M., and, 280
propaganda and, 135–36,
  137–38, 141, 146–65
property and, 1–2, 150, 204
racism and, 152
Reagan, Ronald, and, 124, 135,
  139–42, 282, 284–85
religion and, 2, 132, 138, 151,
  152, 168, 284–85
Roosevelt, Eleanor, and, 91, 95
Roosevelt, Franklin D., and,
  125
school and, 149–50, 151, 163
socialism and, 128
in Soviet Union, 5–14, 72,
  73–76, 168–70
Stalin, Joseph, and, 2
travel and, 151
in Turkey, 32–33, 34–41
United Nations and, 88, 90, 91,
  94, 95
U.S. Congress and, 162, 170–71
West Berlin and, 210
Communist fronts, 157–58
Communist Information Bureau
  (Cominform), 11, 45, 161
Communist Party. *See also* Communism
  communism and, 1, 150

Rusk, Dean, and, 250
SIGINT and, 234, 250
Soviet Union and, 246–49
Turkey and, 234, 255
United Nations and, 241, 248,
249
Culture, 278, 280
Czechoslovakia
communism in, 50, 53, 54, 56,
67
Marshall Plan and, 48, 50

D

Daily Worker, 128
Death, 267–68, 324. *See also* Execution
DEFCON, 253, 260–61
Democracy
communism and, 26, 36, 123,
124, 127, 128, 141, 142, 166,
170, 204, 289
Eastern Bloc and, 54, 56
elections and, 1
Europe and, 2–3
freedom and, 1, 36, 127, 228
Gorbachev, Mikhail, and, 290,
299, 301
imperialism and, 11, 74
peace and, 54–56
perestroika and, 302
power and, 19
press and, 299
Reagan, Ronald, and, 289
religion and, 168
Soviet Union and, 54, 56
United Nations and, 21
Yeltsin, Boris, and, 296
Democratic National Committee
(DNC), 88, 90, 265
Democratic People's Republic of
Korea (DPRK). *See* North
Korea
Détente, 264–65, 282
Deterrence, 53
Dies, Martin, 143 (ill.), 146–47
Diplomacy, 9, 14, 72, 75, 173
Disarmament. *See also* Military
Bush, George, and, 303–4, 305,
308, 311, 322, 323
Eisenhower, Dwight D., and,
102–3, 107–8, 109, 118

Gorbachev, Mikhail, and, 286,
287–96, 299–300, 302–4,
305–6, 308, 314
Khrushchev, Nikita, and, 195,
197, 201, 219
Reagan, Ronald, and, 286,
287–96, 303
Roosevelt, Eleanor, on, 94–95
Shultz, George, and, 303
Soviet Union and, 94–95, 286,
287–96, 299–300, 302–4,
305–6, 314
Yeltsin, Boris, and, 322, 323
DNC. *See* Democratic National
Committee (DNC)
Dobrynin, Anatoly, 250–51,
253–55
Domino theory
Acheson, Dean G., and, 70,
222
China and, 70
communism and, 35–36, 40
Greece and, 35–36, 40
Khrushchev, Nikita, and,
221–22
Soviet Union and, 221–22
Turkey and, 35–36, 40
Vietnam War and, 41
DPRK (North Democratic People's
Republic of Korea). *See* North
Korea
Dulles, John Foster, 110, 119, 169
(ill.), 220

E

East Berlin, 205, 229. *See also*
Berlin
East Germany. *See also* Germany
economy of, 205–7, 223
formation of, 204–5
Gorbachev, Mikhail, and, 230
Khrushchev, Nikita, and, 207,
208, 210
refugees from, 205–7, 209, 210,
215, 221, 223, 224, 225
Soviet Union and, 207, 208,
209, 210, 230
Eastern Bloc. *See also* "Iron Curtain speech"
communism in, 16–24,
295–96, 307, 309, 315

L

Made Before the Women's
Republican Club in Wheel-
ing, West Virginia, Febru-
ary 1950," 166–73
Truman, Harry S., and, 171
U.S. Army and, 172
U.S. State Department and, 69,
73, 123, 166–71
Welch, Joseph N., and, 111,
172
McCarthyism, 166. *See also* Red
Scare
McCloy, John J., 214, 217,
219–20, 221
McCone, John, 238
McDowell, John, 138
McNamara, Robert S., 212, 241,
242, 258, 259
Military. *See also* Disarmament;
U.S. Army
buildup of, 102, 104–5,
186–87, 265
Bush, George, and, 320,
322–23
containment and, 9, 14, 72,
74–78, 119
Cuban Missile Crisis and, 241,
248, 253, 261
economy and, 119–20, 265
Eisenhower, Dwight D., and,
119–20, 191, 202
Gorbachev, Mikhail, and,
312–13, 314
imperialism and, 25, 26, 28–30
Khrushchev, Nikita, and,
190–91, 193–94, 202, 211,
214–15, 221
Marshall Plan and, 54
peace and, 107–8
Reagan, Ronald, and, 265
Soviet Union and, 99, 175,
186–87, 190–91, 193–94,
202, 211, 214–15, 221, 265
Stalin, Joseph, and, 186–87
Truman, Harry S., and, 76–77
U.S. Congress and, 76–77
Warsaw Pact and, 186
Military industrial complex, 191
Missiles
antiballistic missiles, 287–88
ballistic missiles, 287–88,
302–3

Cuban Missile Crisis and, 234,
236, 237–38, 244, 246–47,
251
Molotov Plan, 45
Molotov, Vyacheslav M., 27 (ill.),
45, 48
Mondale, Walter, 283
Morality, 171, 284
"Mrs. Franklin D. Roosevelt's
Address to the Democratic
National Convention on
the Importance of the
United Nations," 90–98

N

National Education Association,
163
National Popular Liberation
Army (ELAS), 34, 41
National Security Council (NSC),
77 (ill.)
containment and, 62, 72,
74–77
Cuba and, 233–34
Cuban Missile Crisis and, 234,
236
NSC-20, 53
NSC-30, 53
NSC-68, 62, 69, 71–77, 119
nuclear weapons and, 53
"National Security Council Re-
port on Soviet Intentions
(NSC-68)," 71–78
Nationalism, 271
Nationalists, 61–62, 64–66
NATO. *See* North Atlantic Treaty
Organization (NATO)
*Nikita Khrushchev and the Creation
of a Superpower*, 175, 199,
250, 256
9/11. *See* September 11, 2001, ter-
rorist attacks
Nitze, Paul H., 62, 69, **71–78**, 73
(ill.)
Nixon Doctrine, 264, **267–73**,
276
Nixon, Pat, 264, 275, 280–81
Nixon, Richard M., 139 (ill.),
196 (ill.), 268 (ill.), 275 (ill.),
277 (ill.)
Asia and, 264, 267–73, 276

Intermediate-range Nuclear Force (INF) treaty, 290, 293, 300, 302–3
Kennan, George F., and, 72
Khrushchev, Nikita, and, 120, 175, 190–91, 220
Kissinger, Henry, and, 280
Korean War and, 63, 80–81
Limited Test-Ban Treaty of 1963, 261
National Security Council and, 53
negotiations concerning, 121, 175, 261, 265–66, 280, 284–92, 293, 320
Nixon, Richard M., and, 280
North Atlantic Treaty Organization and, 120
Outer Space Treaty, 283
peace and, 104–5, 107–8, 109, 113–21
race for, 26, 89, 113, 114, 115–18, 119–21, 168, 190–91, 192, 199, 201, 282–83, 284
Reagan, Ronald, and, 265–66, 284–92, 293, 300, 303
Roosevelt, Eleanor, and, 94–95
Shevardnadze, Eduard, and, 291
Shultz, George, and, 300, 303
Soviet Union and, 69, 71, 94–95, 102, 113, 114, 116–17, 120–21, 175, 190–91, 220, 265–66, 280, 284–92, 293, 295, 296, 299–300, 302–4, 308, 314
Strategic Arms Limitation Talks (SALT), 280, 285, 287–92
Strategic Defense Initiative (SDI), 282–83, 285, 287–92, 320, 323
strength of, 101, 115, 242–43
testing of, 101, 113, 115, 116, 121
threats and, 29, 119
treaties concerning, 261, 280, 283, 287, 290, 293, 300, 302–3
Truman, Harry S., and, 69
United Nations and, 94–95, 102, 108, 118
Yeltsin, Boris, and, 319, 320, 323

O

OAS. *See* Organization of American States (OAS)
October Revolution. *See* Bolshevik Revolution
Oil, 12, 23
"Old Soldiers Never Die; They Just Fade Away" speech, 63, **79–87**
"One Hundred Things You Should Know About Communism in the U.S.A.," 124, **146–65**
"Open Skies" plan, 102–3, 188–89
Oppenheimer, J. Robert, 49
Organization of American States (OAS), 241, 248
Orlov, Vadim, 259
"Our First Line of Defense," 62, **64–70**
Outer Space Treaty, 283

P

Pacific Rim, 268–69
Peace
Adenauer, Konrad, and, 110
Asia and, 107, 270–71, 277
Berlin and, 213–14
China and, 277–78, 279
Churchill, Winston, and, 110
Cuban Missile Crisis and, 246–47, 248–49, 256, 258, 260
democracy and, 54–56
Dulles, John Foster, and, 110
Eastern Bloc and, 107, 108
Eisenhower, Dwight D., and, 88–89, 99–111, 113–21, 188, 192
freedom and, 54–55, 57
Gorbachev, Mikhail, and, 294, 298–99, 300–302, 314
Kennedy, John F., and, 213–14, 246–47, 248–49
Khrushchev, Nikita, and, 175, 187–88, 192, 195–203, 256, 258, 260
Korean War and, 106–7, 108

communism and, 124, 135, 139–42, 282, 284–85

democracy and, 289

détente and, 265, 282

disarmament and, 286, 287–96, 303

economy and, 265

election of, 142, 265, 283, 284

freedom and, 284–85, 289

Gorbachev, Mikhail, and, 265–66, 282–92, 293–94, 295, 300, 303, 312

Hoover, J. Edgar, and, 132

House Un-American Activities Committee testimony and, 124, **135–45**

Intermediate-range Nuclear Force treaty and, 290, 293

military and, 265

nuclear weapons and, 265–66, 284–92, 293, 300, 303

peace and, 284–85

religion and, 284–85

Shultz, George, and, 283

Soviet Union and, 282–92, 293–94, 295, 312

Strategic Defense Initiative and, 282–83, 285, 287–92

Reconnaissance, 236, 246, 247, 255. *See also* Espionage; Intelligence

Red Scare. *See also* McCarthyism

fear and, 123

Hollywood and, 132

House Un-American Activities Committee and, 124, 129–30

McCarthy, Joseph R., and, 110, 124, 163, 166–73

overview of, 71, 123–24

Religion

communism and, 2, 132, 138, 151, 152, 168, 284–85

democracy and, 168

Eisenhower, Dwight D., and, 111

Reagan, Ronald, and, 284–85

Soviet Union and, 138, 151

"Remarks at Andrews Air Force Base on Returning from the People's Republic of China, February 28, 1972," 274–81

"Remarks by the Honorable George C. Marshall, Secre-tary of State, at Harvard University on June 5, 1947," 43–51

"Remarks in the Rudolph Wild Platz, Berlin, June 26, 1963" 207, **224–31**

Republic of China (ROC), 66, 69, 70. *See also* China; People's Republic of China (PRC); Taiwan

Republic of Korea. *See* South Korea

Robinson, Jackie, 163

ROC. *See* Republic of China (ROC)

Rockefeller, Nelson A., 188

Rogers, William, 277 (ill.)

Roosevelt, Eleanor, 88, **90–98**, 92 (ill.), 93 (ill.), 95 (ill.), 96 (ill.)

Roosevelt, Franklin D., 19 (ill.)

communism and, 125

Eisenhower, Dwight D., and, 100

health of, 97–98

Hoover, J. Edgar, and, 125

peace and, 91, 92

Roosevelt, Eleanor, and, 97–98

World War II and, 92, 100

Yalta Conference and, 18

Rosenberg, Ethel, 133

Rosenberg, Julius, 133

Rusk, Dean, 250

Russia, 2, 250 (ill.), 323, 324. *See also* Commonwealth of Independent States (CIS); Soviet Union

S

SALT. *See* Strategic Arms Limitation Talks (SALT)

Schlesinger, Arthur M., Jr., 258

School, 149–50, 151, 163. *See also* Education

Schorr, Daniel, 225, 225 (ill.)

Scowcroft, Brent, 312

Screen Actors Guild, 124, 132, 136, 139–41

SDI. *See* Strategic Defense Initiative (SDI)

T

U

V

W

Warsaw Pact, 186, 317
Watergate scandal, 264–65, 282
Weapons. *See also* Missiles; Nuclear weapons
  chemical, 311
  cost of, 104–5, 324
  inspections of, 95, 102–3, 108, 188–89, 201
  peace and, 104–5, 107–8, 109
Welch, Joseph N., 111, 172
West Berlin, 205, 210, 211–14, 222 (ill.), 224–31, 226 (ill.), 249. *See also* Berlin
West Germany, 204–5, 205–7. *See also* Germany
White Paper, 65, 67–68, 81
World Bank, 23
World War I, 20
World War II, 49 (ill.)
  battles of, 100
  Big Three and, 28
  Churchill, Winston, and, 16–17, 21
  Eisenhower, Dwight D., and, 99–100, 103
  end of, 100, 103
  Europe and, 27
  Germany and, 100
  Great Britain and, 16–17
  Hitler, Adolf, and, 8, 21
  Kennan, George F., and, 13–14
  Khrushchev, Nikita, and, 174, 187
  MacArthur, Douglas, and, 81, 83–84
  peace and, 53–54, 55–56
  Roosevelt, Franklin D., and, 92, 100

  Soviet Union and, 7, 13–14, 100
  United States of America and, 7, 13–14
  Yalta Conference and, 18
World War III, 26, 29, 94, 95, 105. *See also* Nuclear war

X

"X" article. *See* "The Sources of Soviet Conduct"

Y

Yalta Conference, 18, 38
Yeltsin, Boris
  Bush, George, and, 322, 323
  constitution and, 324
  coup attempt and, 320
  democracy and, 296
  disarmament and, 322, 323
  economy and, 296, 323, 324
  election of, 304–5
  nuclear weapons and, 319, 320, 323
  resignation of, 324
Young Communist League, 132
Yugoslavia, 34, 41, 180, 323–24

Z

Zhdanov, Andrei, 11
Zhou Enlai, 275 (ill.), 277 (ill.)